Emma Frost

Emma Frost

writer: **Karl Bollers**

pencils: **Carlo Pagulayan**

inks: **Dennis Crisostomo**

colors: Pete Pantazis & Transparency Digital

letters: Virtual Calligraphy's Cory Petit
& Dave Sharpe

cover art: Greg Horn

assistant editors: Cory Sedlmeier
& Stephanie Moore

editor: Mike Marts

collections editor: Jeff Youngquist

assistant editor: Jennifer Grünwald

book designer: Carrie Beadle

editor in chief: Joe Quesada

publisher: Dan Buckley

PREVIOUSLY...

Emma Frost has discovered she's not like other girls. She has the ability to hear the thoughts and see memories of othe people. She is a mutant.

Although Emma's wonderous gifts unwittingly earn her the respect of her enormously wealthy and equally domineering father, Winston, she is unable to prevent him from exiling her brother, Christian, to a mental institution.

This is the final straw for the embittered Emma, and rather than accept Winston's offer of steering the Frost family fortune into the future, she leaves home instead. Now, out on her own, without the benefit of her parents' wealth, Emma finds she isn't repared for such a dramatic change in lifestyle...

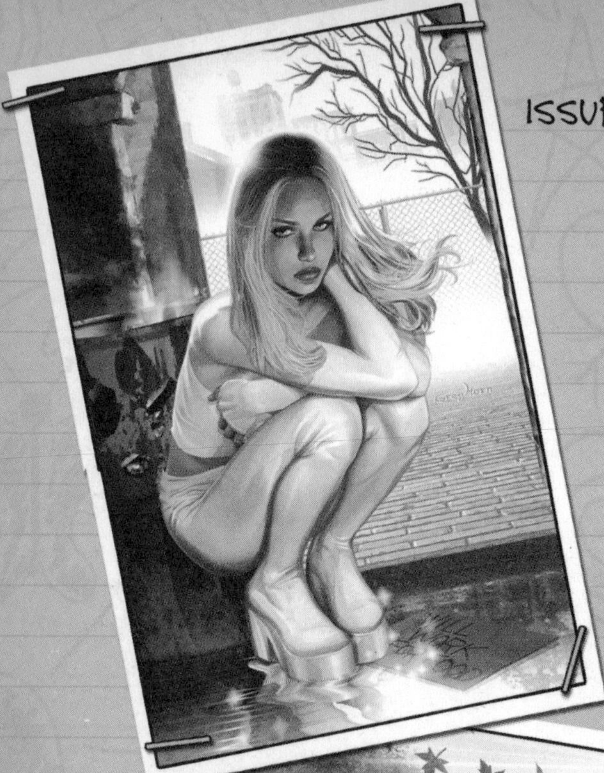

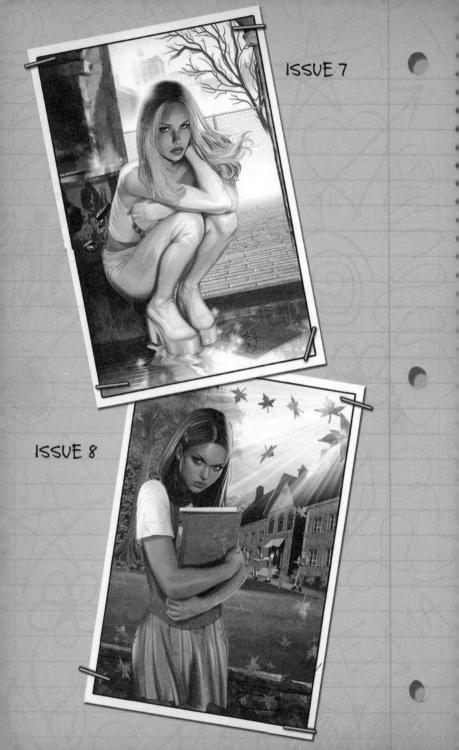

ISSUE 7

ISSUE 8

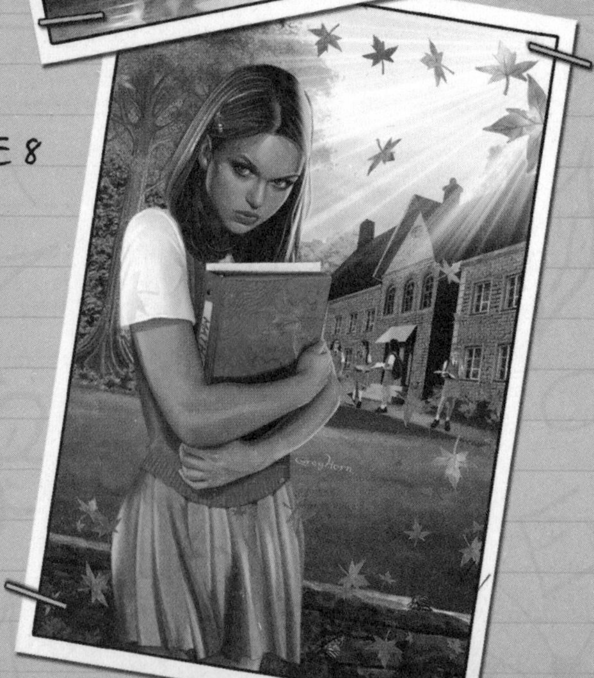

Mind Games

1 of 6

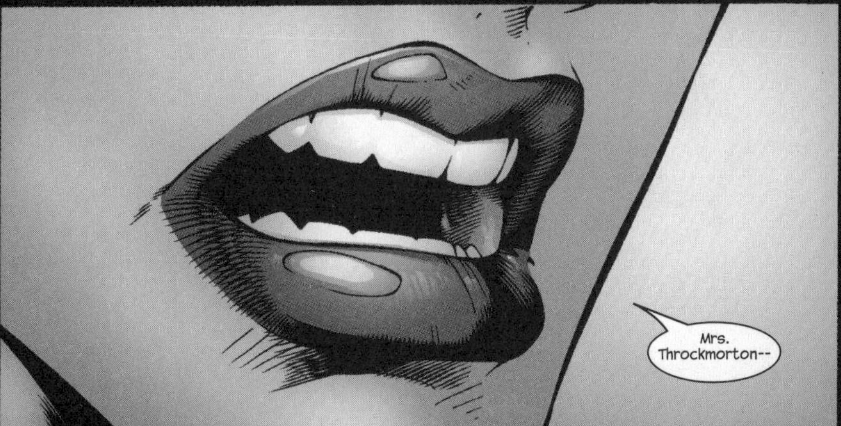
Mrs. Throckmorton--

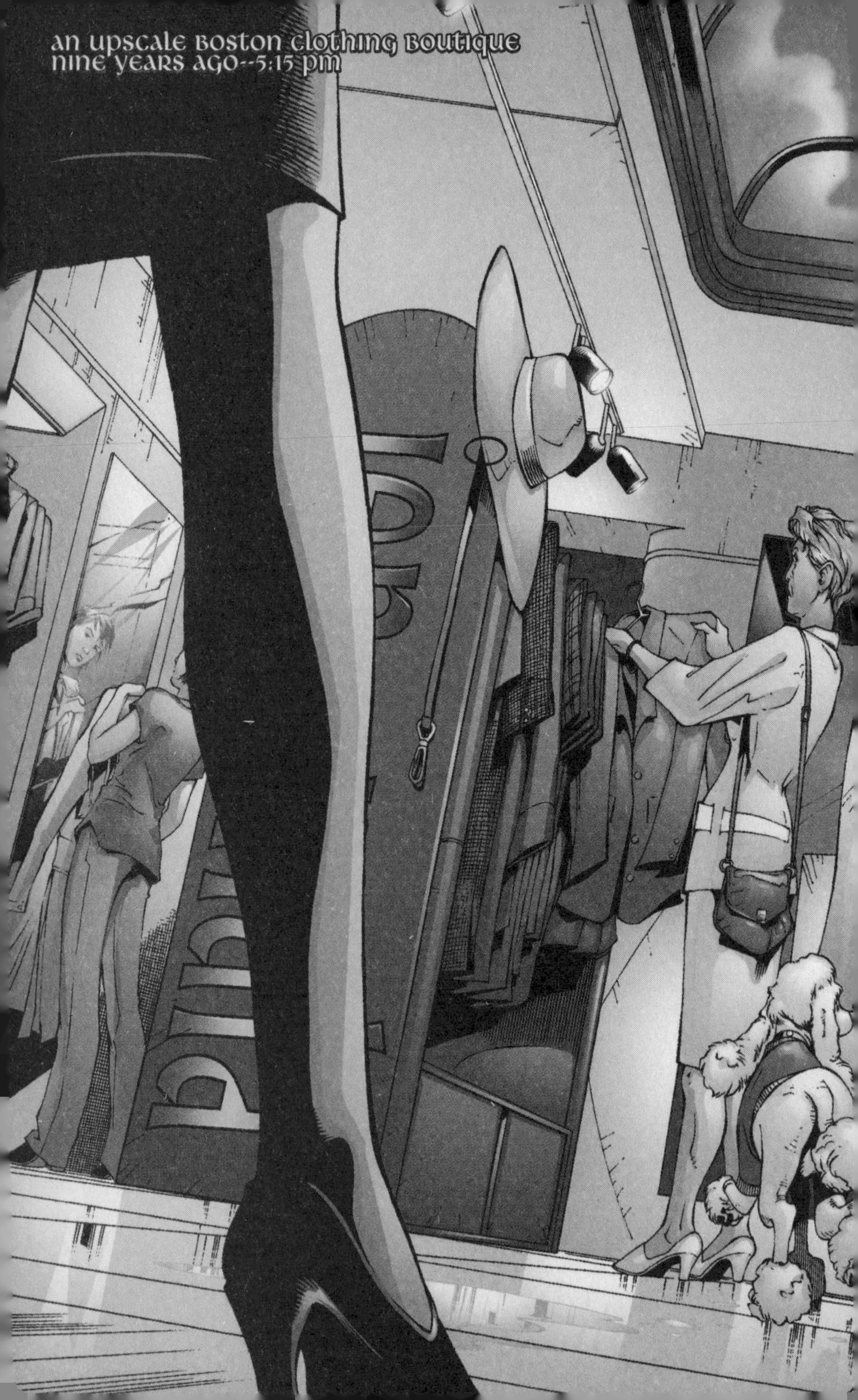
an upscale boston clothing boutique
nine years ago--5:15 pm

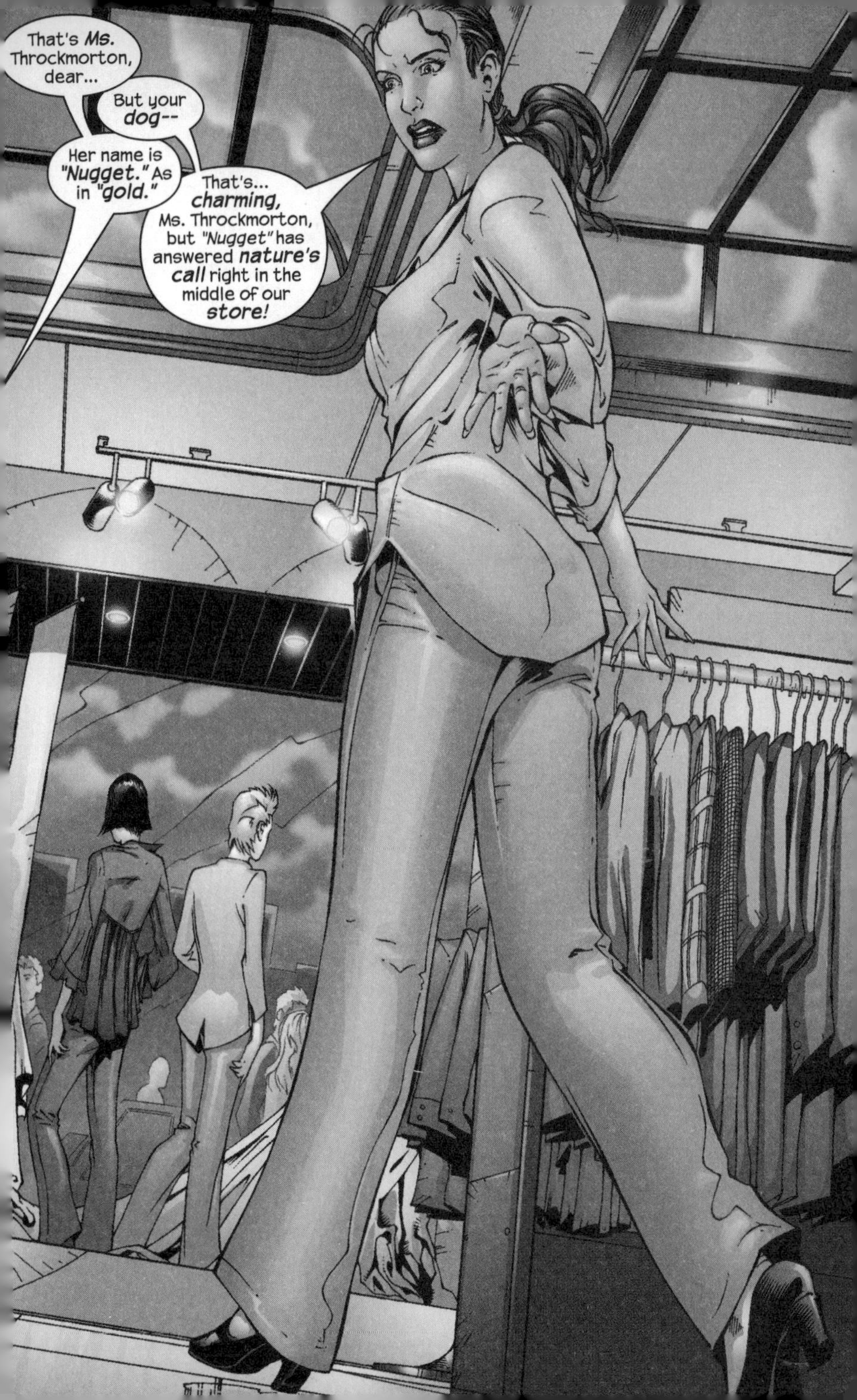
That's *Ms.* Throckmorton, dear...
But your *dog--*
Her name is *"Nugget."* As in *"gold."*
That's... *charming,* Ms. Throckmorton, but *"Nugget"* has answered *nature's call* right in the middle of our *store!*

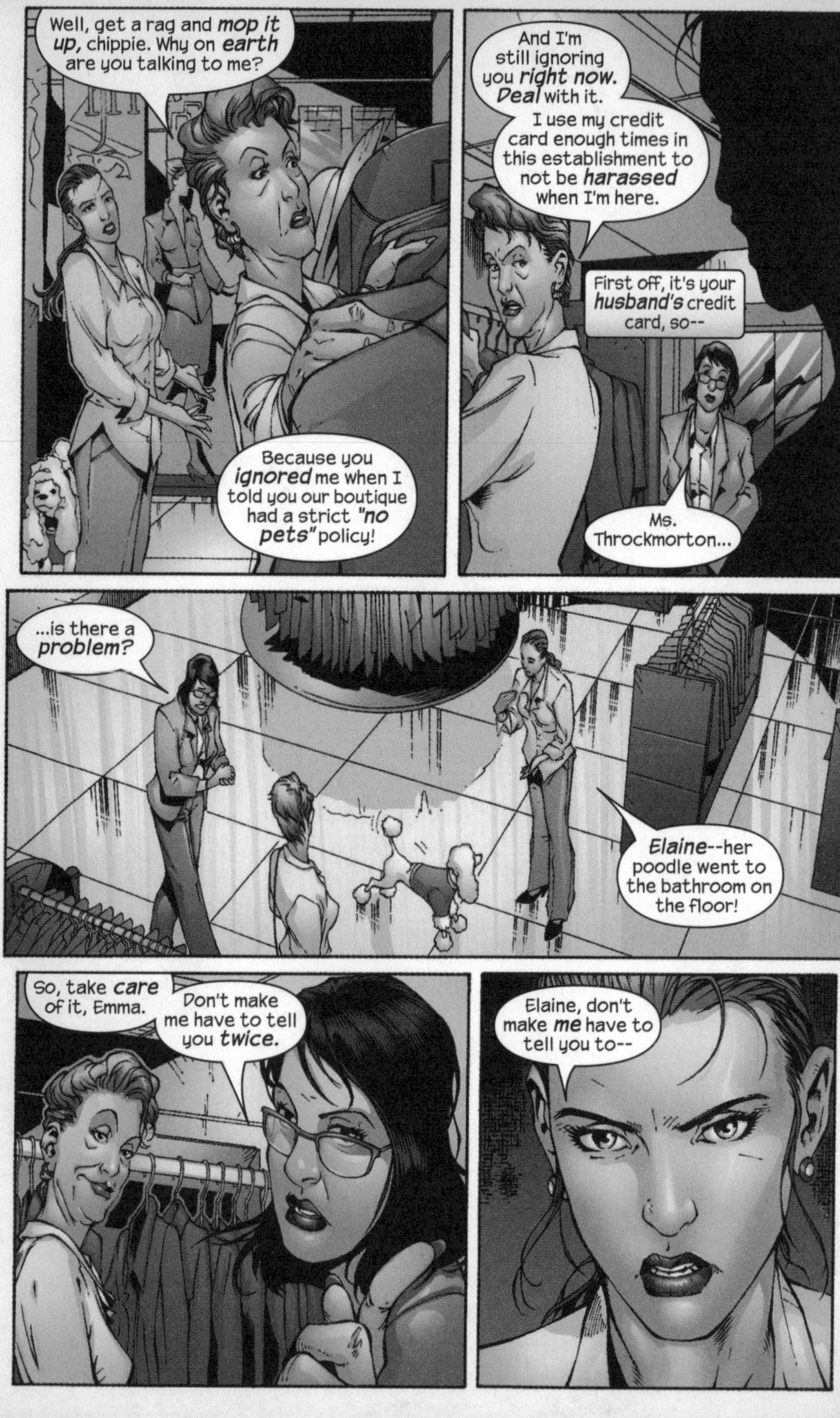
Well, get a rag and mop it up, chippie. Why on earth are you talking to me?
Because you ignored me when I told you our boutique had a strict "no pets" policy!
And I'm still ignoring you right now. Deal with it.
I use my credit card enough times in this establishment to not be harassed when I'm here.
First off, it's your husband's credit card, so--
Ms. Throckmorton...
...is there a problem?
Elaine--her poodle went to the bathroom on the floor!
So, take care of it, Emma.
Don't make me have to tell you twice.
Elaine, don't make me have to tell you to--

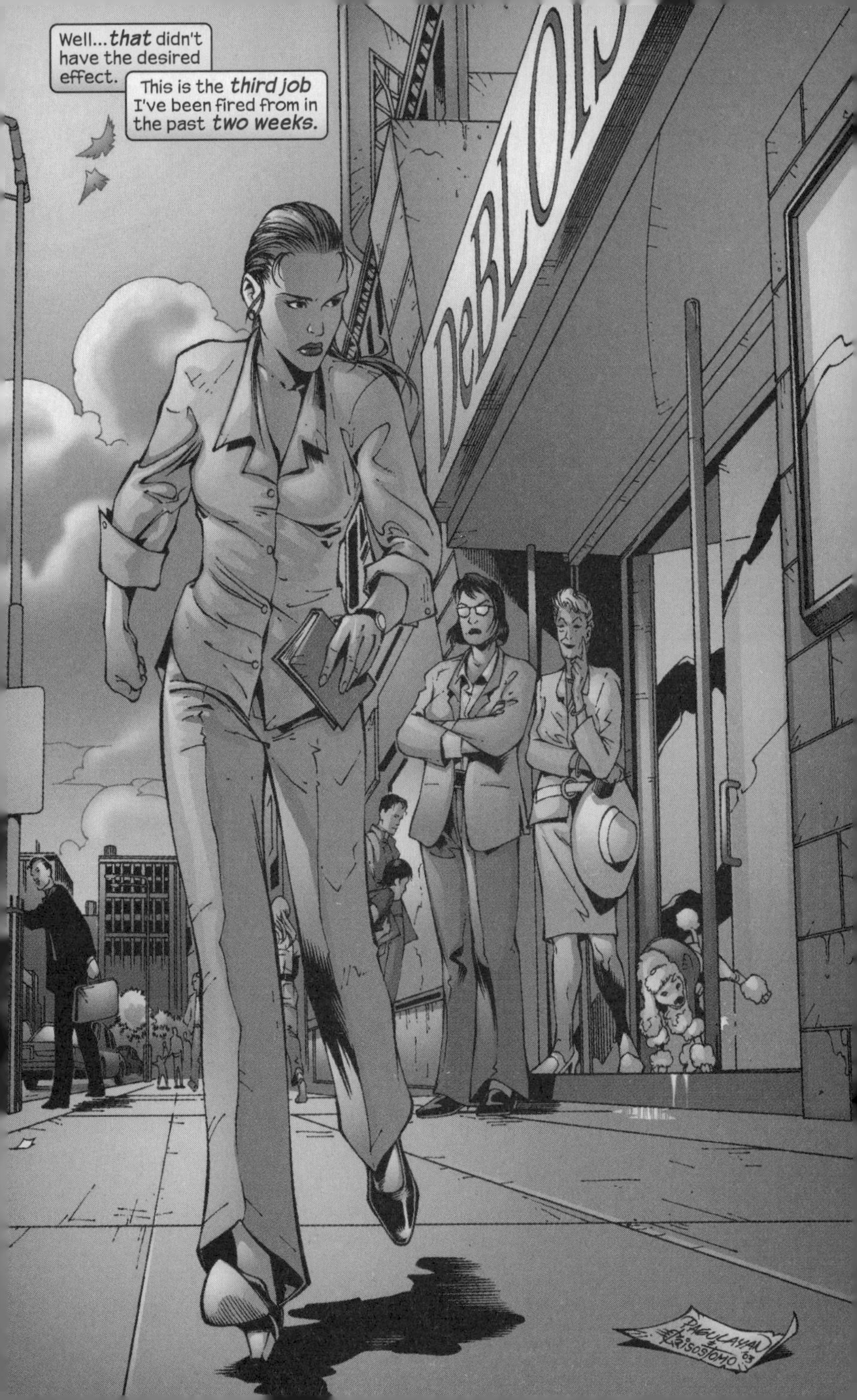
Well...that didn't have the desired effect.
This is the third job I've been fired from in the past two weeks.
DeBLO
PAGULAYAN & CRISOSTOMO '03

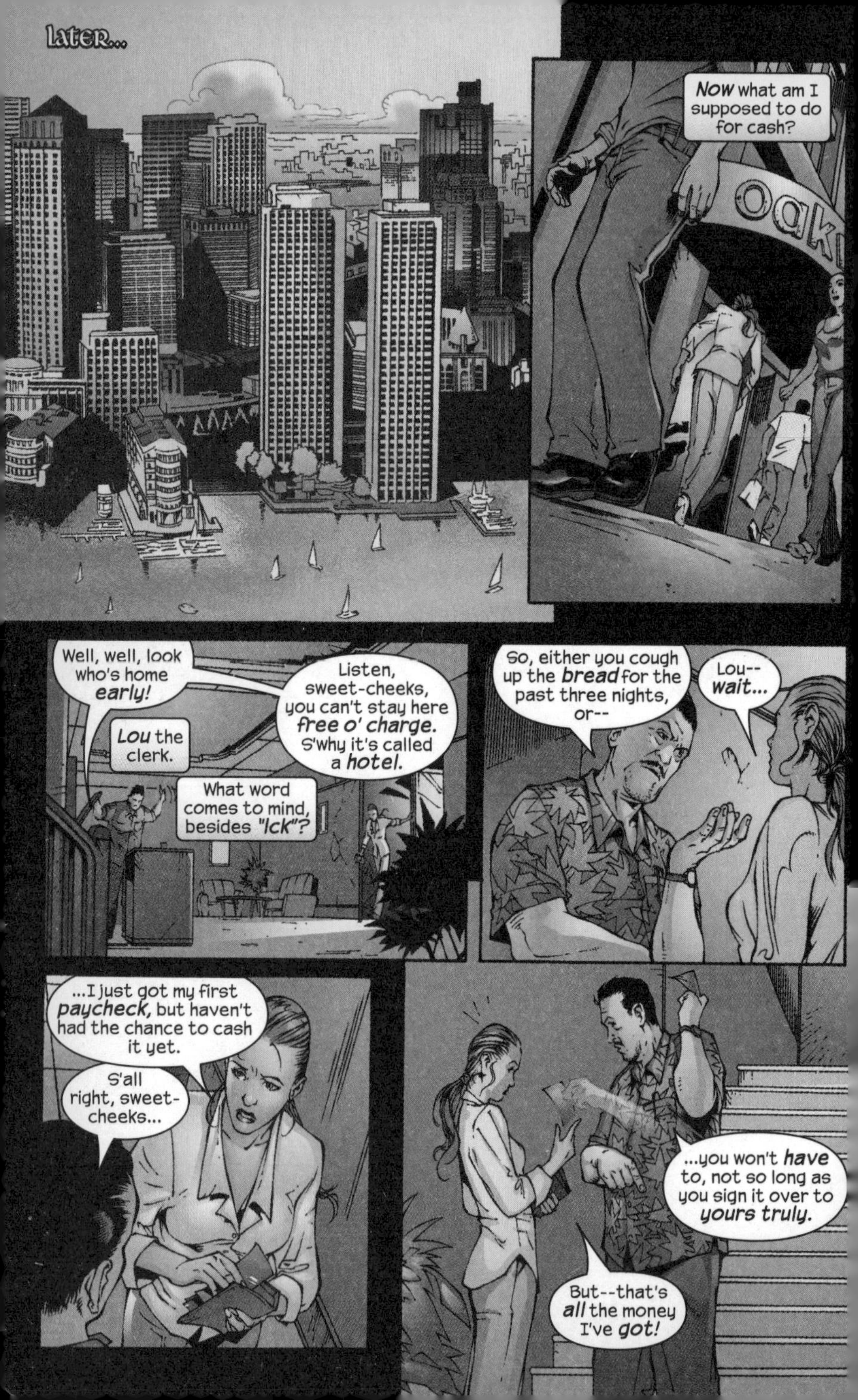
Later...
Now what am I supposed to do for cash?
oak
Well, well, look who's home early!
Lou the clerk.
What word comes to mind, besides "Ick"?
Listen, sweet-cheeks, you can't stay here free o' charge. S'why it's called a hotel.
So, either you cough up the bread for the past three nights, or--
Lou-- wait...
...I just got my first paycheck, but haven't had the chance to cash it yet.
S'all right, sweet-cheeks...
...you won't have to, not so long as you sign it over to yours truly.
But--that's all the money I've got!

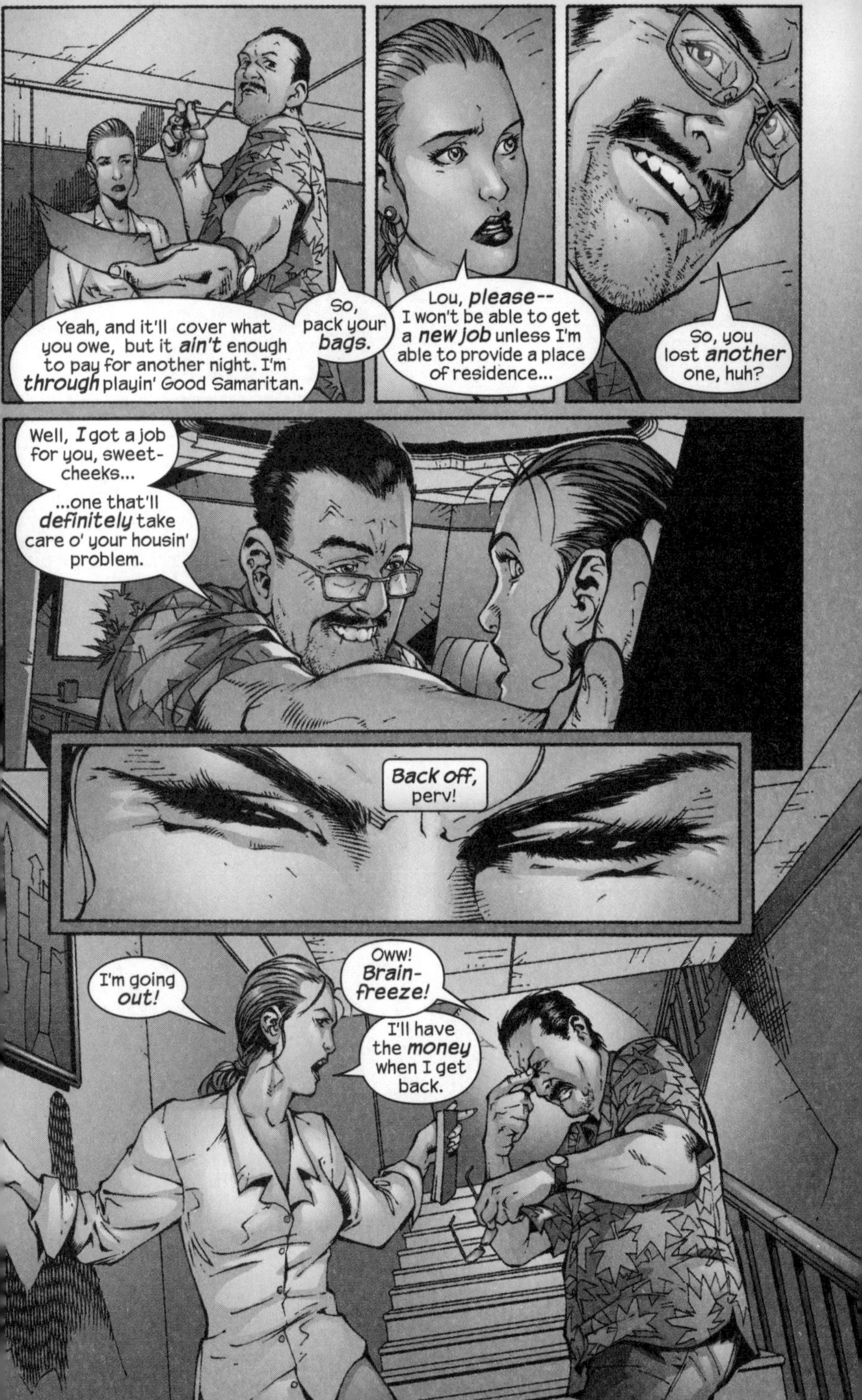

Yeah, and it'll cover what you owe, but it *ain't* enough to pay for another night. I'm *through* playin' Good Samaritan.
So, pack your *bags.*
Lou, *please--* I won't be able to get a *new job* unless I'm able to provide a place of residence...
So, you lost *another* one, huh?
Well, *I* got a job for you, sweet-cheeks...
...one that'll *definitely* take care o' your housin' problem.
Back off, perv!
I'm going *out!*
Oww! *Brain-freeze!*
I'll have the *money* when I get back.

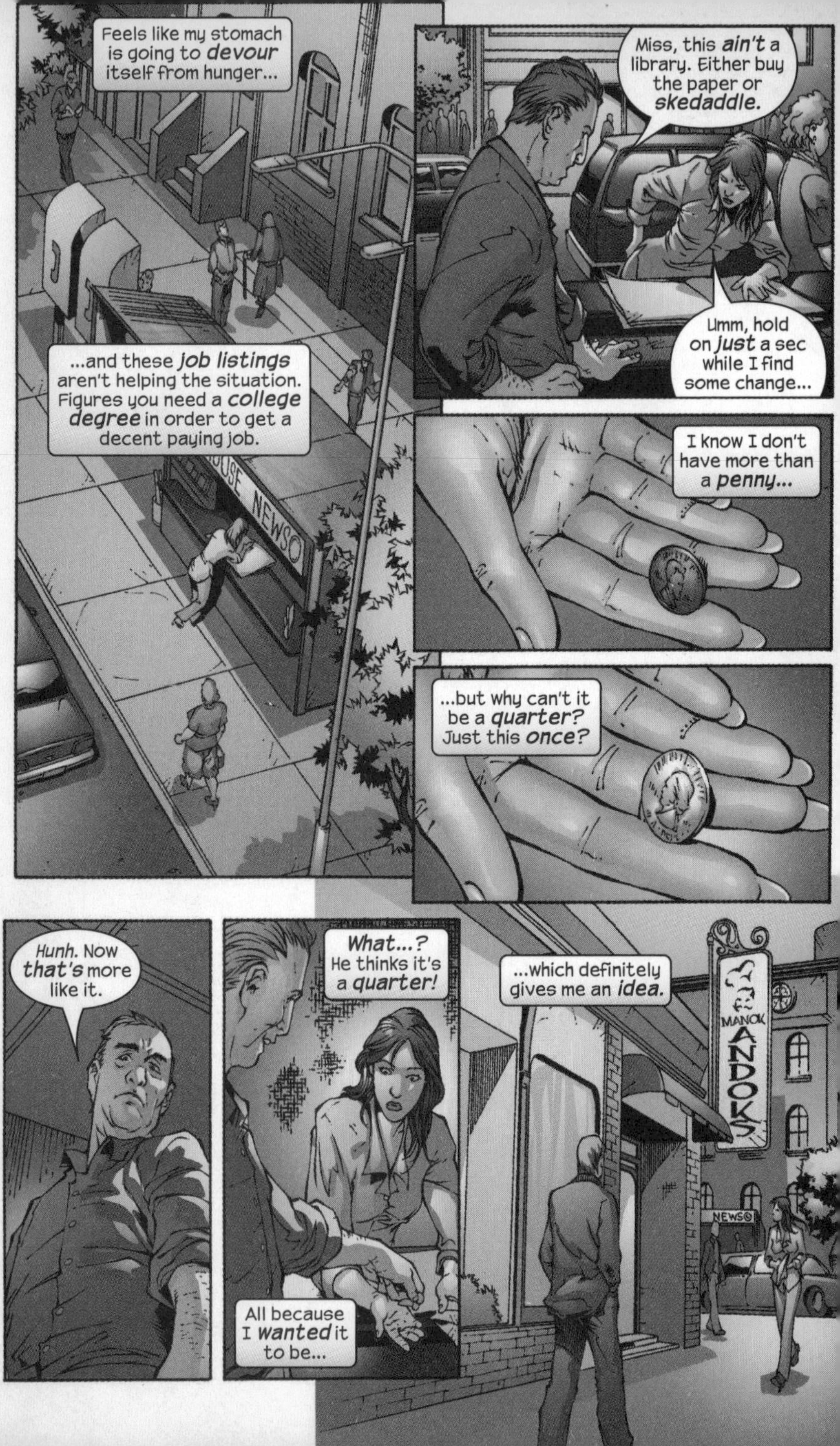

Feels like my stomach is going to devour itself from hunger...
...and these job listings aren't helping the situation. Figures you need a college degree in order to get a decent paying job.
NEWSO
Miss, this ain't a library. Either buy the paper or skedaddle.
Umm, hold on just a sec while I find some change...
I know I don't have more than a penny...
...but why can't it be a quarter? Just this once?
Hunh. Now that's more like it.
What...? He thinks it's a quarter!
All because I wanted it to be...
...which definitely gives me an idea.
MANOK
ANDOKS
NEWS

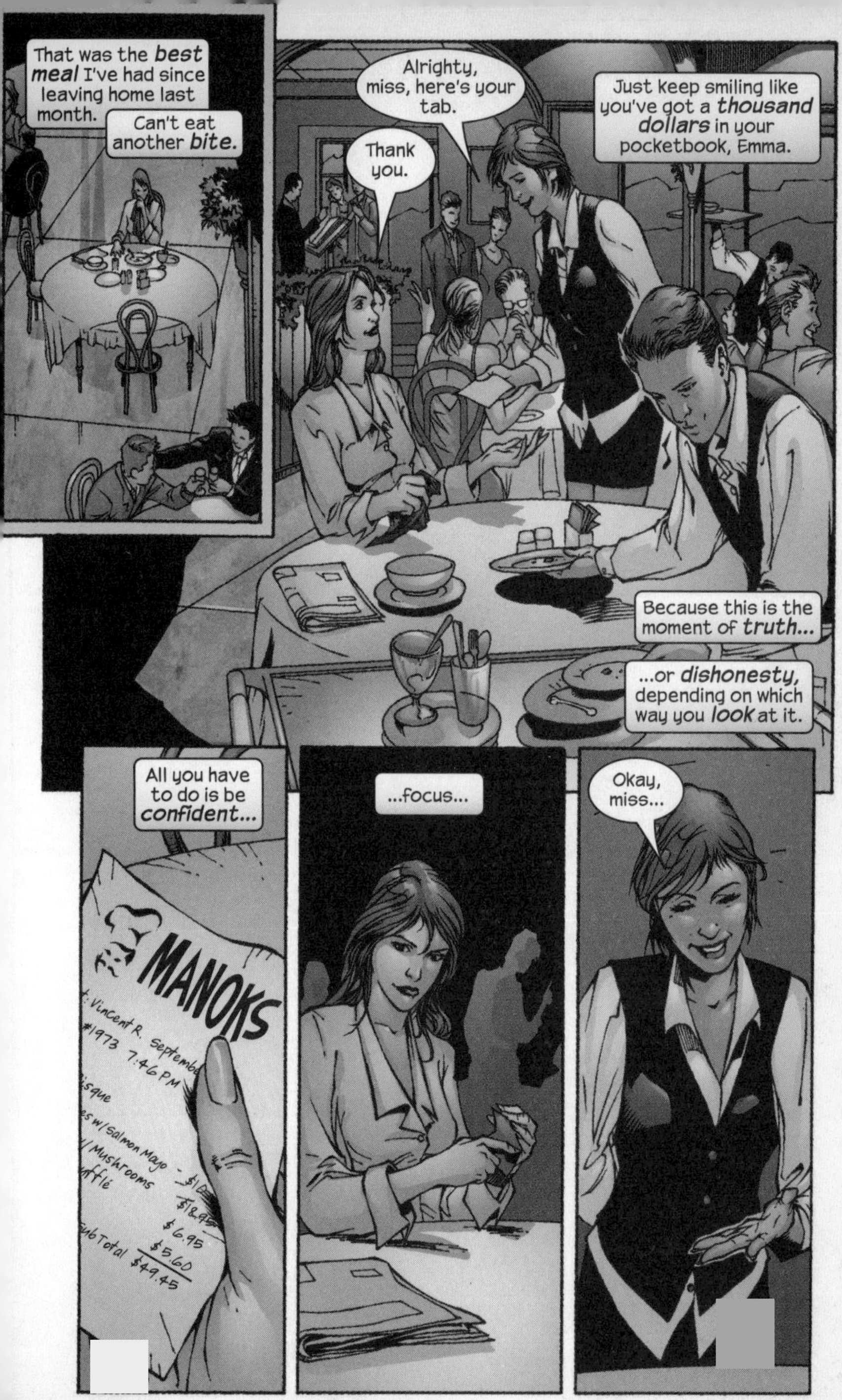
That was the best meal I've had since leaving home last month.
Can't eat another bite.
Alrighty, miss, here's your tab.
Thank you.
Just keep smiling like you've got a thousand dollars in your pocketbook, Emma.
Because this is the moment of truth...
...or dishonesty, depending on which way you look at it.
All you have to do is be confident...
MANOKS
#1973 7:46 PM
$6.95
$5.60
$49.45
...focus...
Okay, miss...

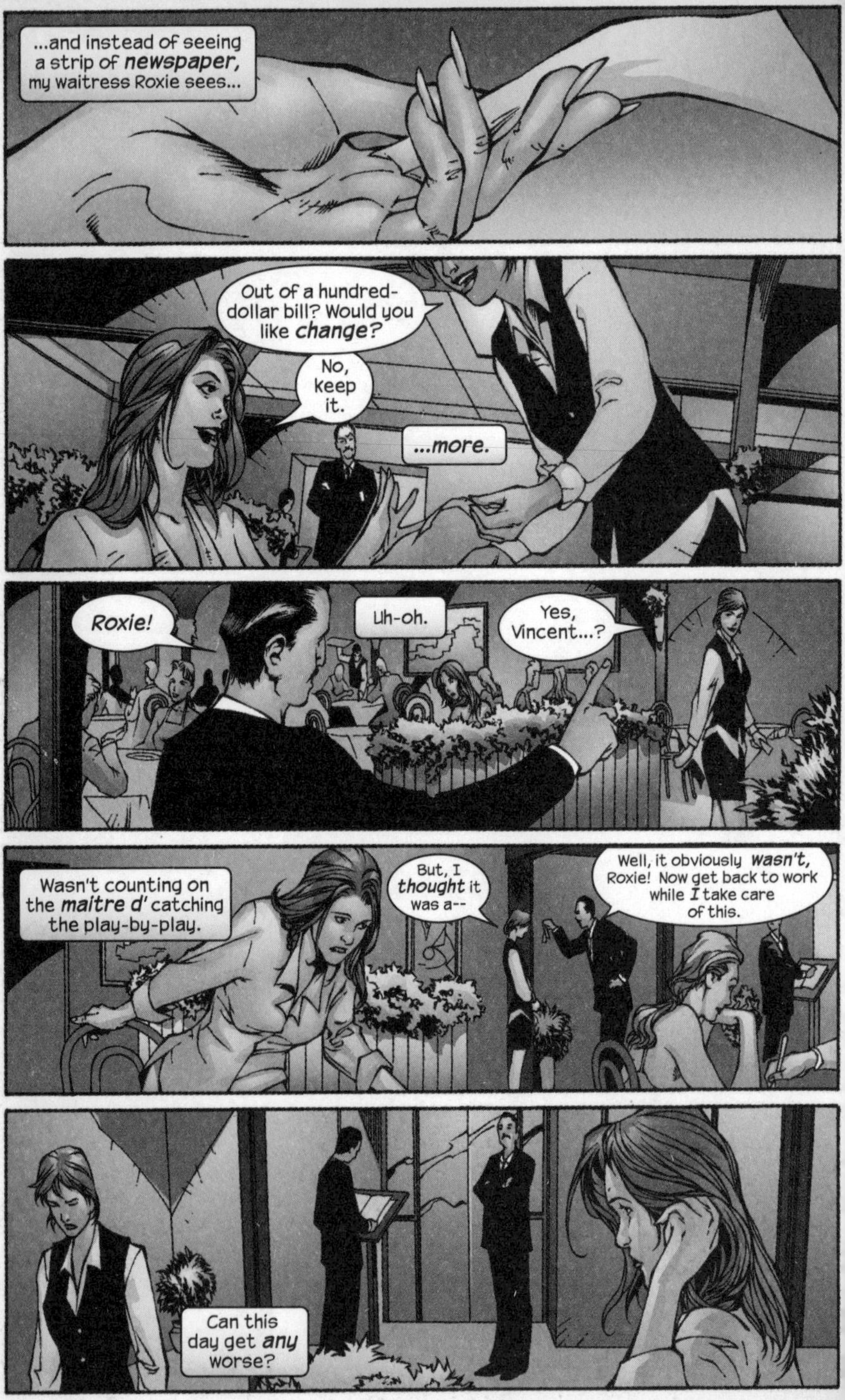

...and instead of seeing a strip of newspaper, my waitress Roxie sees...
Out of a hundred-dollar bill? Would you like change?
No, keep it.
...more.
Roxie!
Uh-oh.
Yes, Vincent...?
Wasn't counting on the maitre d' catching the play-by-play.
But, I thought it was a--
Well, it obviously wasn't, Roxie! Now get back to work while I take care of this.
Can this day get any worse?

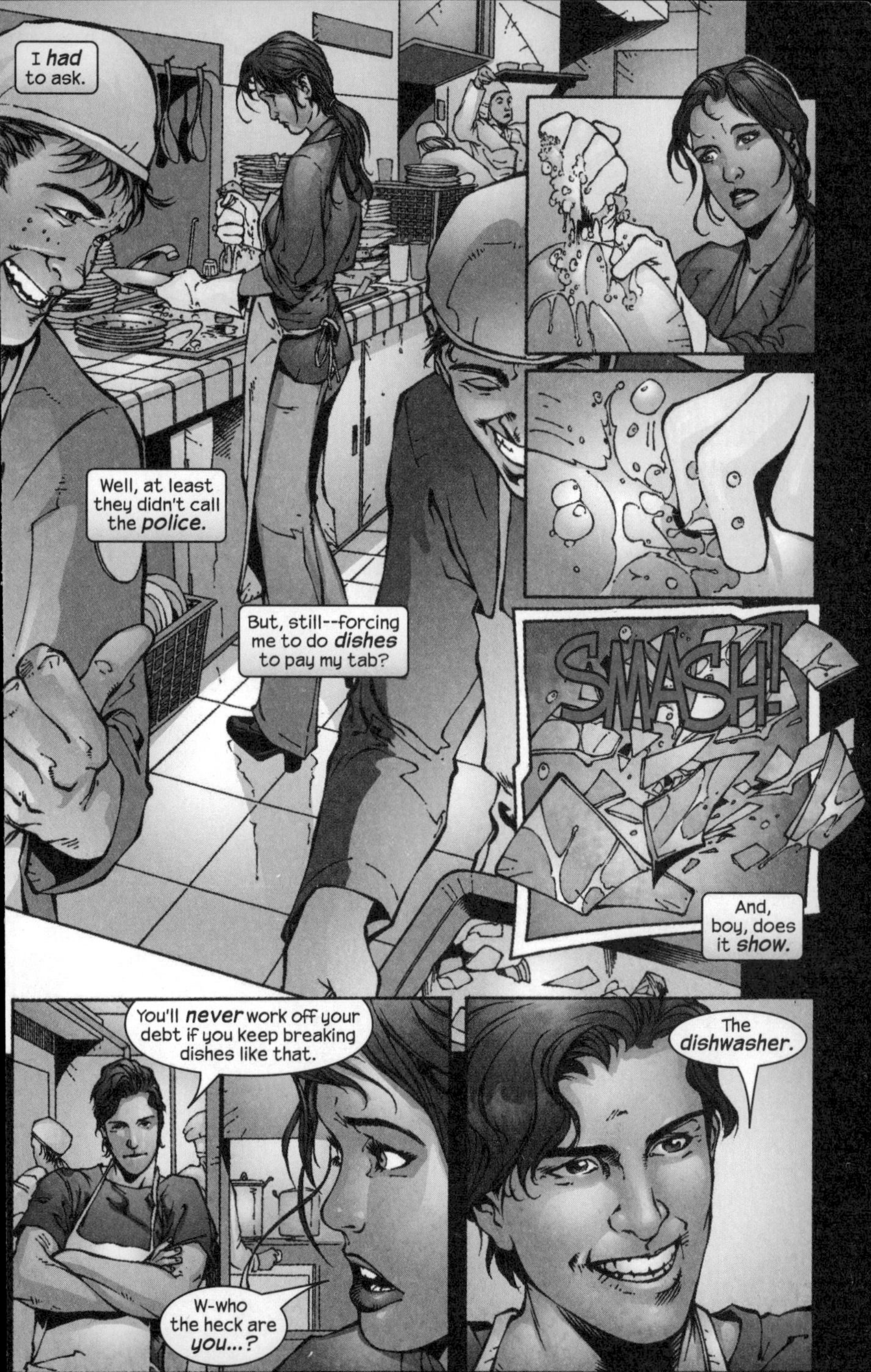
I had to ask.
Well, at least they didn't call the police.
But, still--forcing me to do dishes to pay my tab?
SMASH!
And, boy, does it show.
You'll never work off your debt if you keep breaking dishes like that.
W-who the heck are you...?
The dishwasher.

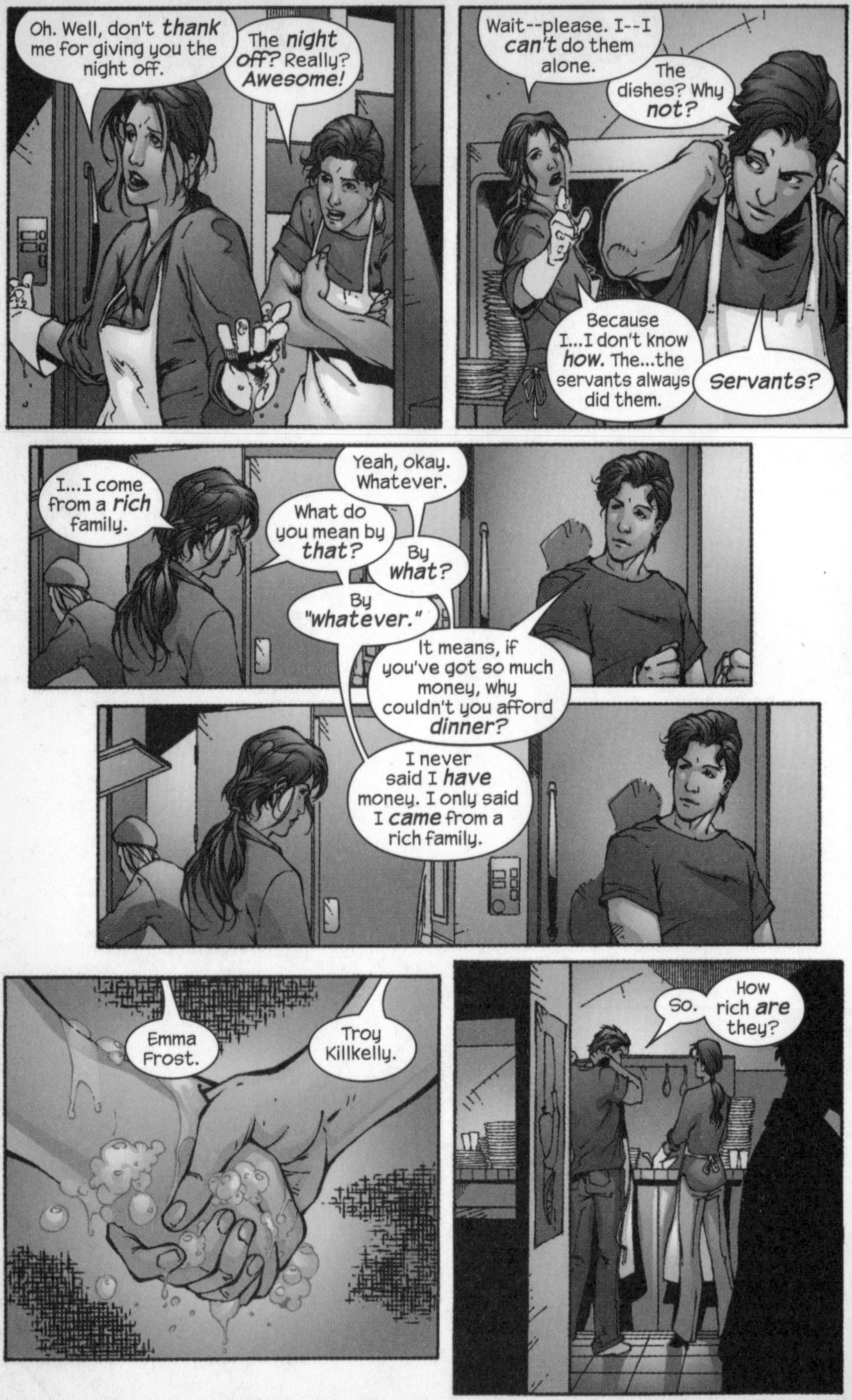
Oh. Well, don't *thank* me for giving you the night off.
The *night off?* Really? *Awesome!*
Wait--please. I--I *can't* do them alone.
The dishes? Why *not?*
Because I...I don't know *how.* The...the servants always did them.
Servants?
I...I come from a *rich* family.
Yeah, okay. Whatever.
What do you mean by *that?*
By *what?*
By *"whatever."*
It means, if you've got so much money, why couldn't you afford *dinner?*
I never said I *have* money. I only said I *came* from a rich family.
Emma Frost.
Troy Killkelly.
So.
How rich *are* they?

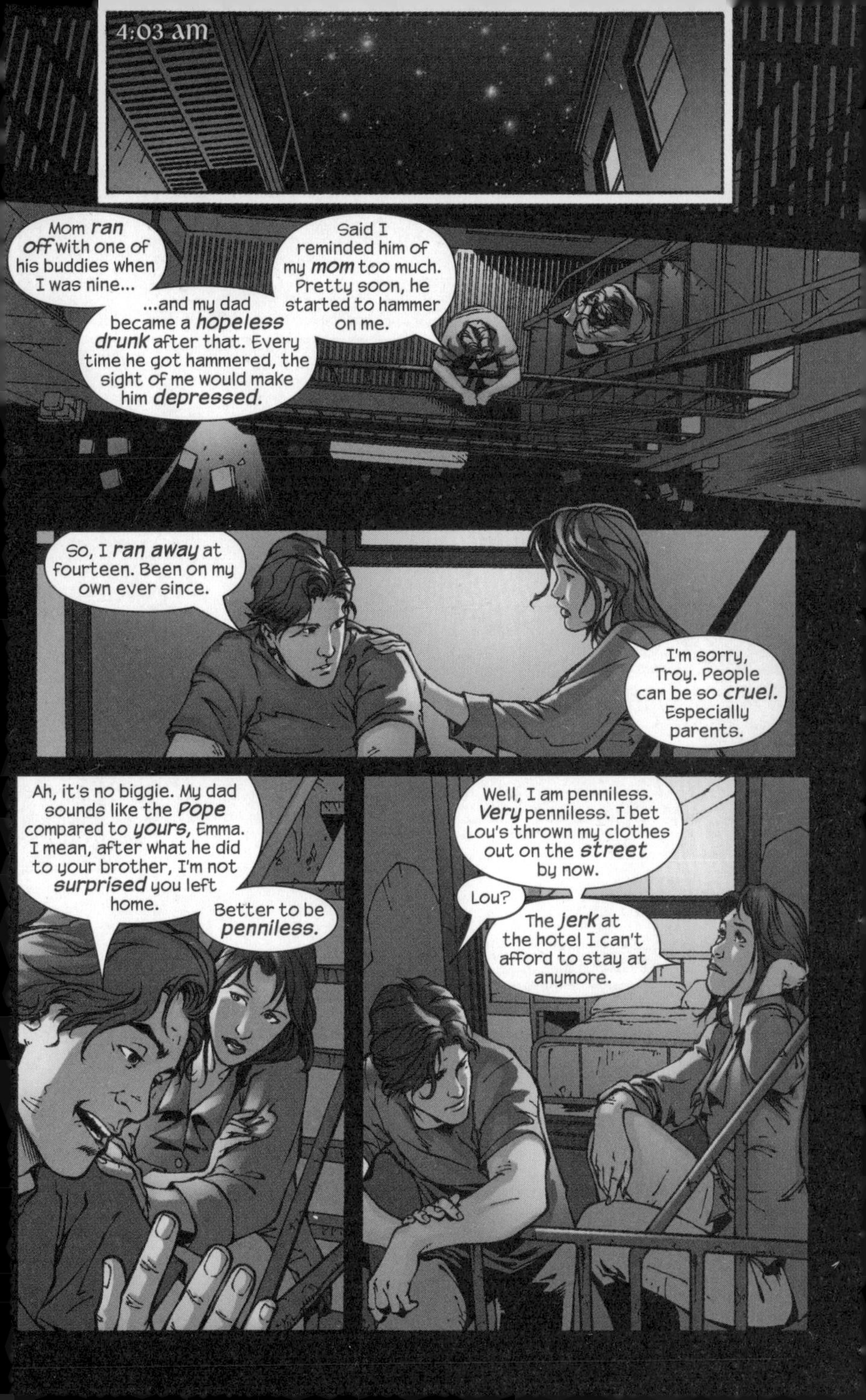
4:03 AM
Mom ran off with one of his buddies when I was nine...
...and my dad became a hopeless drunk after that. Every time he got hammered, the sight of me would make him depressed.
Said I reminded him of my mom too much. Pretty soon, he started to hammer on me.
So, I ran away at fourteen. Been on my own ever since.
I'm sorry, Troy. People can be so cruel. Especially parents.
Ah, it's no biggie. My dad sounds like the Pope compared to yours, Emma. I mean, after what he did to your brother, I'm not surprised you left home.
Better to be penniless.
Well, I am penniless. Very penniless. I bet Lou's thrown my clothes out on the street by now.
Lou?
The jerk at the hotel I can't afford to stay at anymore.

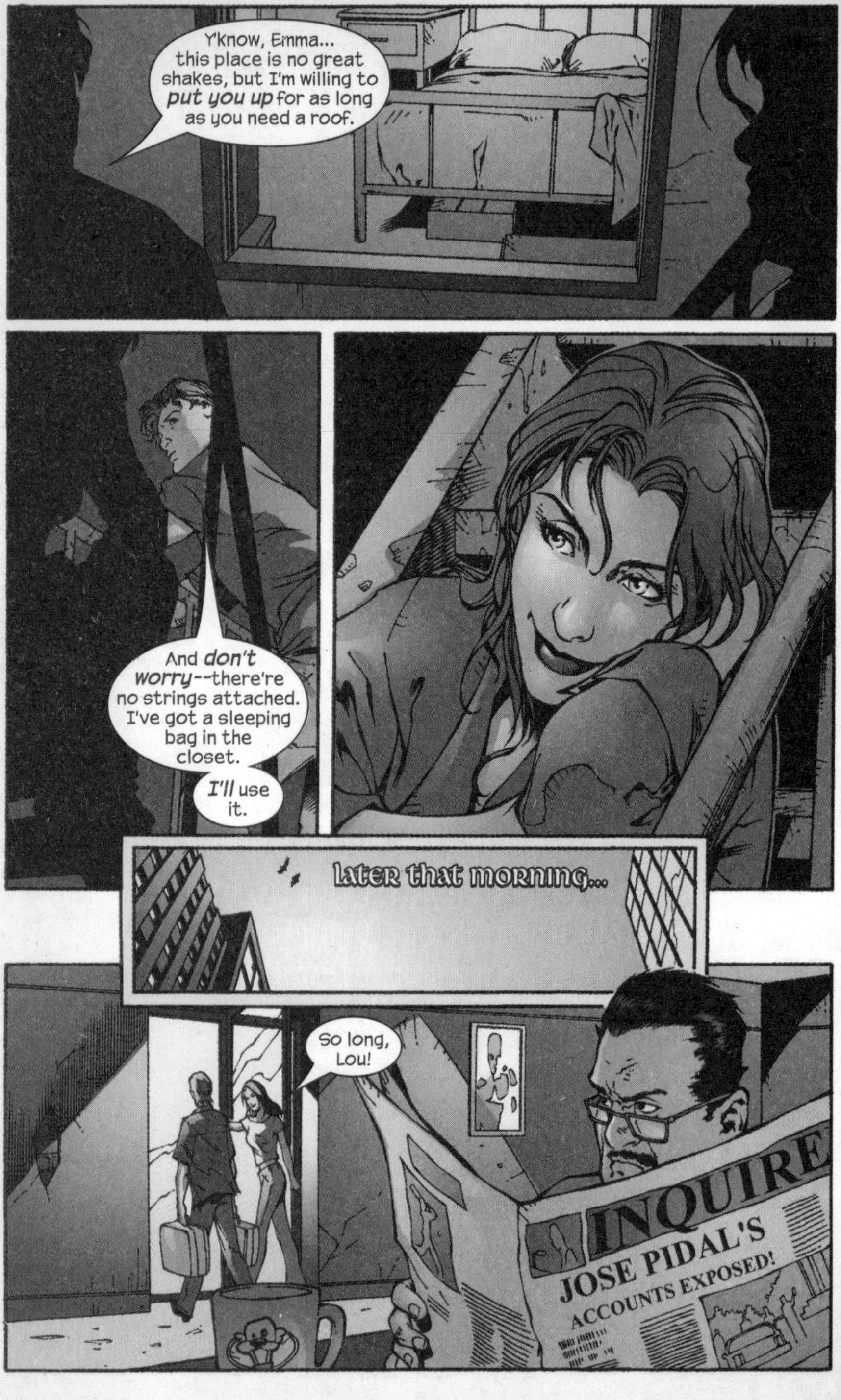
Y'know, Emma... this place is no great shakes, but I'm willing to *put you up* for as long as you need a roof.
And *don't worry*--there're no strings attached. I've got a sleeping bag in the closet.
I'll use it.
later that morning...
So long, Lou!
INQUIRE
JOSE PIDAL'S ACCOUNTS EXPOSED!

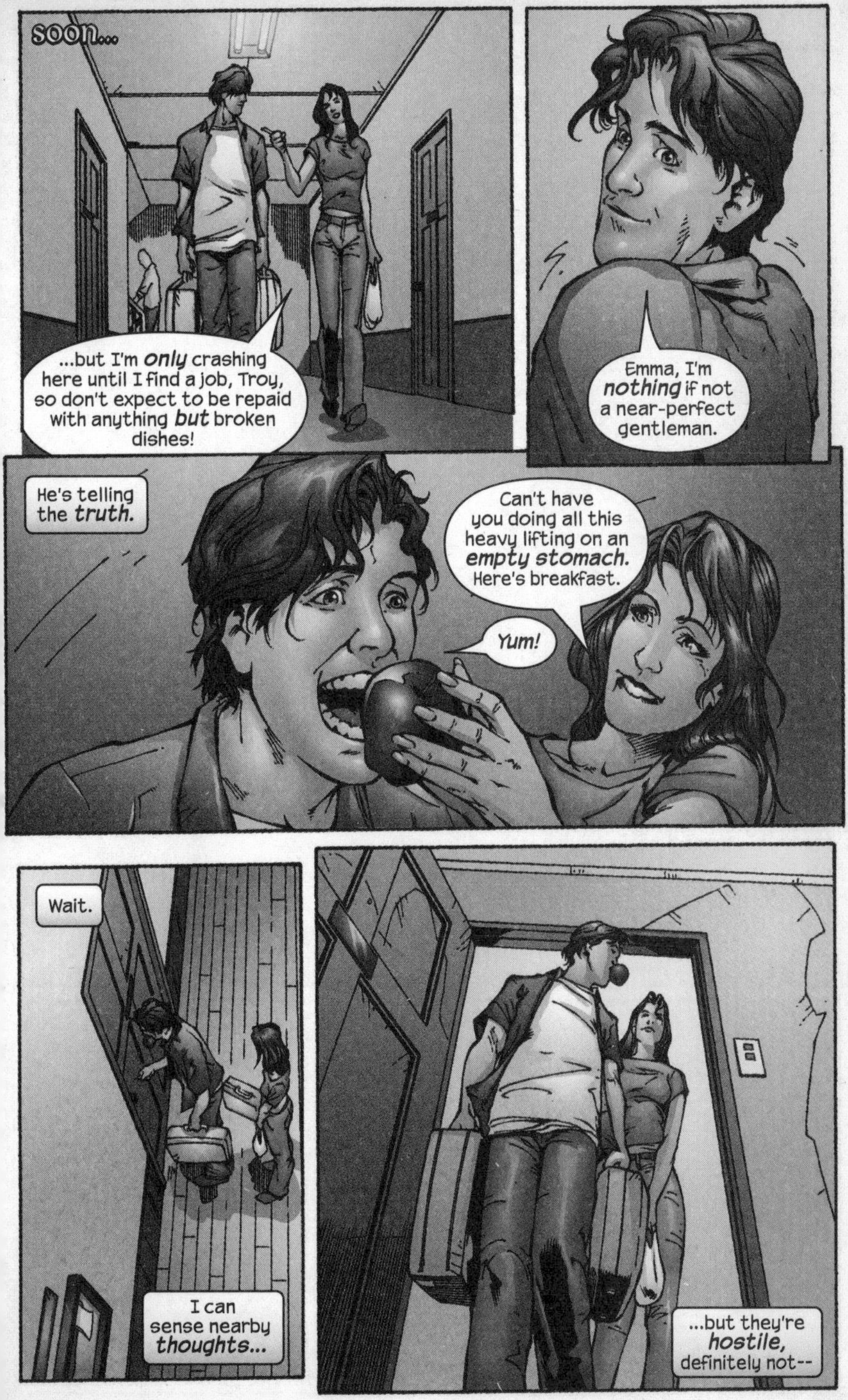
soon...
...but I'm *only* crashing here until I find a job, Troy, so don't expect to be repaid with anything *but* broken dishes!
Emma, I'm *nothing* if not a near-perfect gentleman.
He's telling the *truth.*
Can't have you doing all this heavy lifting on an *empty stomach.* Here's breakfast.
Yum!
Wait.
I can sense nearby *thoughts...*
...but they're *hostile,* definitely not--

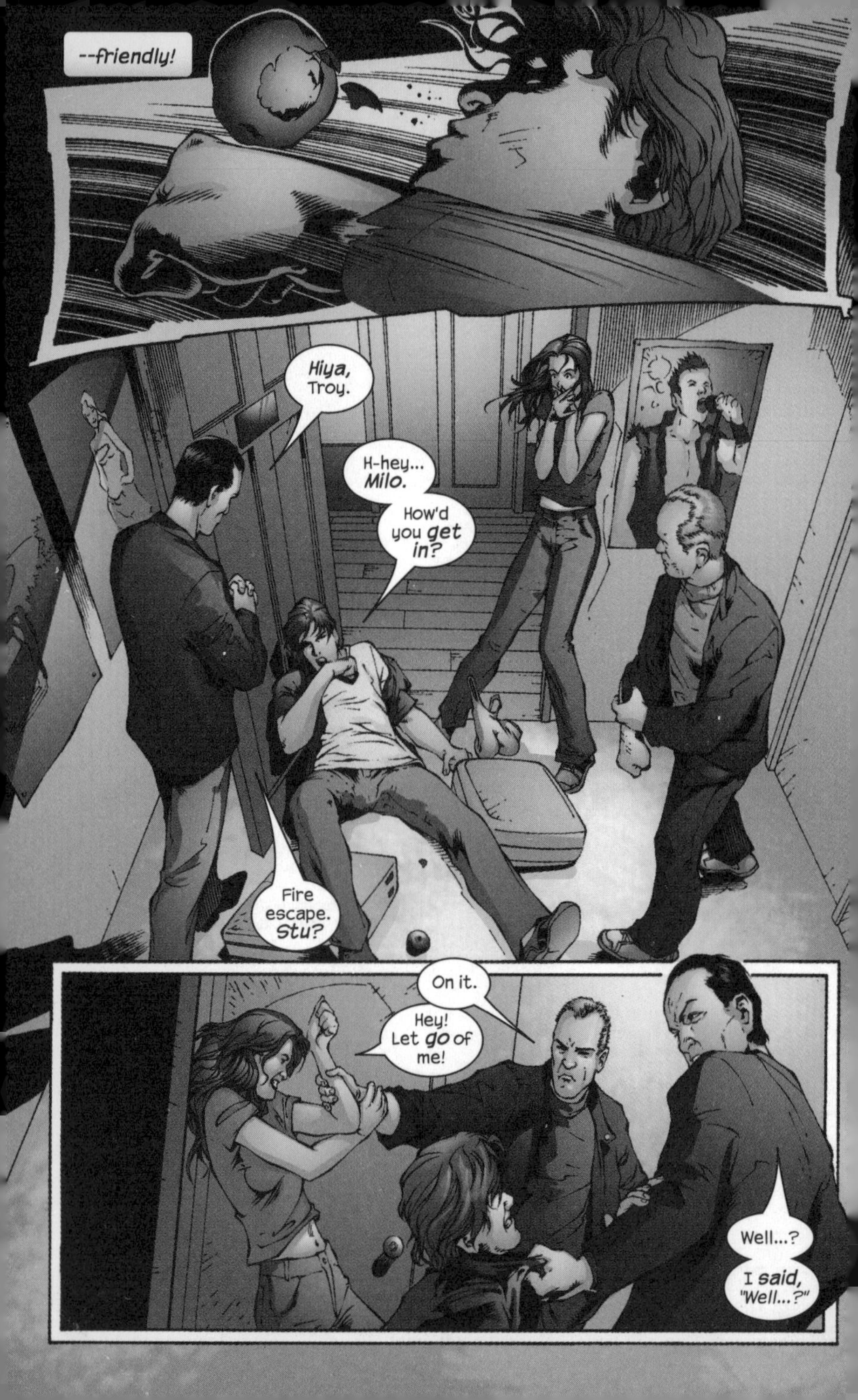
--friendly!
Hiya, Troy.
H-hey... Milo.
How'd you get in?
Fire escape. Stu?
On it.
Hey! Let go of me!
Well...?
I said, "Well...?"

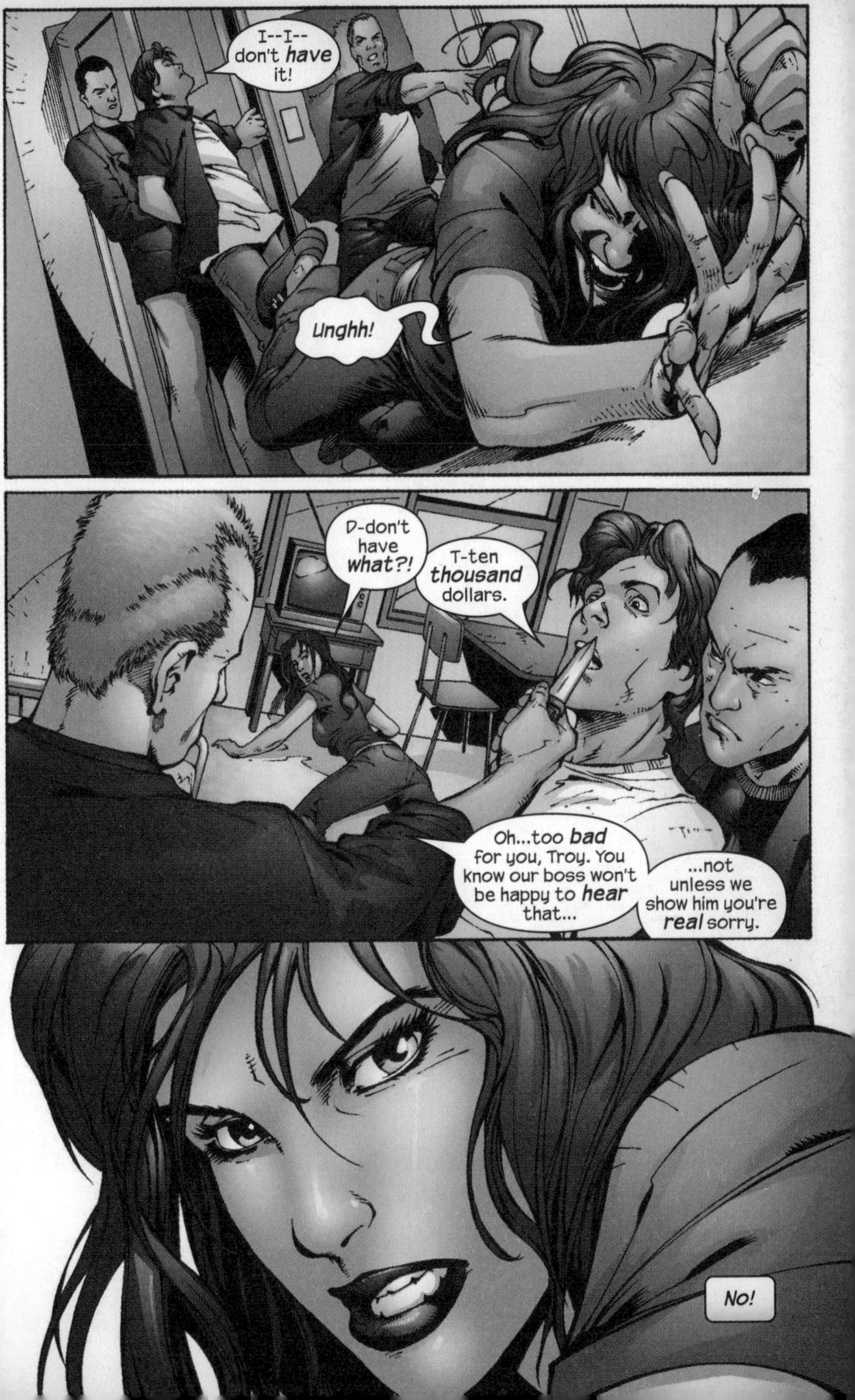

I--I-- don't *have* it!
Unghh!
D-don't have *what?!*
T-ten *thousand* dollars.
Oh...too *bad* for you, Troy. You know our boss won't be happy to *hear* that...
...not unless we show him you're *real* sorry.
No!

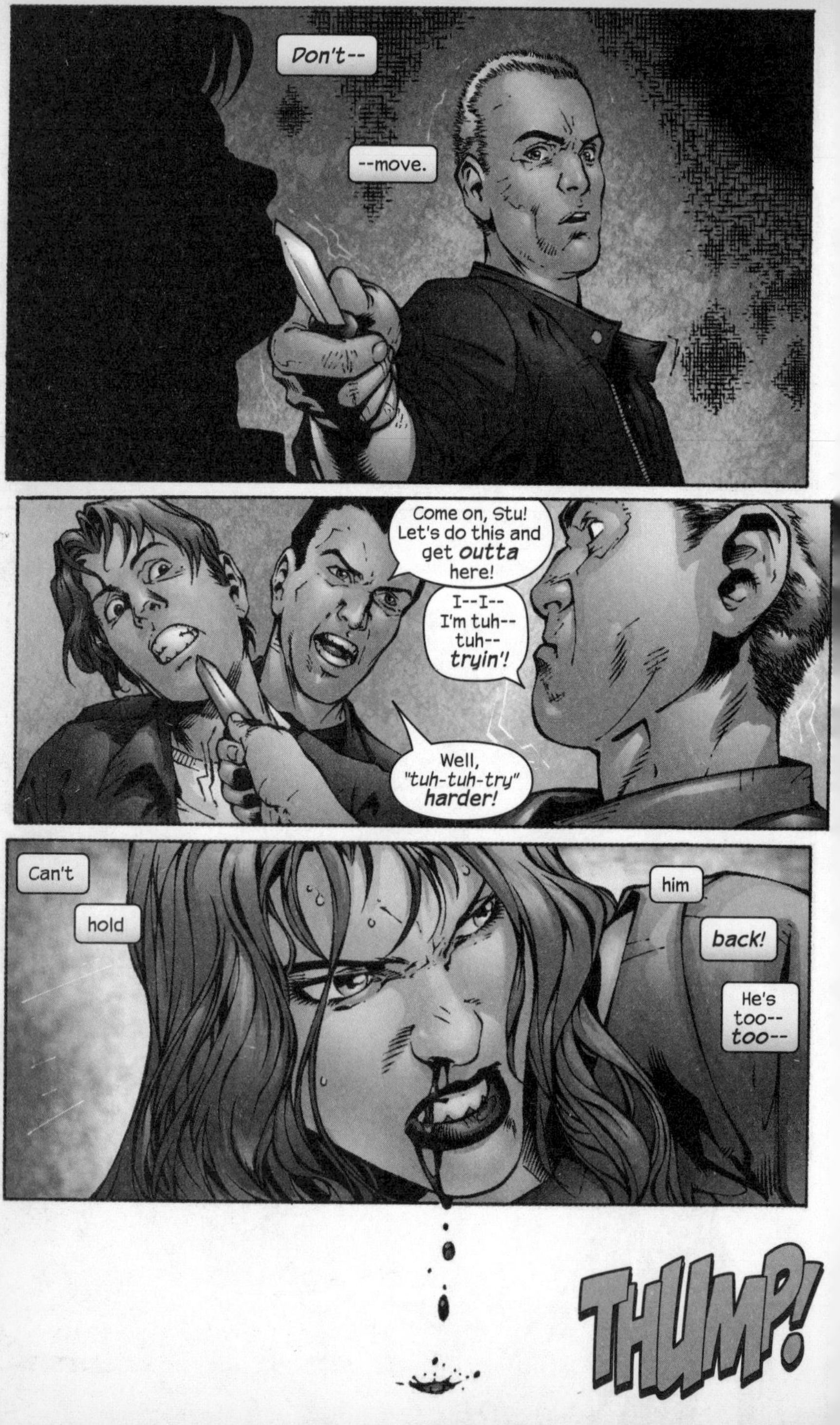
Don't--
--move.
Come on, Stu! Let's do this and get *outta* here!
I--I-- I'm tuh-- tuh-- tuh-- *tryin'*!
Well, "tuh-tuh-try" **harder**!
Can't
hold
him
back!
He's too-- *too--*
THUMP!

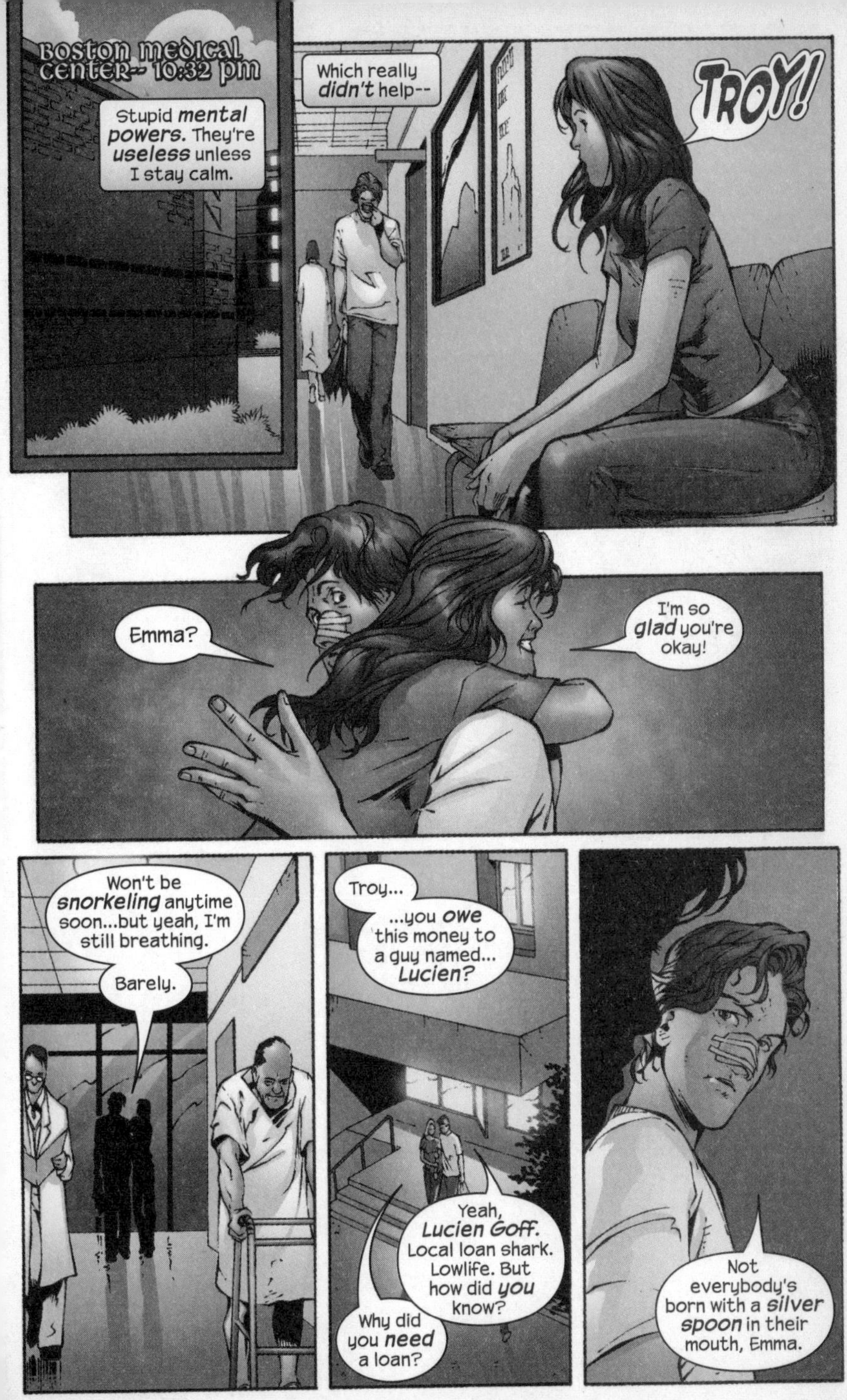
Boston Medical Center-- 10:32 pm
Stupid mental powers. They're useless unless I stay calm.
Which really didn't help--
TROY!
Emma?
I'm so glad you're okay!
Won't be snorkeling anytime soon...but yeah, I'm still breathing.
Barely.
Troy...
...you owe this money to a guy named... Lucien?
Yeah, Lucien Goff. Local loan shark. Lowlife. But how did you know?
Why did you need a loan?
Not everybody's born with a silver spoon in their mouth, Emma.

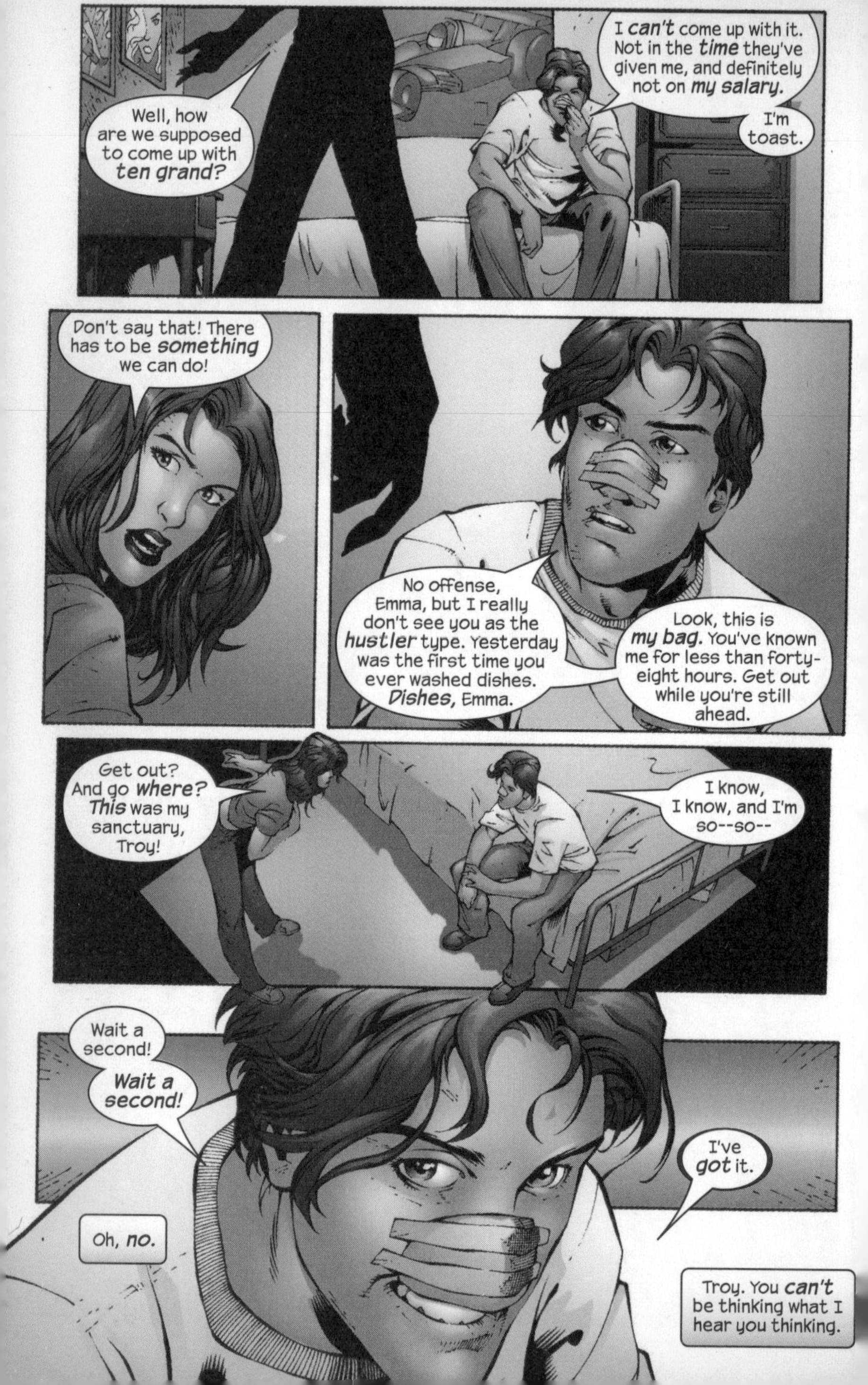
Well, how are we supposed to come up with ten grand?
I can't come up with it. Not in the time they've given me, and definitely not on my salary.
I'm toast.
Don't say that! There has to be something we can do!
No offense, Emma, but I really don't see you as the hustler type. Yesterday was the first time you ever washed dishes. Dishes, Emma.
Look, this is my bag. You've known me for less than forty-eight hours. Get out while you're still ahead.
Get out? And go where? This was my sanctuary, Troy!
I know, I know, and I'm so--so--
Wait a second!
Wait a second!
I've got it.
Oh, no.
Troy. You can't be thinking what I hear you thinking.

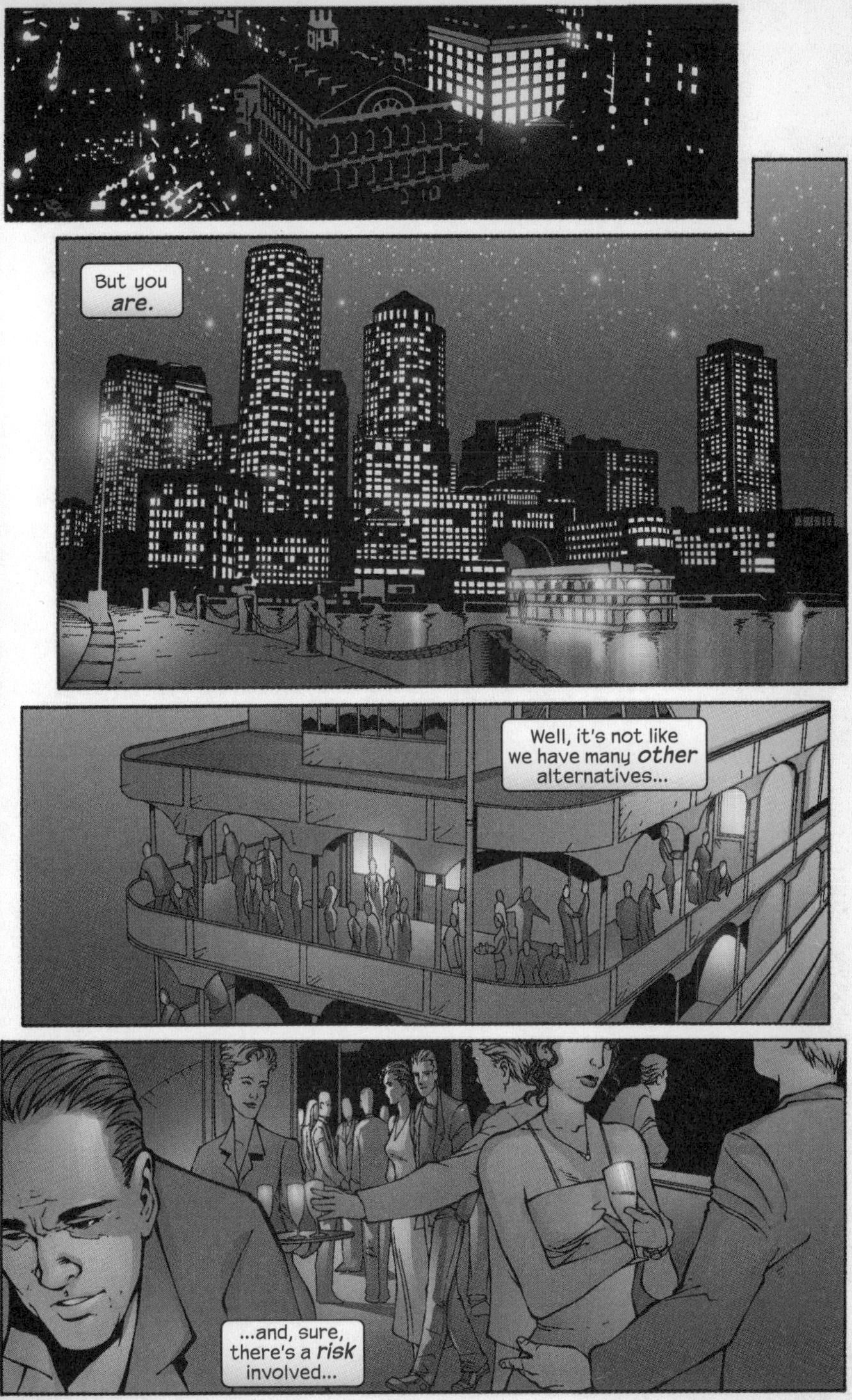
But you *are.*
Well, it's not like we have many *other* alternatives...
...and, sure, there's a *risk* involved...

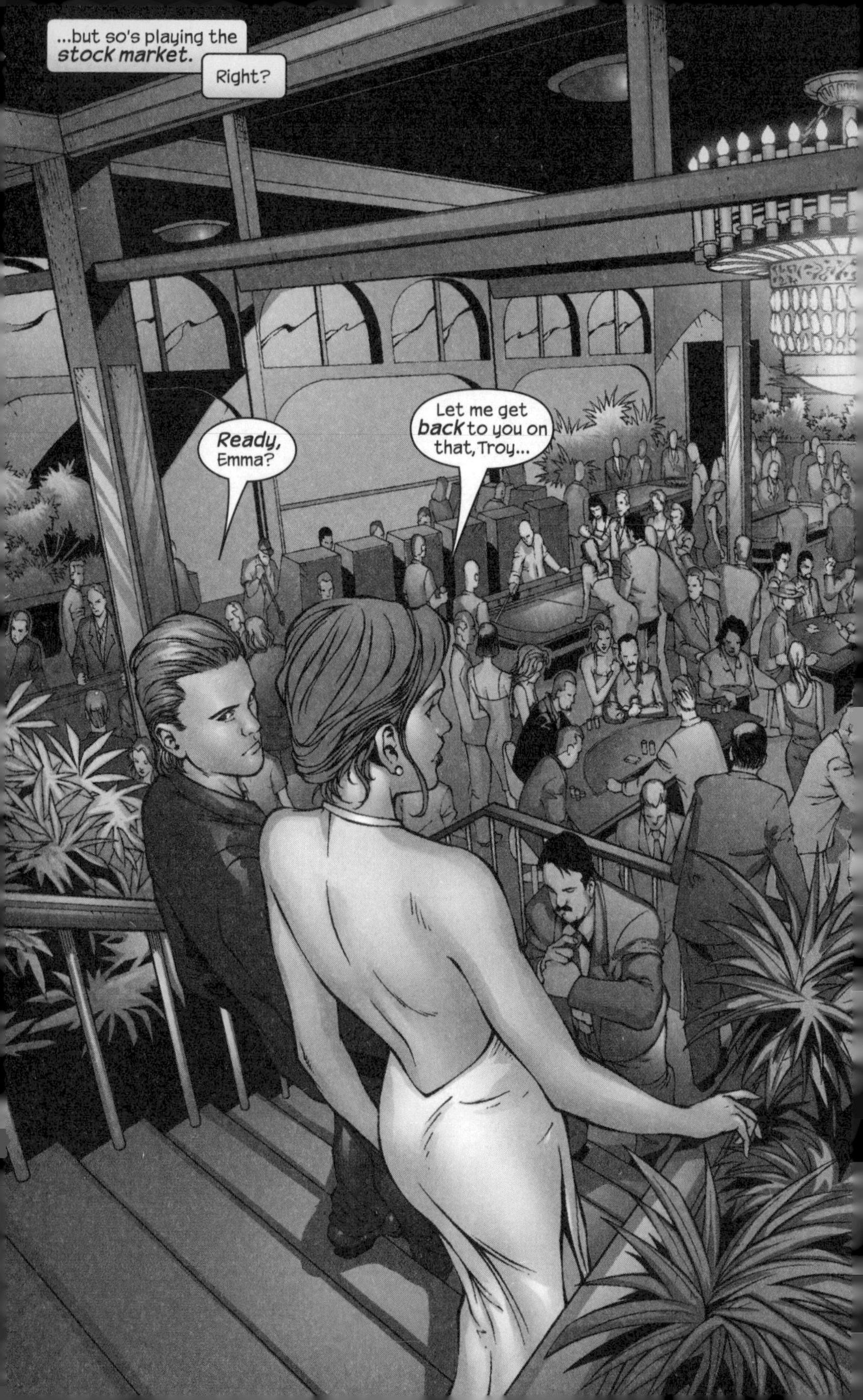

...but so's playing the *stock market.*
Right?
Ready, Emma?
Let me get *back* to you on that, Troy...

MIND GAMES 2 of 6

[redacted]UCK BE A [redacted]ADY

All right, gentlemen...

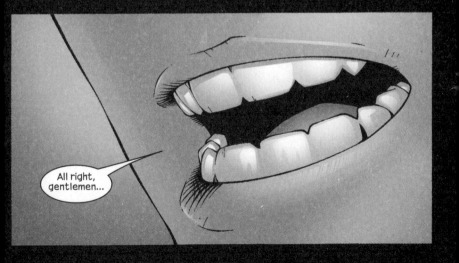

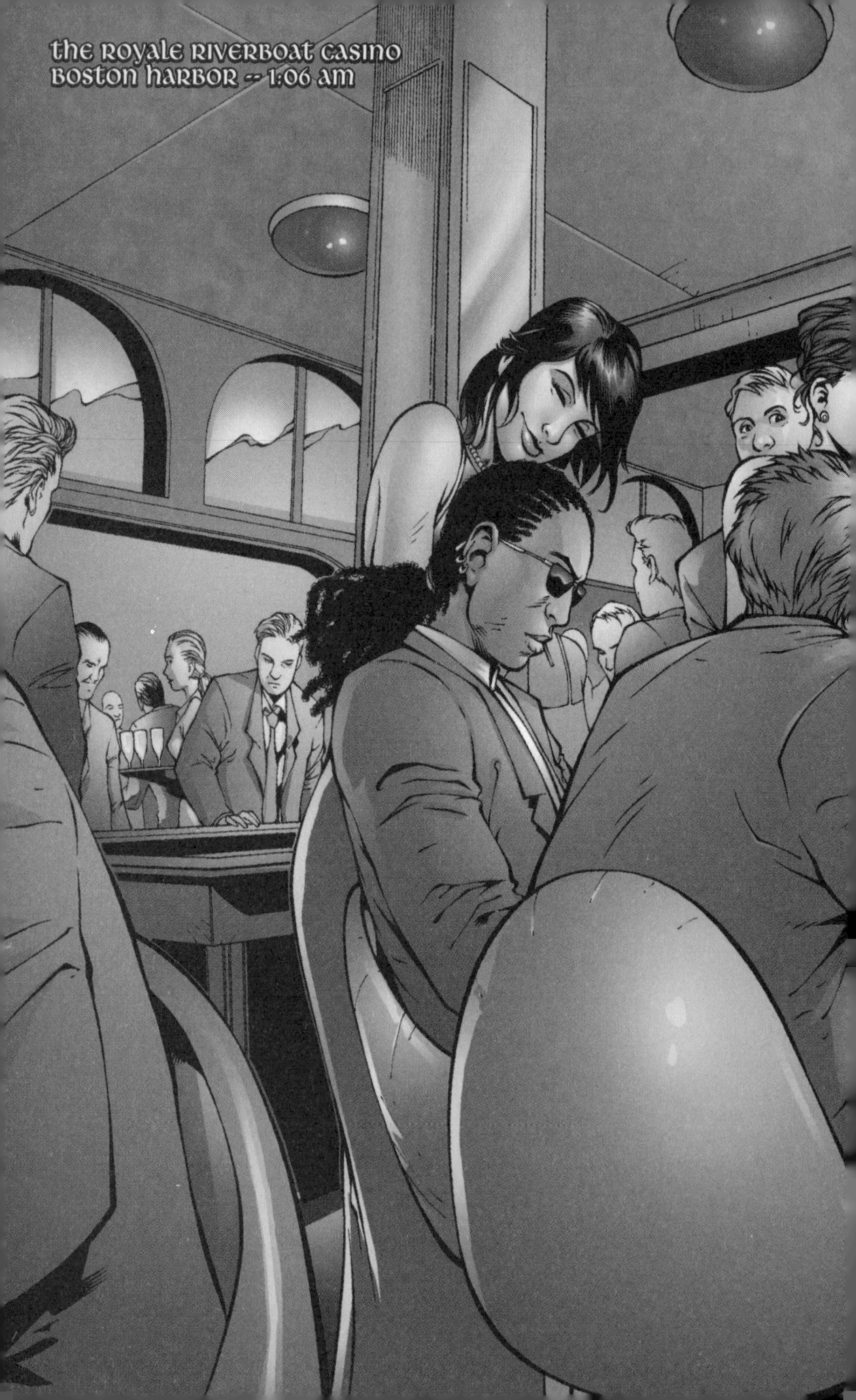
THE ROYALE RIVERBOAT CASINO
BOSTON HARBOR -- 1:06 AM

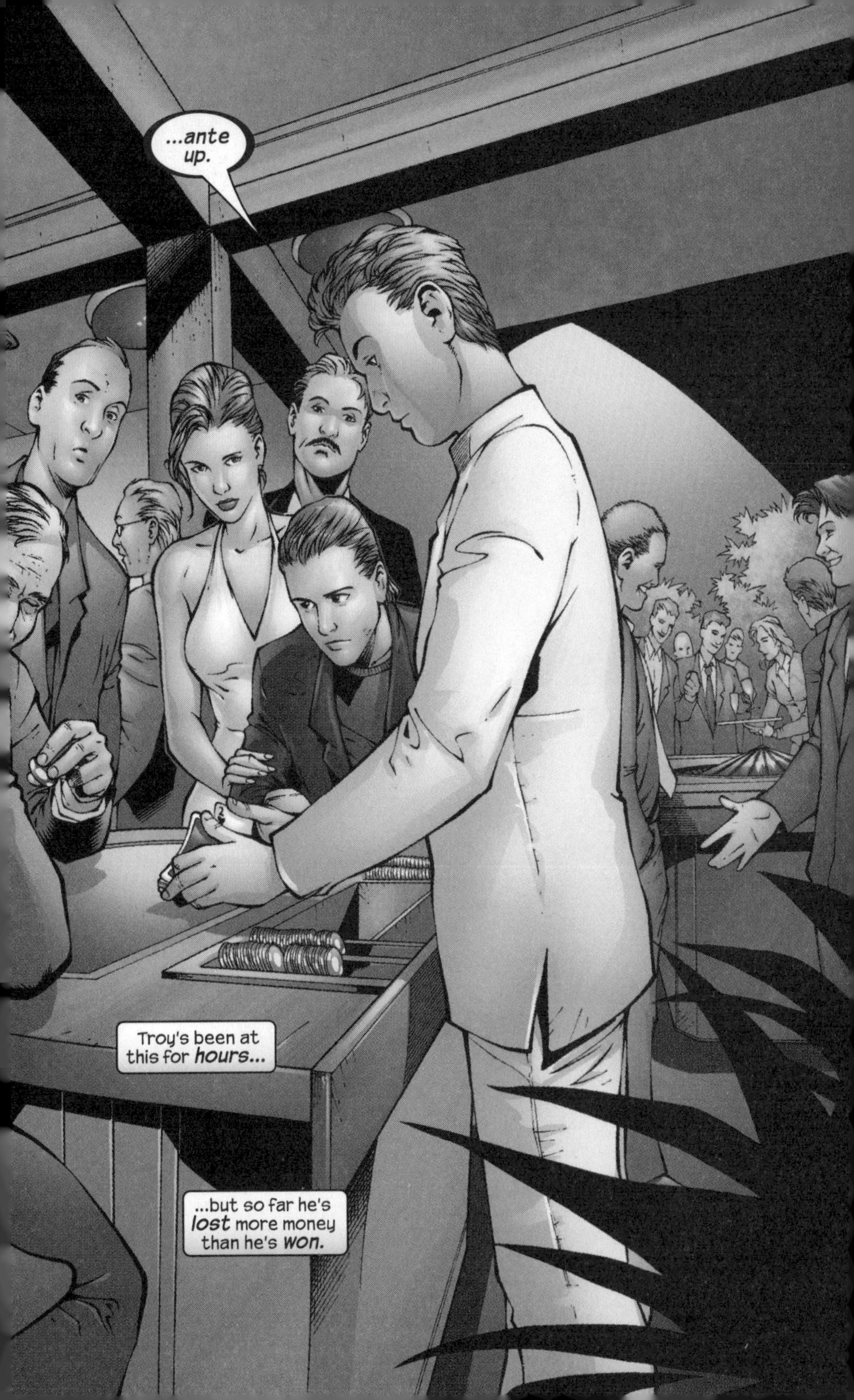
...ante up.
Troy's been at this for *hours*...
...but so far he's *lost* more money than he's *won*.

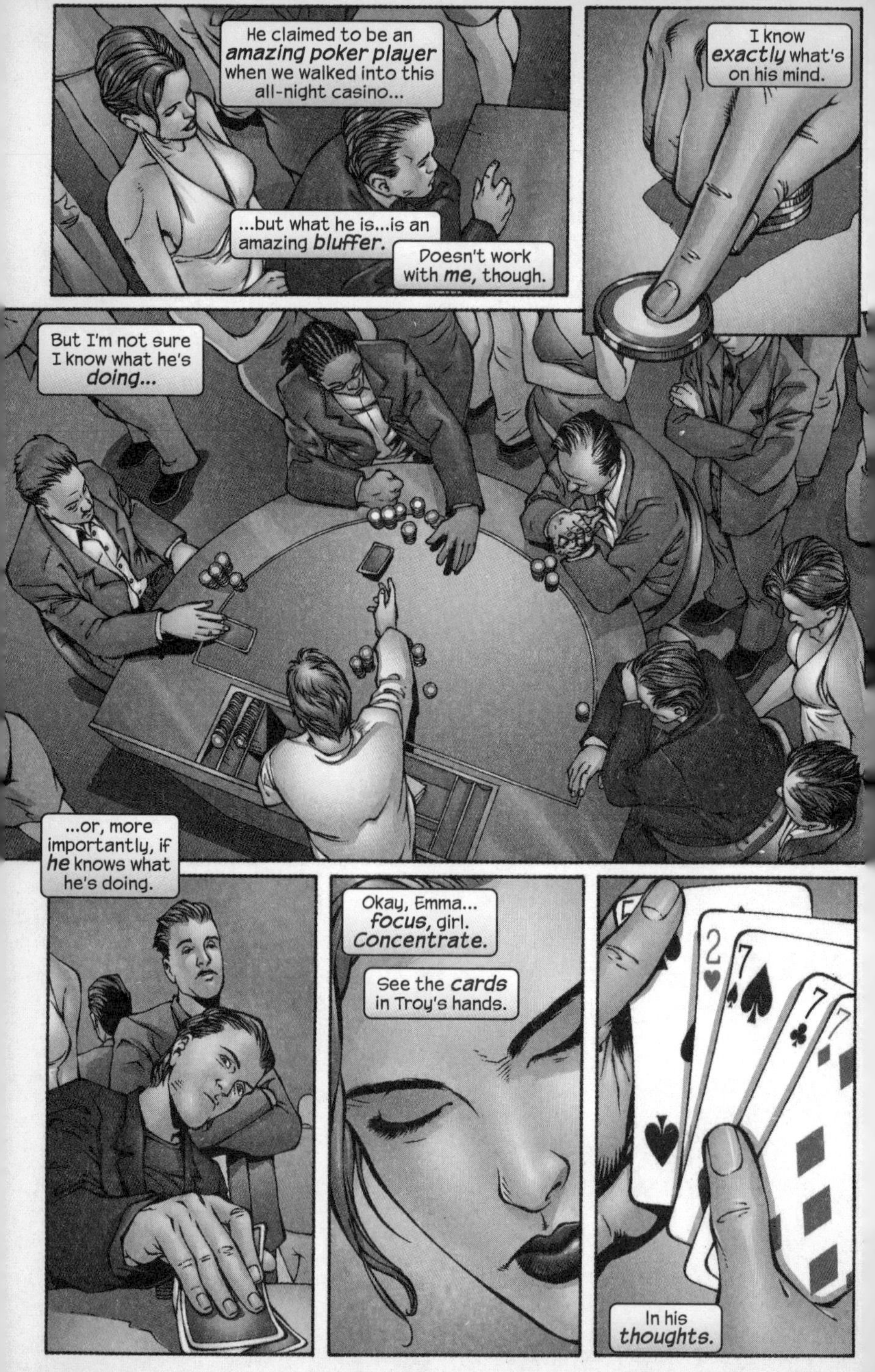
He claimed to be an amazing poker player when we walked into this all-night casino...
...but what he is...is an amazing bluffer.
Doesn't work with me, though.
I know exactly what's on his mind.
But I'm not sure I know what he's doing...
...or, more importantly, if he knows what he's doing.
Okay, Emma... focus, girl. Concentrate.
See the cards in Troy's hands.
In his thoughts.

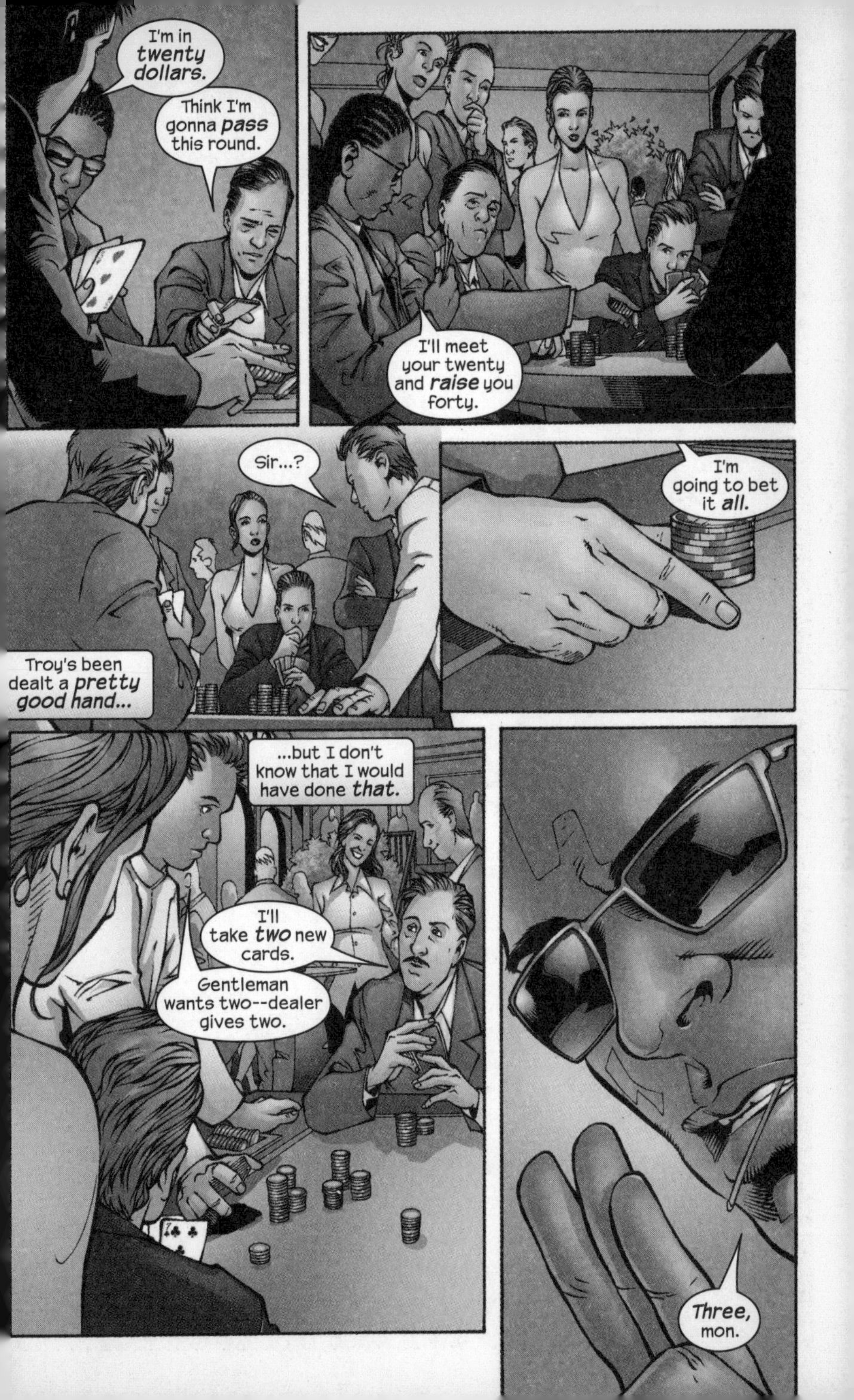
I'm in twenty dollars.
Think I'm gonna pass this round.
I'll meet your twenty and raise you forty.
Sir...?
I'm going to bet it all.
Troy's been dealt a pretty good hand...
...but I don't know that I would have done that.
I'll take two new cards.
Gentleman wants two--dealer gives two.
Three, mon.

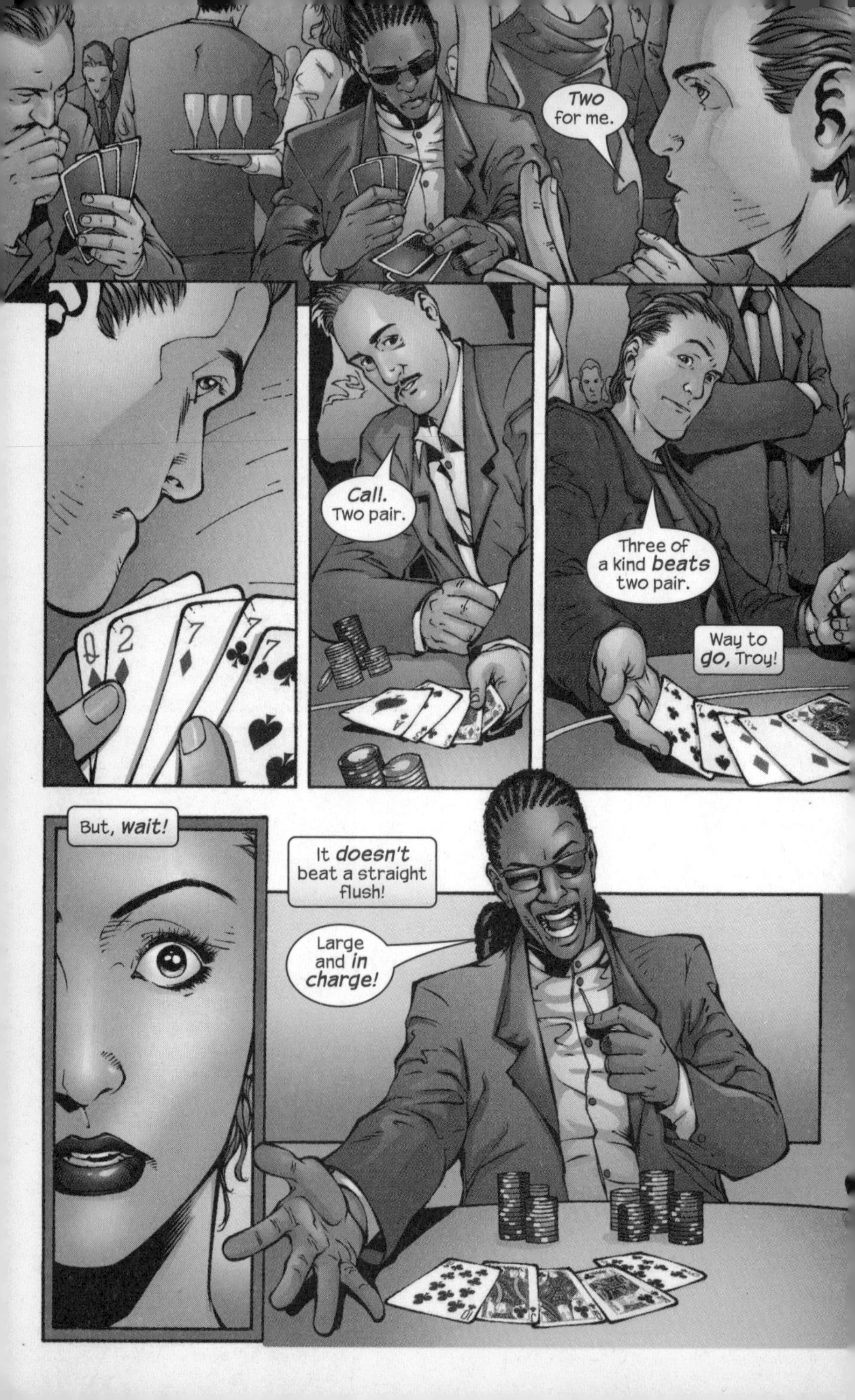
Two for me.
Call. Two pair.
Three of a kind beats two pair.
Way to go, Troy!
But, wait!
It doesn't beat a straight flush!
Large and in charge!

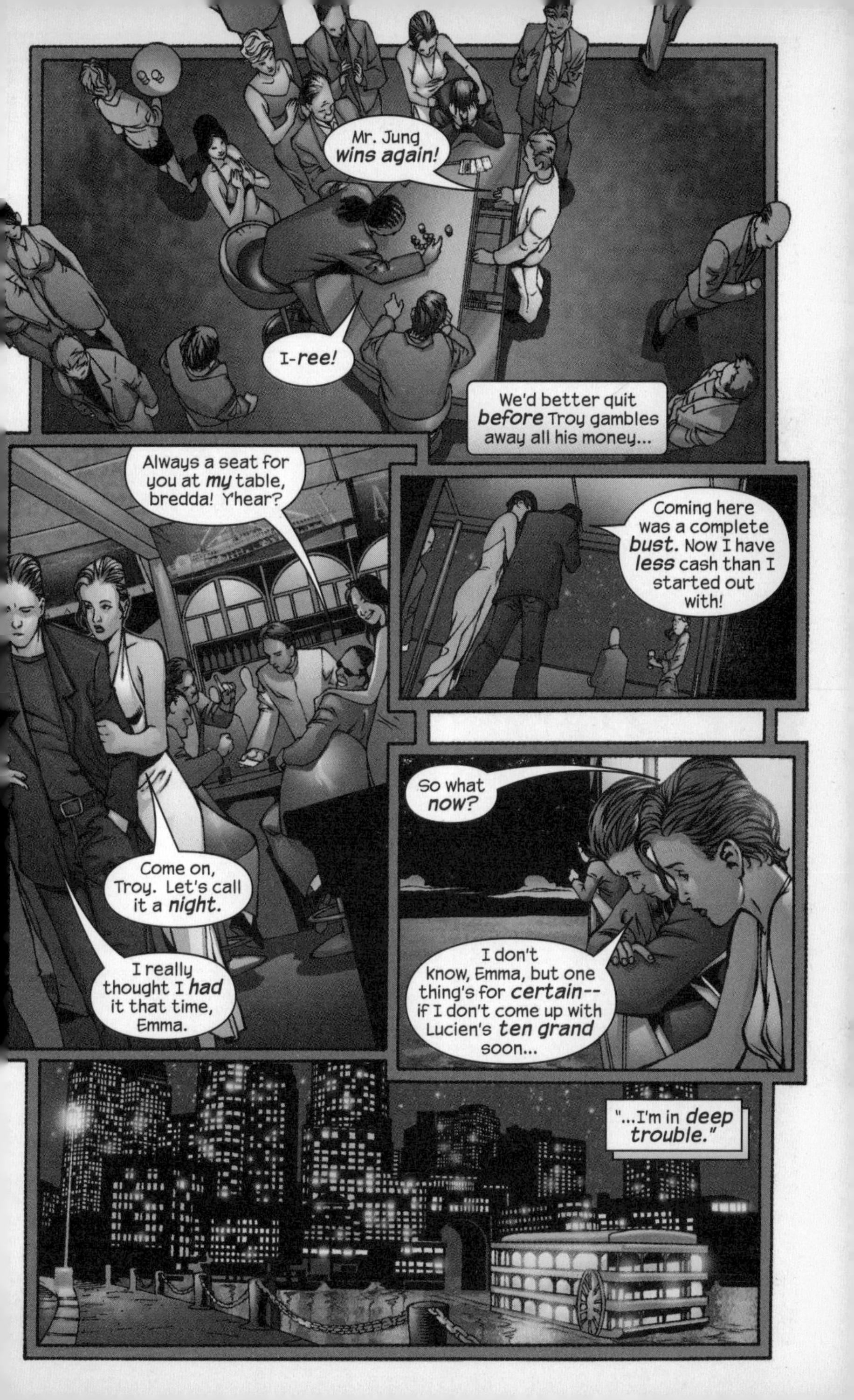

Mr. Jung wins again!
I-ree!
We'd better quit before Troy gambles away all his money...
Always a seat for you at my table, bredda! Y'hear?
Come on, Troy. Let's call it a night.
I really thought I had it that time, Emma.
Coming here was a complete bust. Now I have less cash than I started out with!
So what now?
I don't know, Emma, but one thing's for certain-- if I don't come up with Lucien's ten grand soon...
"...I'm in deep trouble."

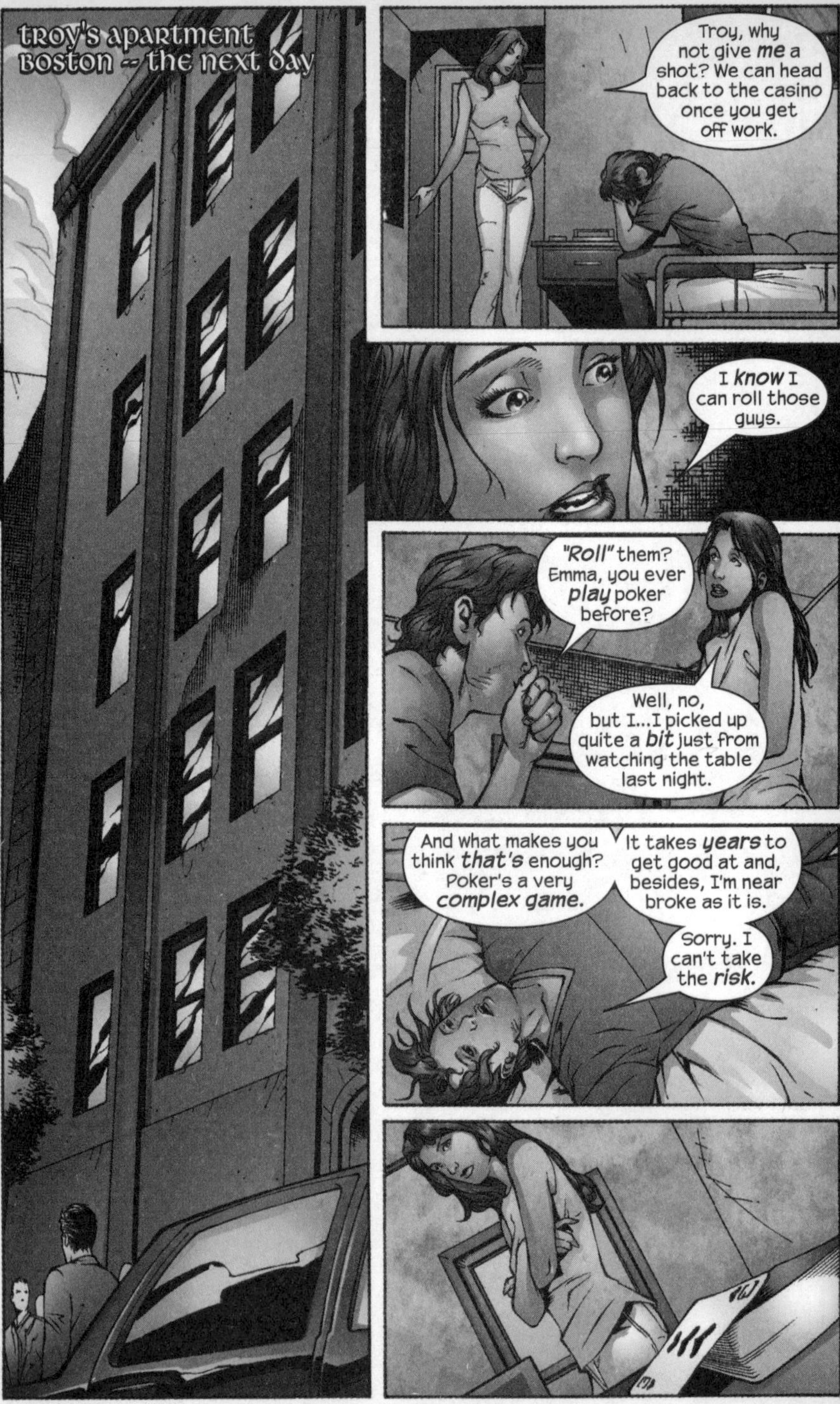
troy's apartment
boston -- the next day
Troy, why not give *me* a shot? We can head back to the casino once you get off work.
I *know* I can roll those guys.
"*Roll*" them? Emma, you ever *play* poker before?
Well, no, but I...I picked up quite a *bit* just from watching the table last night.
And what makes you think *that's* enough? Poker's a very *complex game.*
It takes *years* to get good at and, besides, I'm near broke as it is.
Sorry. I can't take the *risk.*

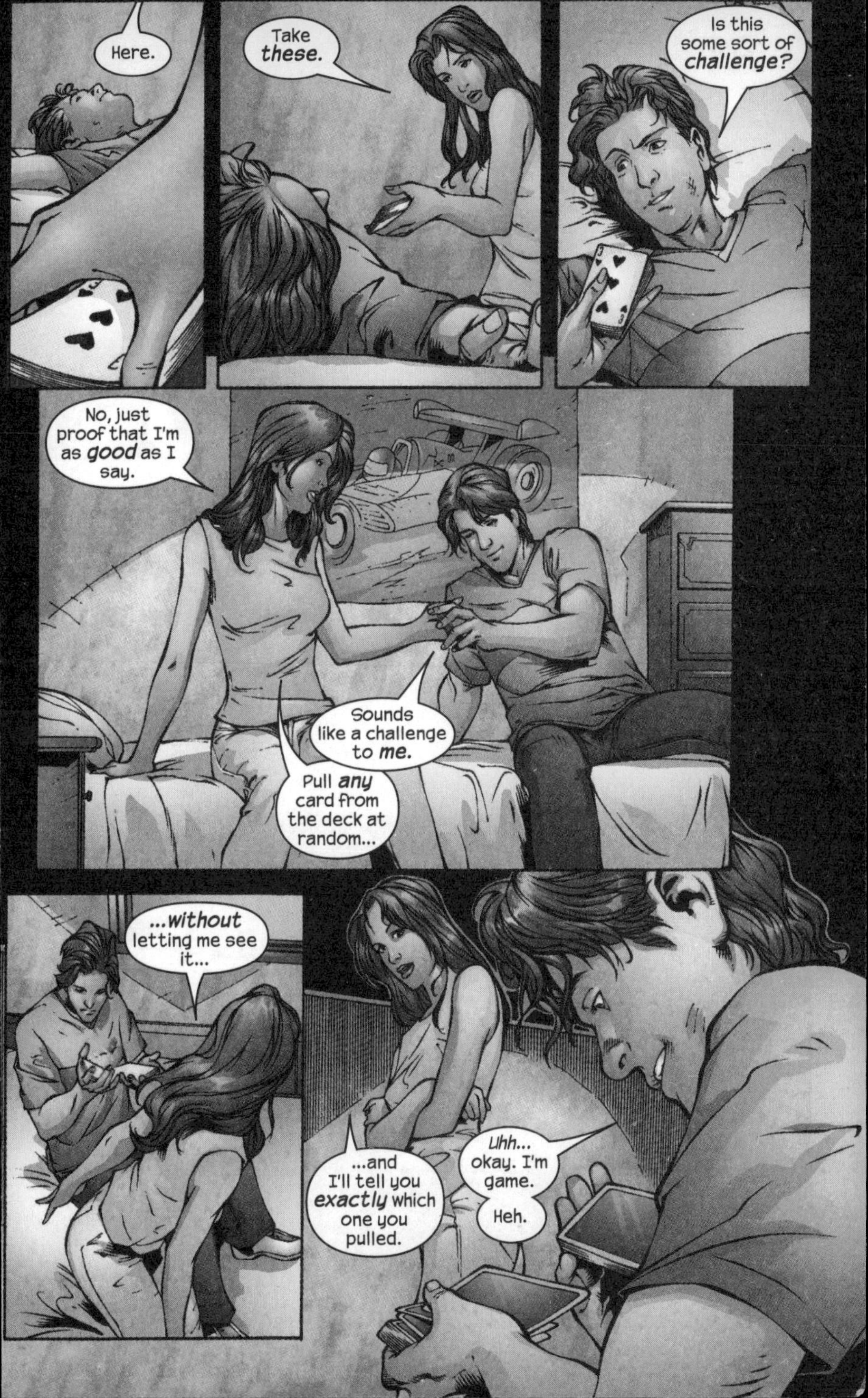
Here.
Take these.
Is this some sort of challenge?
No, just proof that I'm as good as I say.
Sounds like a challenge to me.
Pull any card from the deck at random...
...without letting me see it...
...and I'll tell you exactly which one you pulled.
Uhh... okay. I'm game.
Heh.

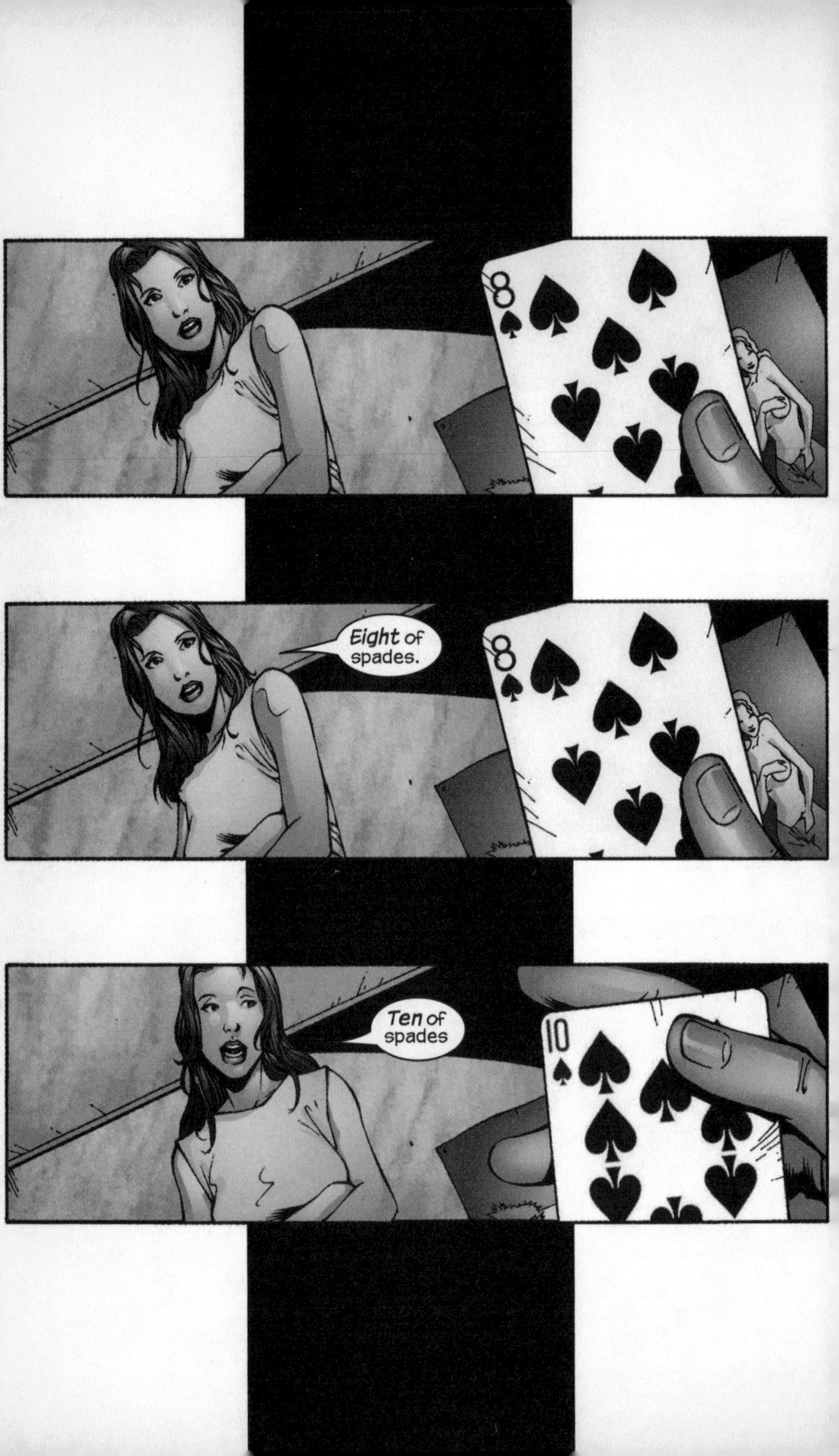
Eight of spades.
Ten of spades

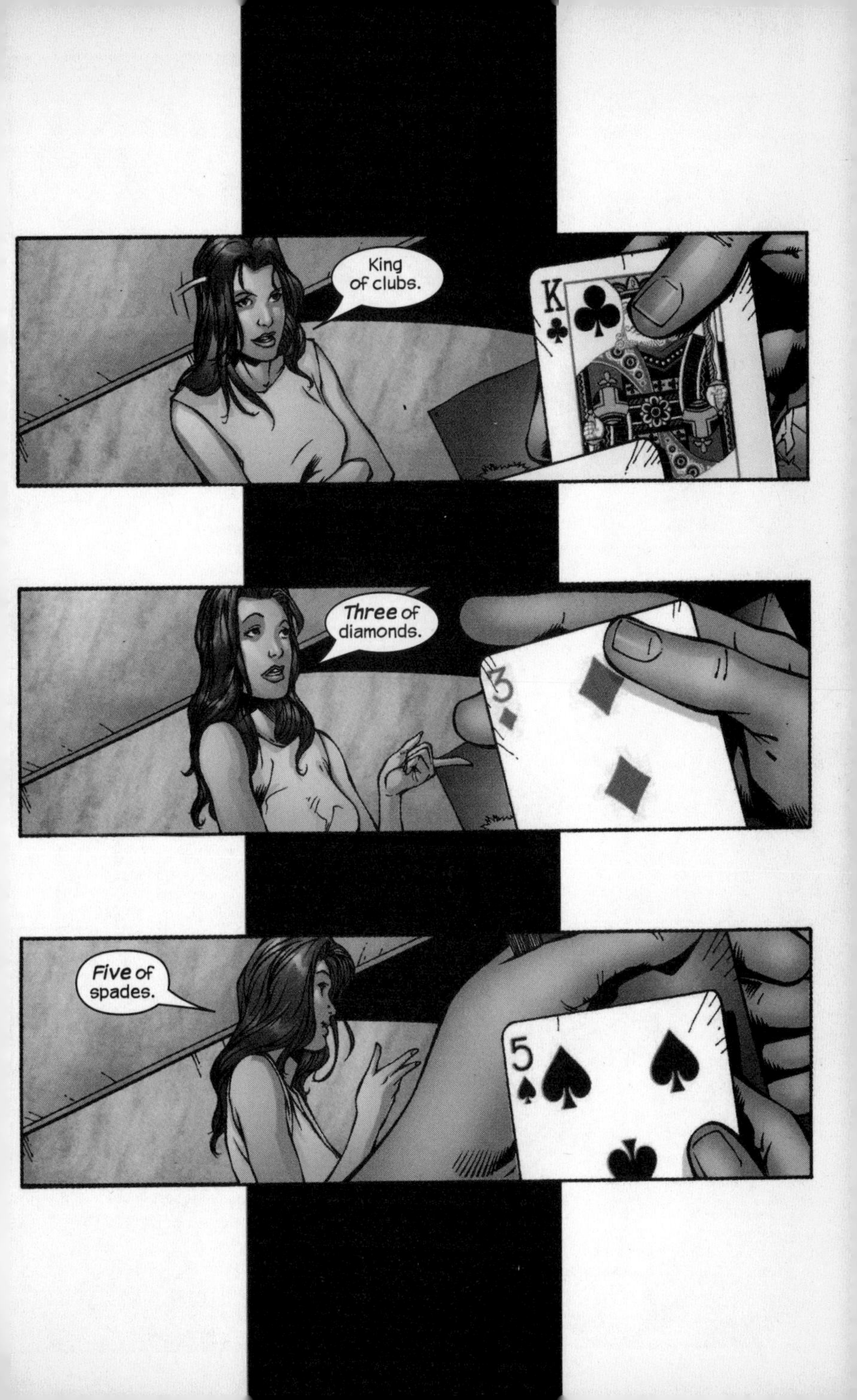
King of clubs.
Three of diamonds.
Five of spades.

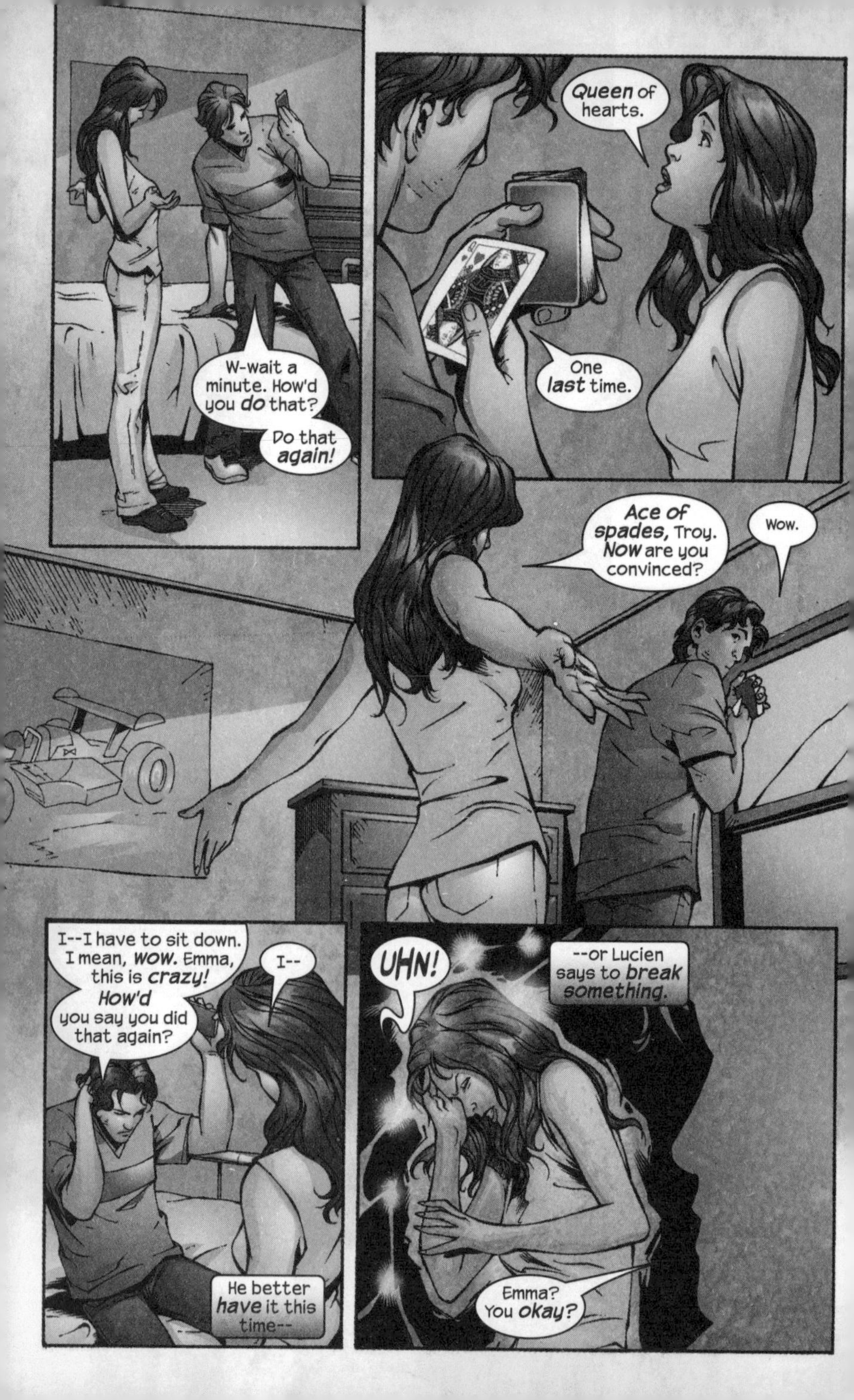
W-wait a minute. How'd you do that?
Do that again!
Queen of hearts.
One last time.
Ace of spades, Troy. NOW are you convinced?
Wow.
I--I have to sit down. I mean, WOW. Emma, this is crazy! How'd you say you did that again?
I--
He better have it this time--
UHN!
--or Lucien says to break something.
Emma? You okay?

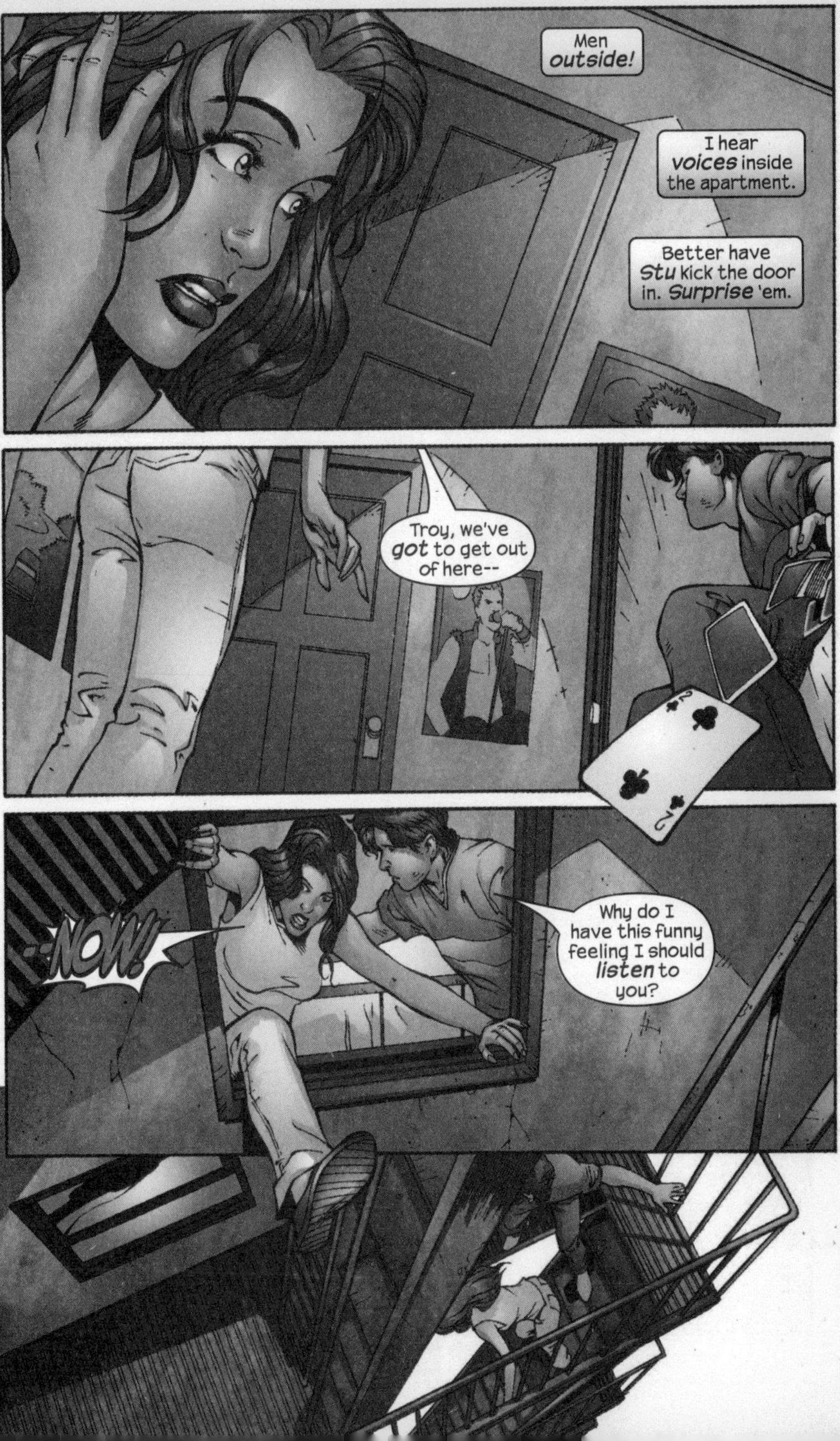
Men outside!
I hear voices inside the apartment.
Better have Stu kick the door in. Surprise 'em.
Troy, we've got to get out of here--
--NOW!
Why do I have this funny feeling I should listen to you?

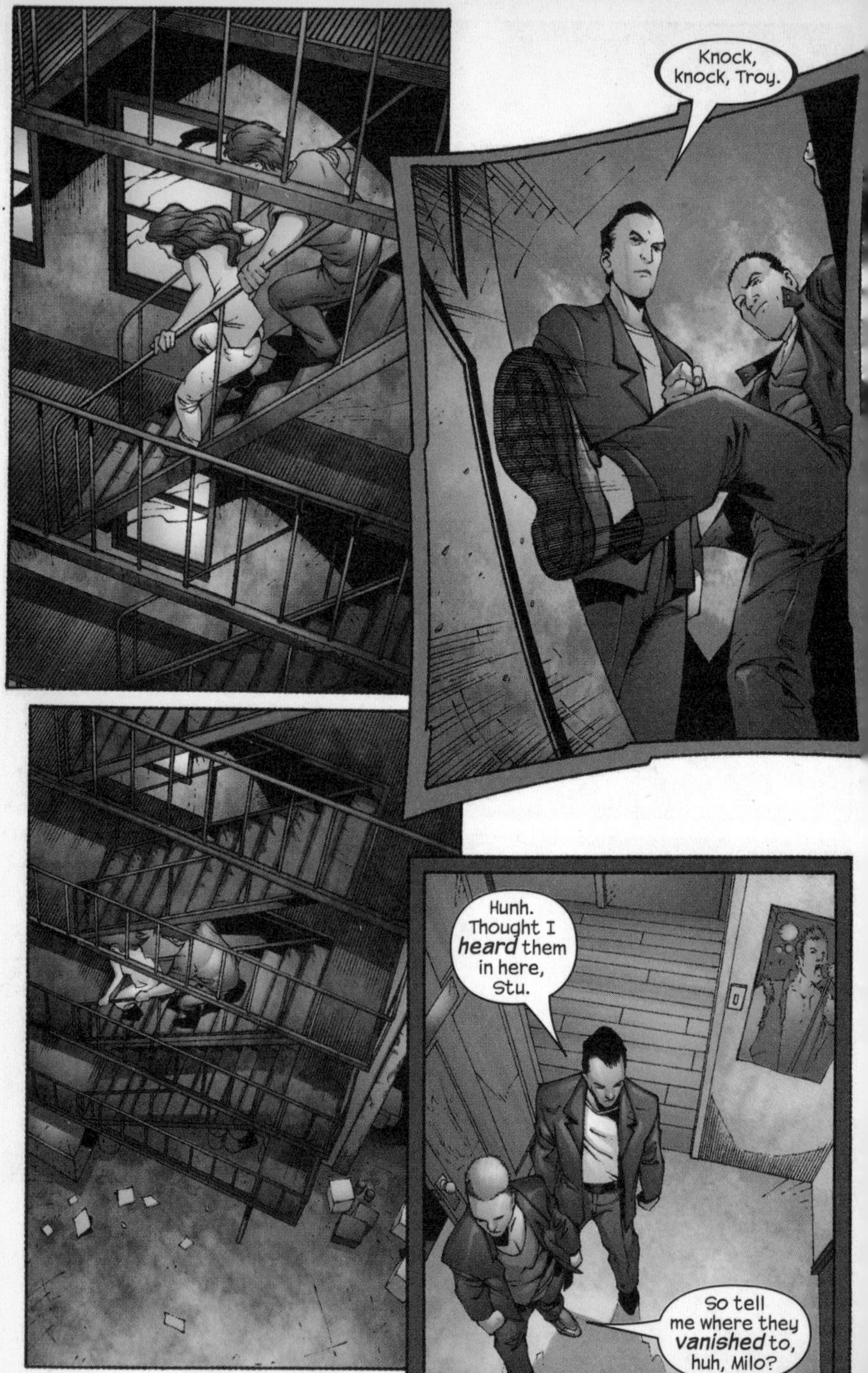
Knock, knock, Troy.
Hunh. Thought I *heard* them in here, Stu.
So tell me where they *vanished* to, huh, Milo?

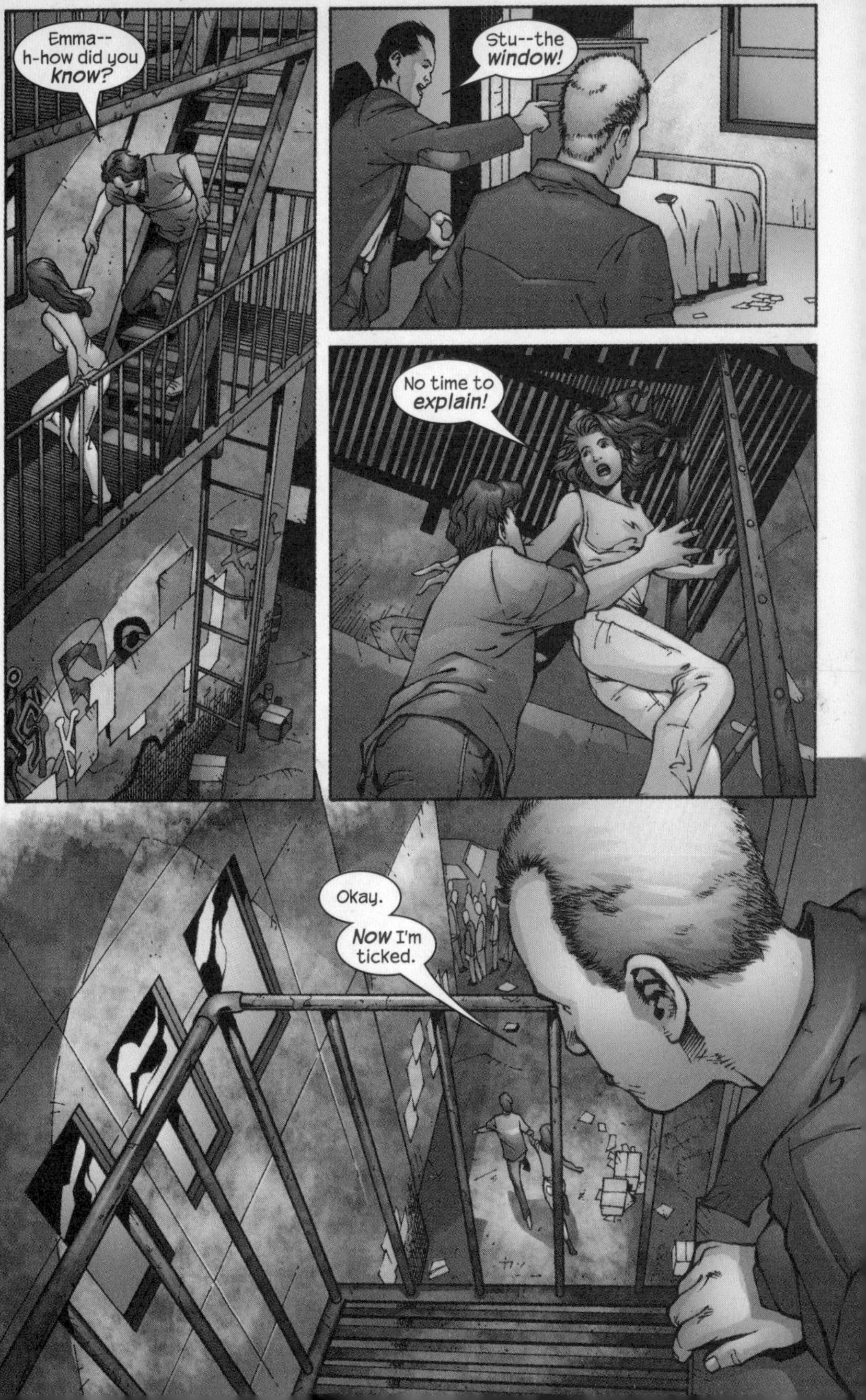
Emma--
h-how did you
know?
Stu--the
window!
No time to
explain!
Okay.
Now I'm
ticked.

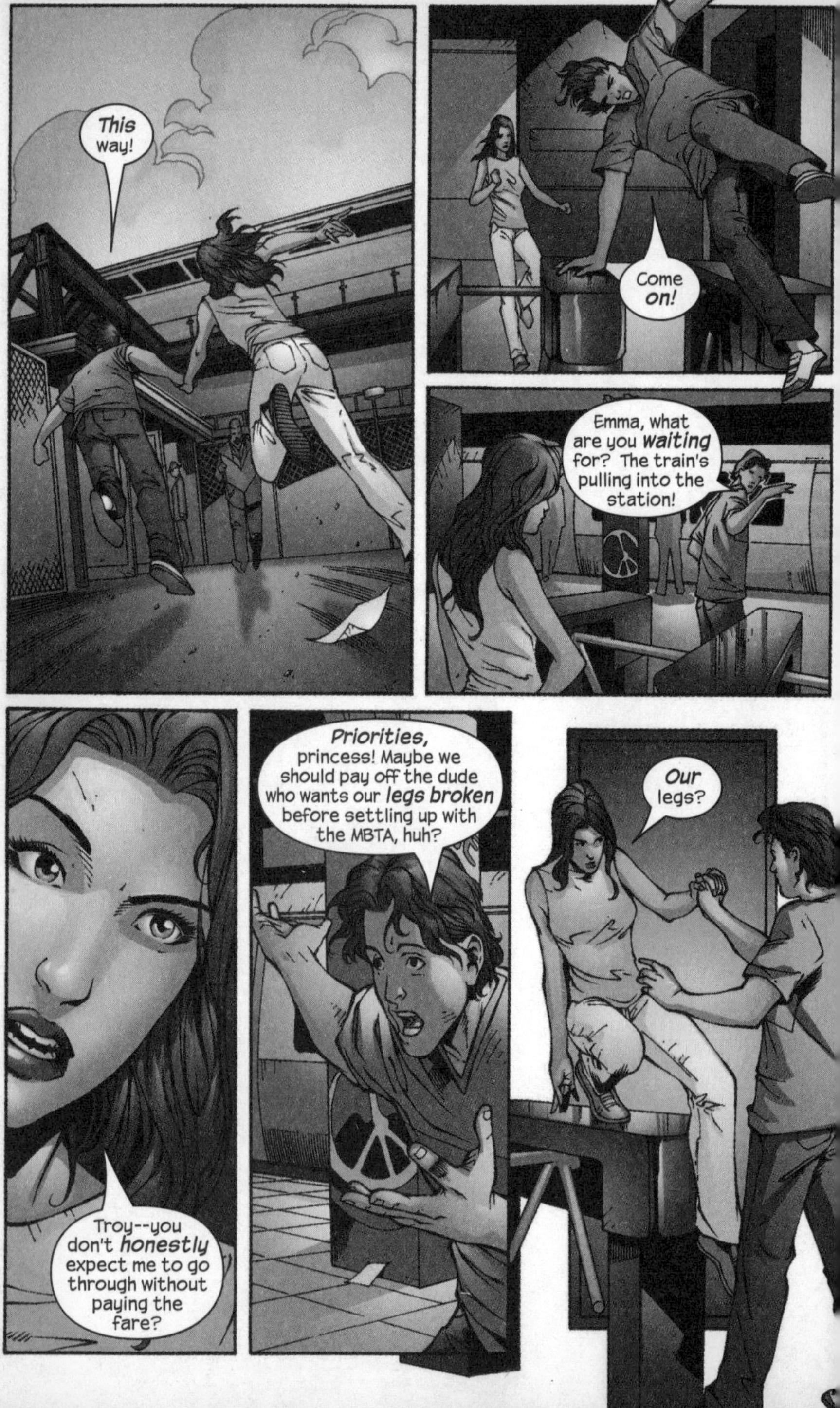
This way!
Come on!
Emma, what are you waiting for? The train's pulling into the station!
Troy--you don't honestly expect me to go through without paying the fare?
Priorities, princess! Maybe we should pay off the dude who wants our legs broken before settling up with the MBTA, huh?
Our legs?

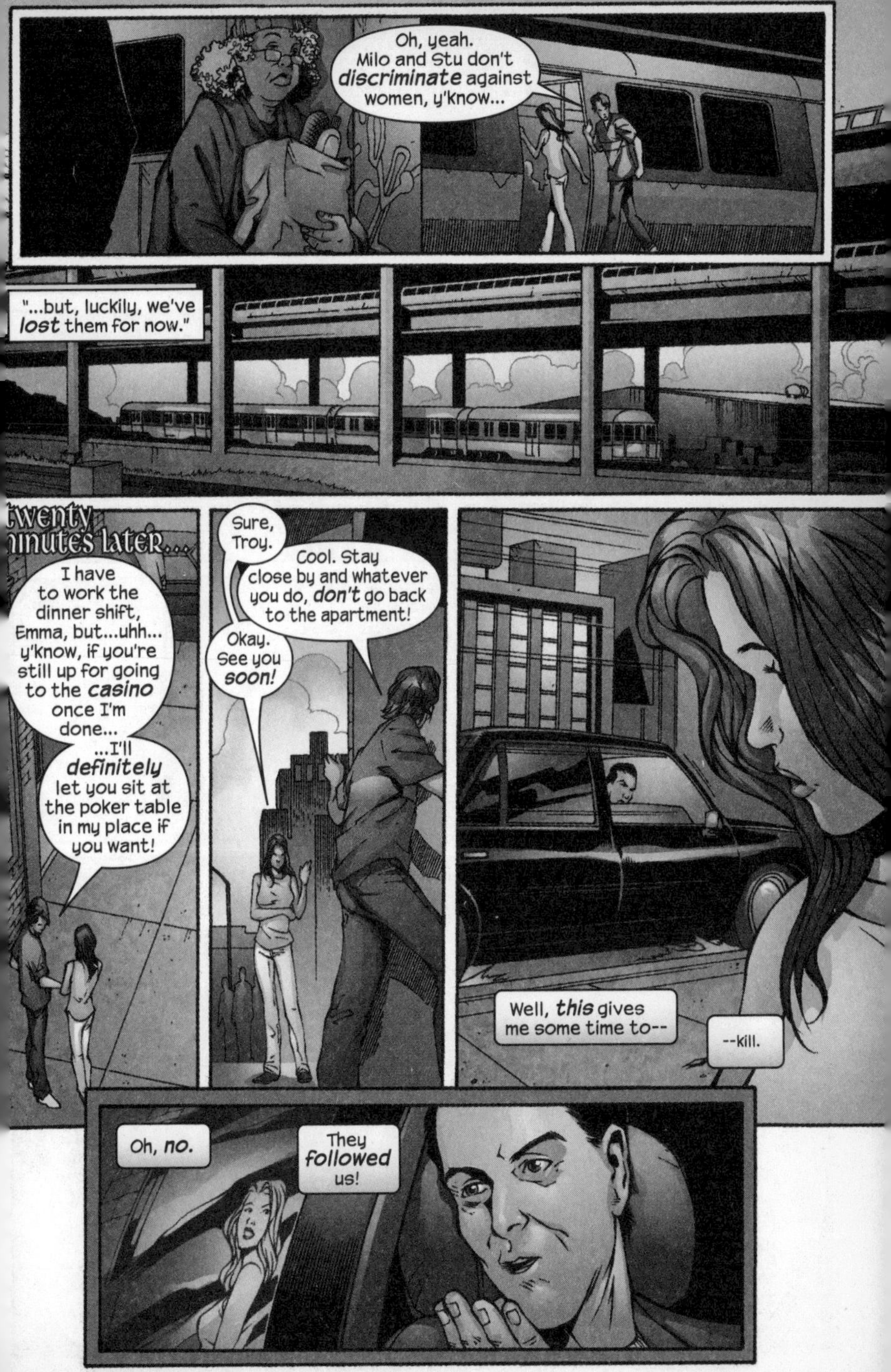
Oh, yeah. Milo and Stu don't *discriminate* against women, y'know...
"...but, luckily, we've *lost* them for now."
twenty minutes later...
I have to work the dinner shift, Emma, but...uhh... y'know, if you're still up for going to the *casino* once I'm done...
...I'll *definitely* let you sit at the poker table in my place if you want!
Sure, Troy.
Cool. Stay close by and whatever you do, *don't* go back to the apartment!
Okay. See you *soon!*
Well, *this* gives me some time to--
--kill.
Oh, *no.*
They *followed* us!

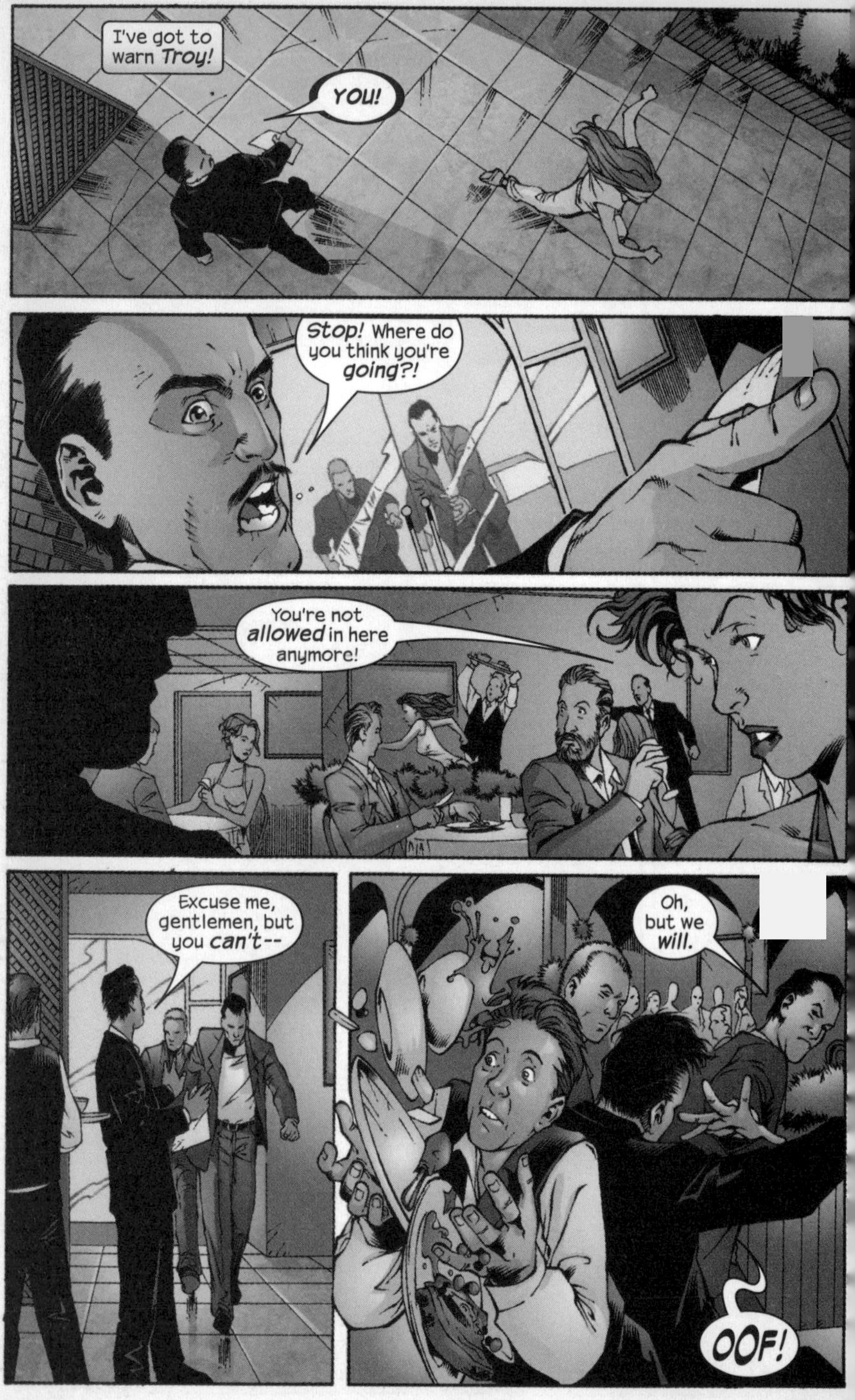
I've got to warn Troy!
YOU!
Stop! Where do you think you're going?!
You're not allowed in here anymore!
Excuse me, gentlemen, but you can't--
Oh, but we will.
OOF!

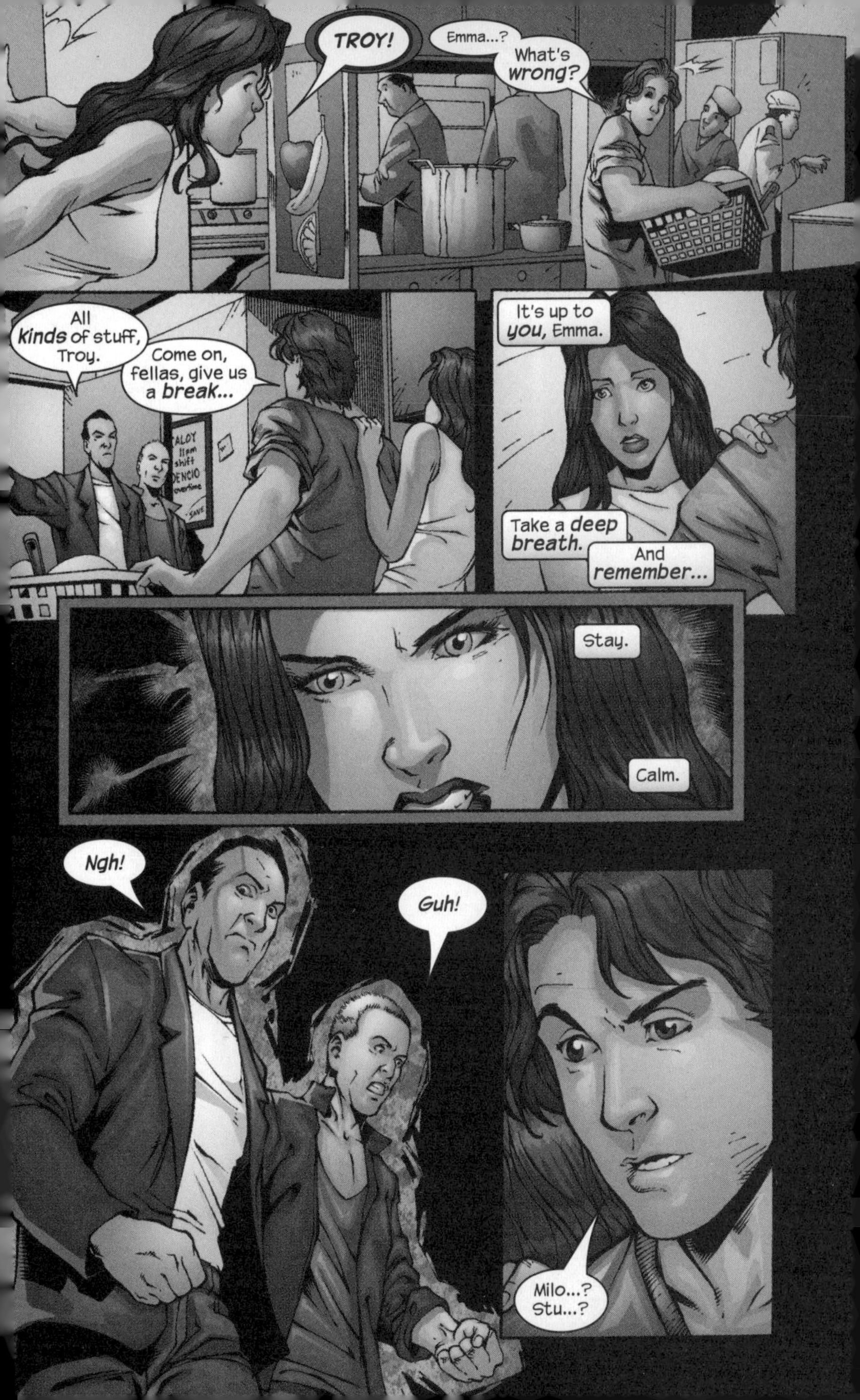
TROY!
Emma...? What's wrong?
All kinds of stuff, Troy.
Come on, fellas, give us a break...
It's up to you, Emma.
Take a deep breath.
And remember...
Stay.
Calm.
Ngh!
Guh!
Milo...? Stu...?

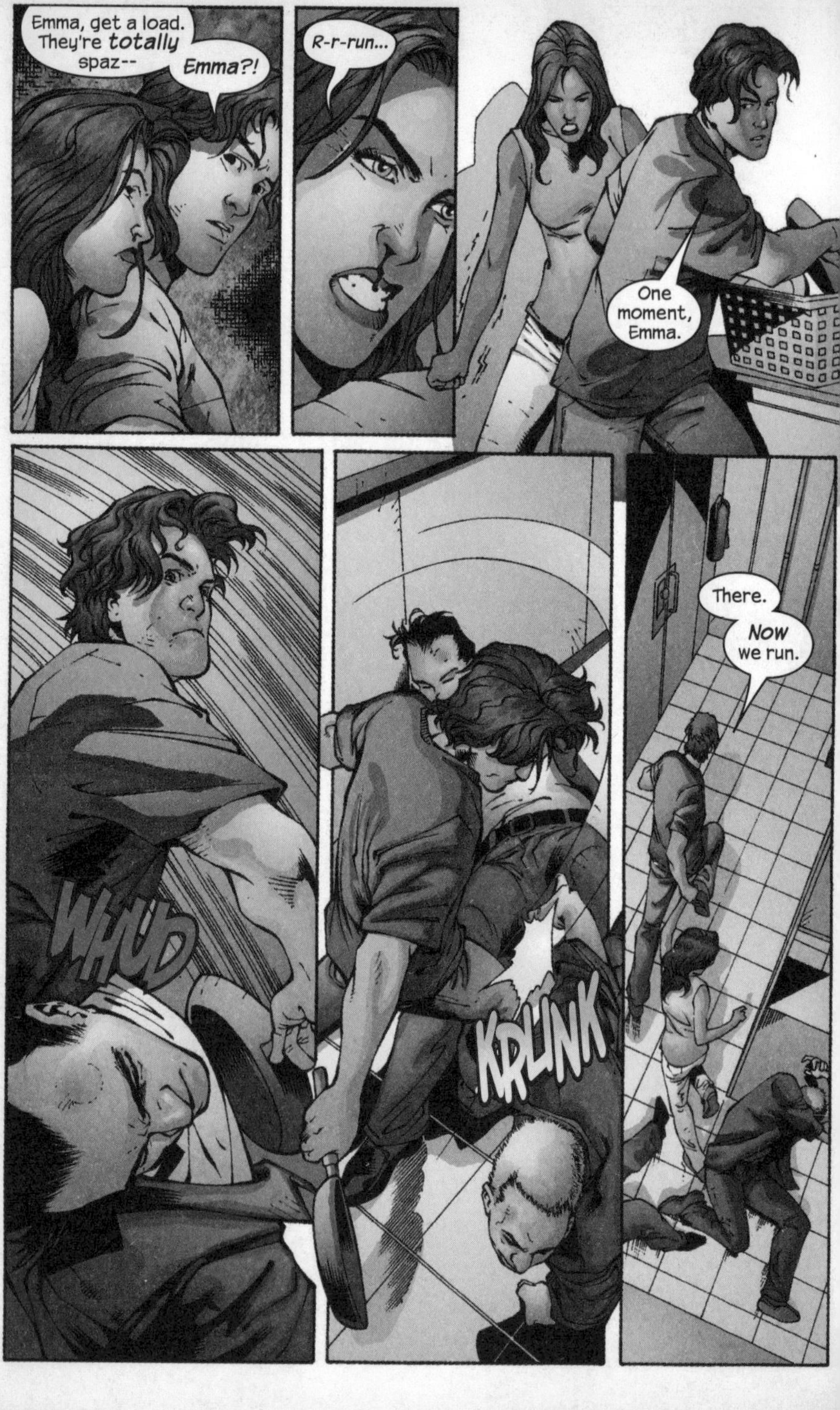
Emma, get a load. They're totally spaz--
Emma?!
R-r-run...
One moment, Emma.
WHUD
KRUNK
There. NOW we run.

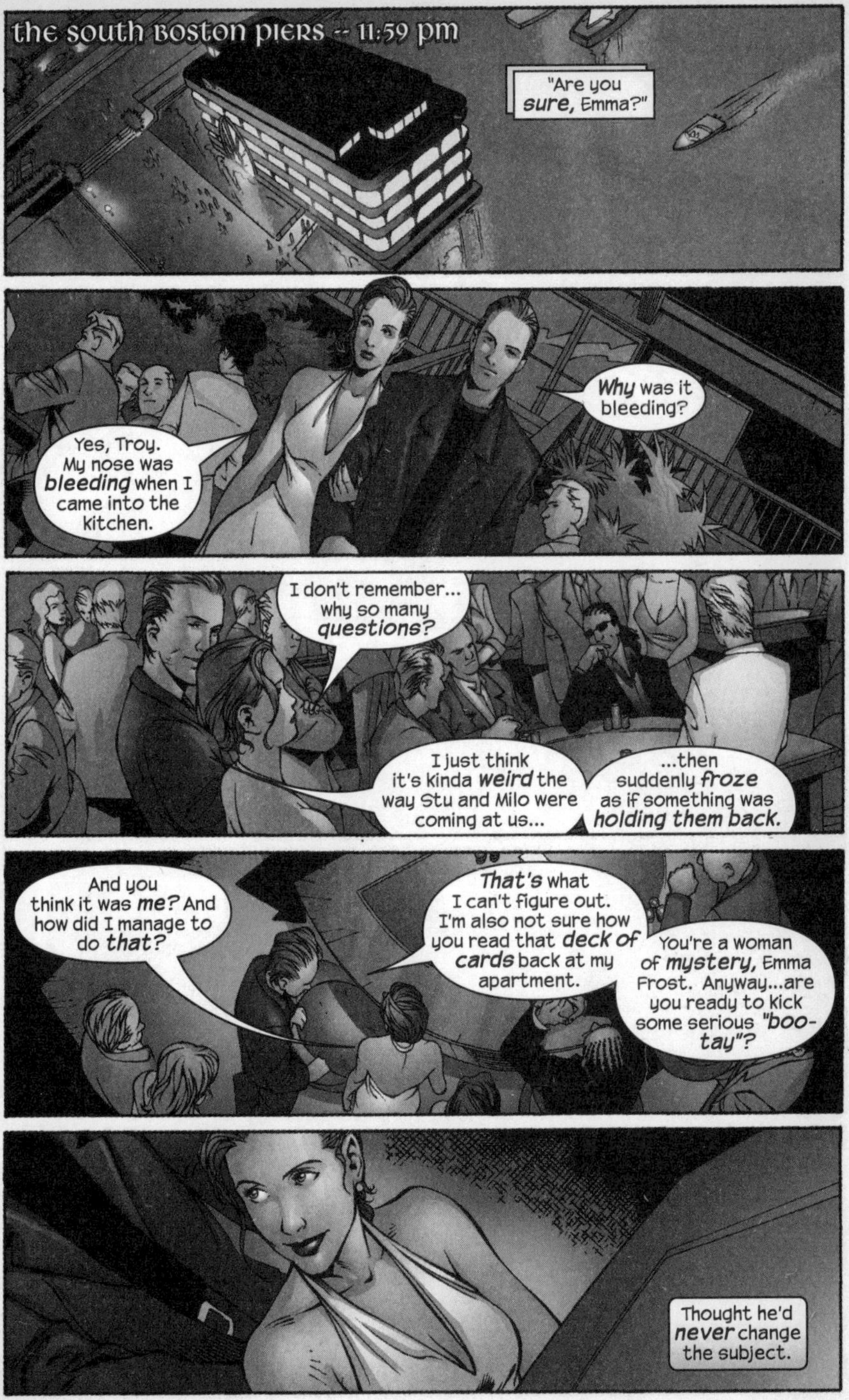
the south boston piers -- 11:59 pm
"Are you sure, Emma?"
Yes, Troy. My nose was bleeding when I came into the kitchen.
Why was it bleeding?
I don't remember... why so many questions?
I just think it's kinda weird the way Stu and Milo were coming at us...
...then suddenly froze as if something was holding them back.
And you think it was me? And how did I manage to do that?
That's what I can't figure out. I'm also not sure how you read that deck of cards back at my apartment.
You're a woman of mystery, Emma Frost. Anyway...are you ready to kick some serious "boo-tay"?
Thought he'd never change the subject.

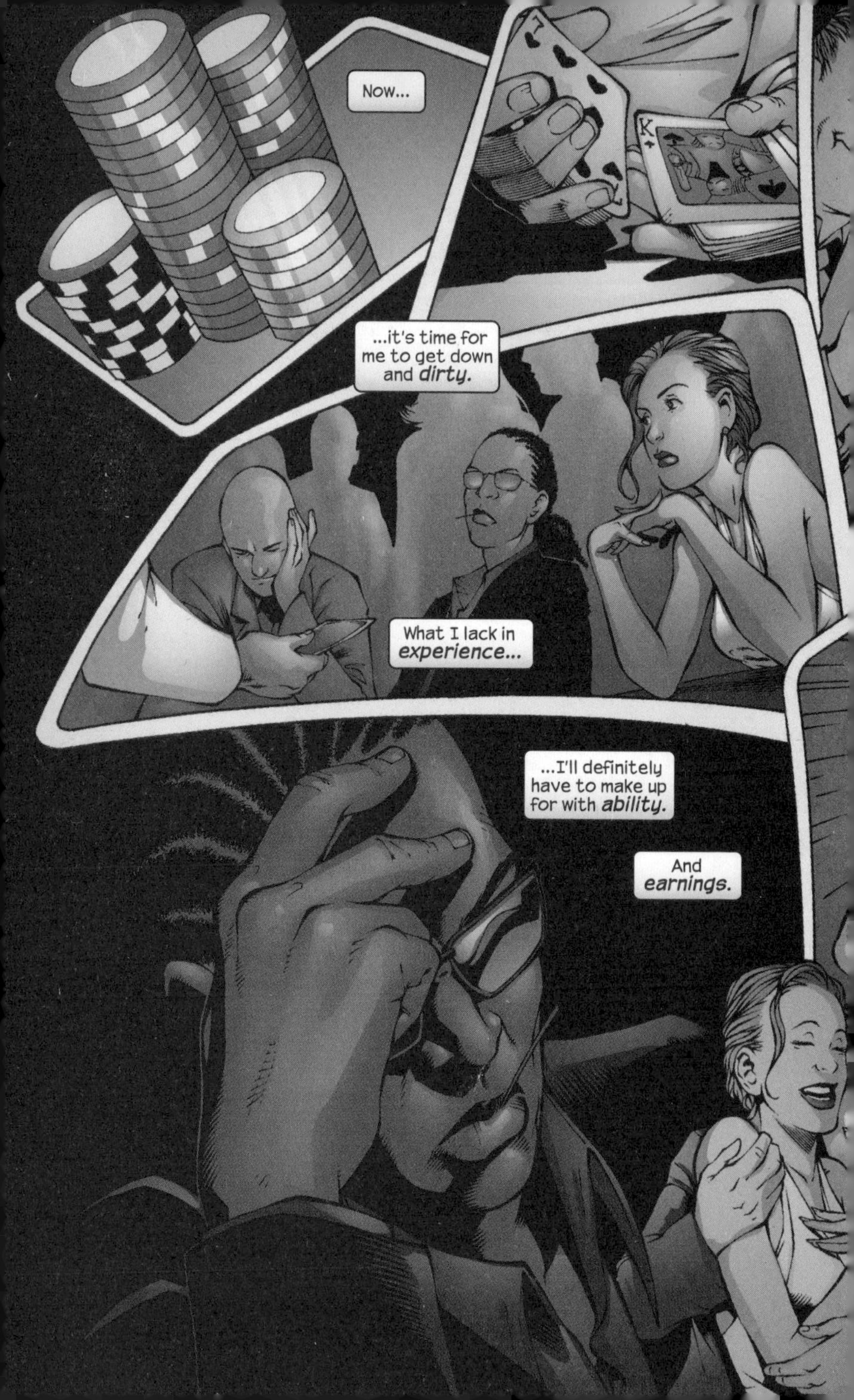
Now...
...it's time for me to get down and dirty.
What I lack in experience...
...I'll definitely have to make up for with ability.
And earnings.

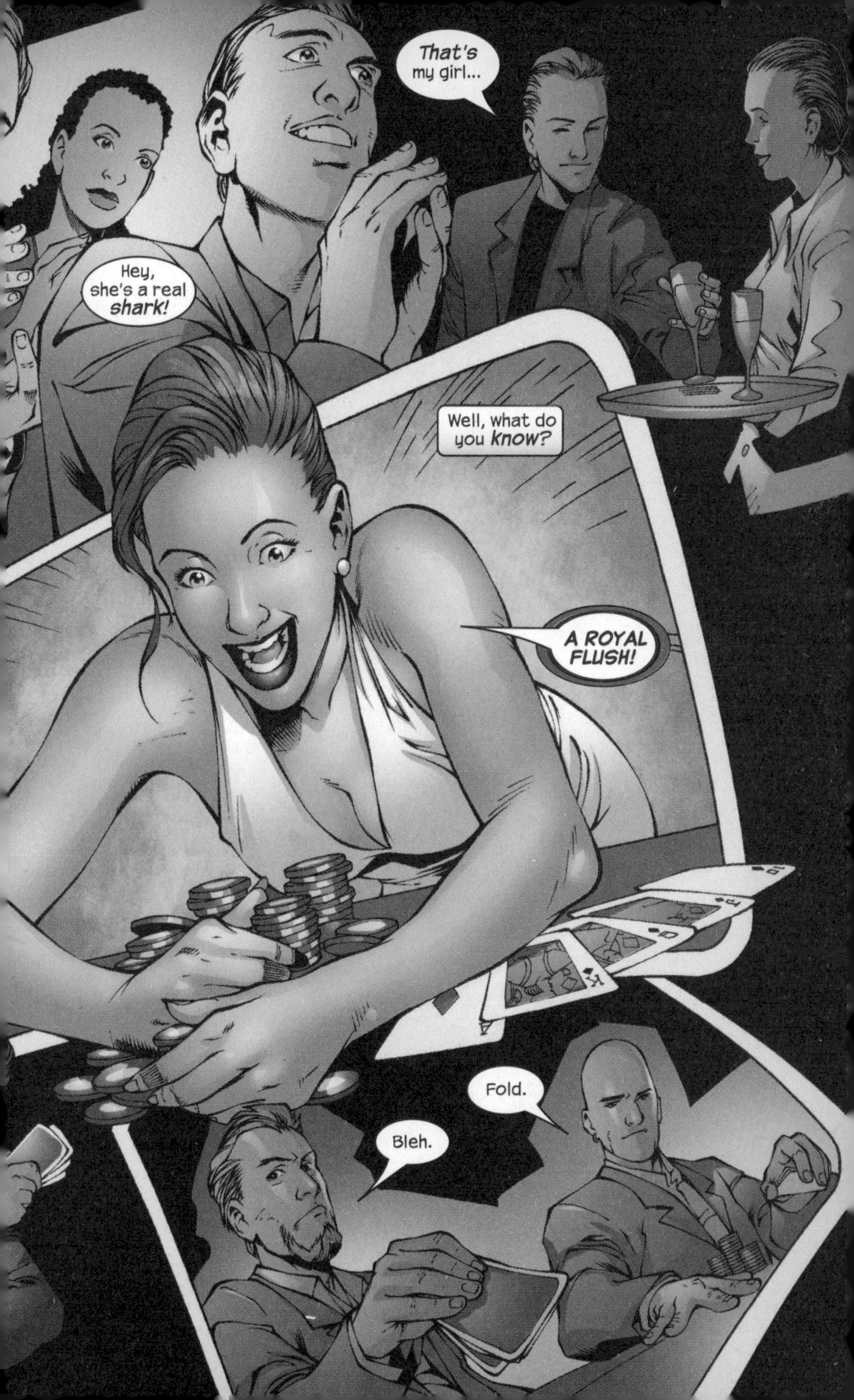
That's my girl...
Hey, she's a real shark!
Well, what do you know?
A ROYAL FLUSH!
Fold.
Bleh.

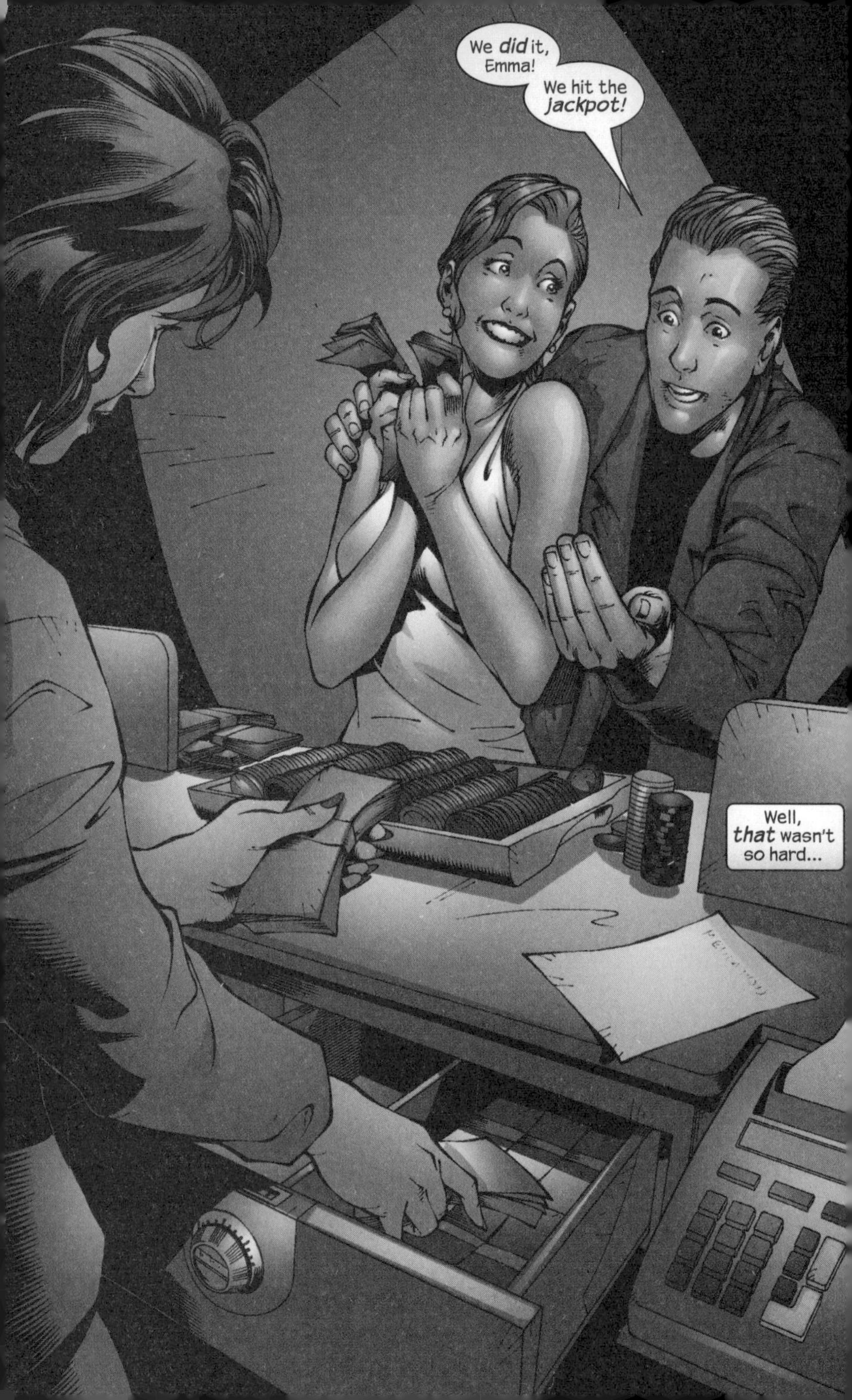
We *did* it, Emma!
We hit the *jackpot!*
Well, *that* wasn't so hard...

MIND GAMES 3 OF 6

OUTRAGEOUS FORTUNE

Where to, kids?

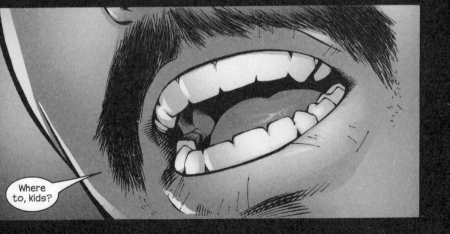

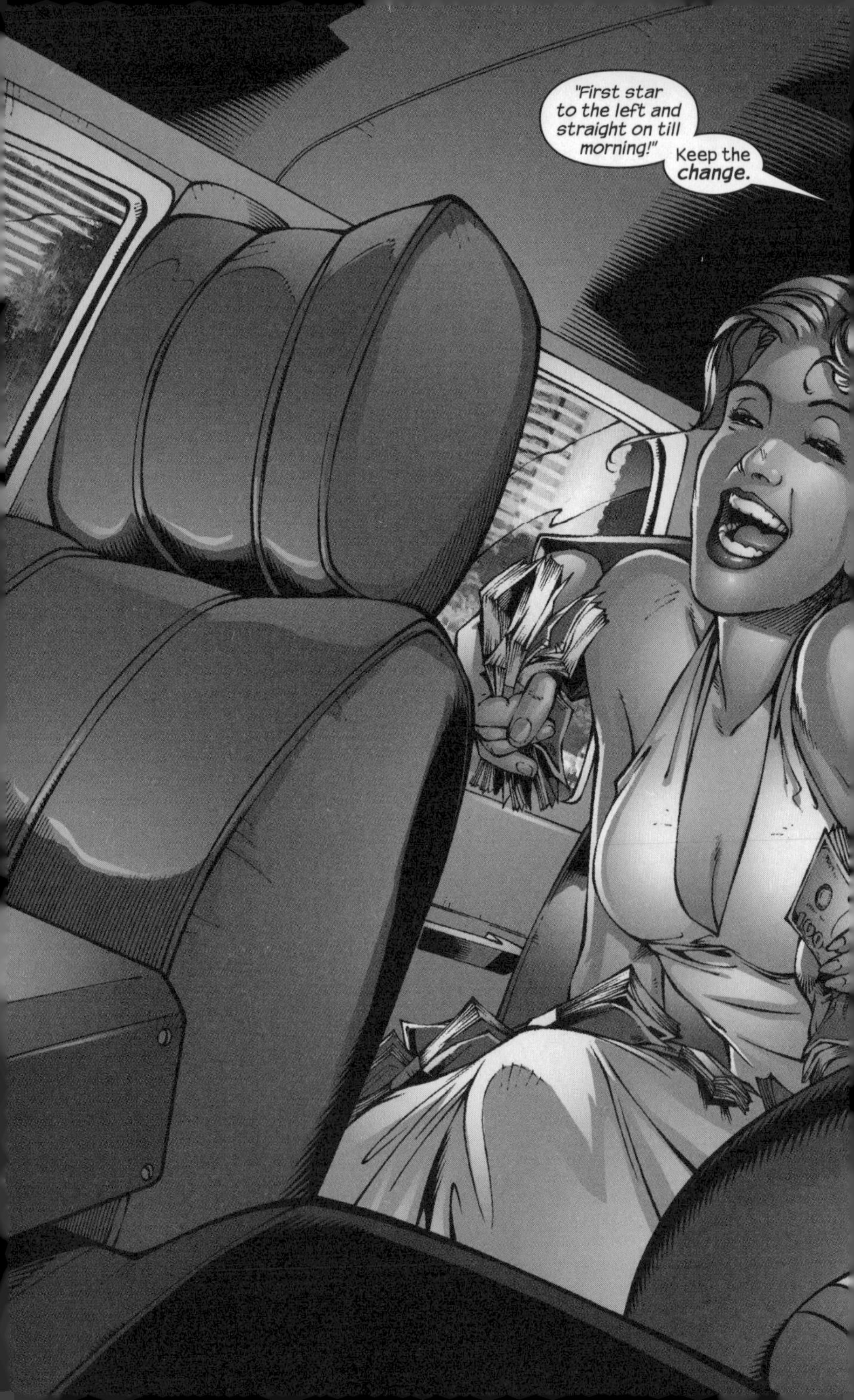
"First star to the left and straight on till morning!"
Keep the *change.*

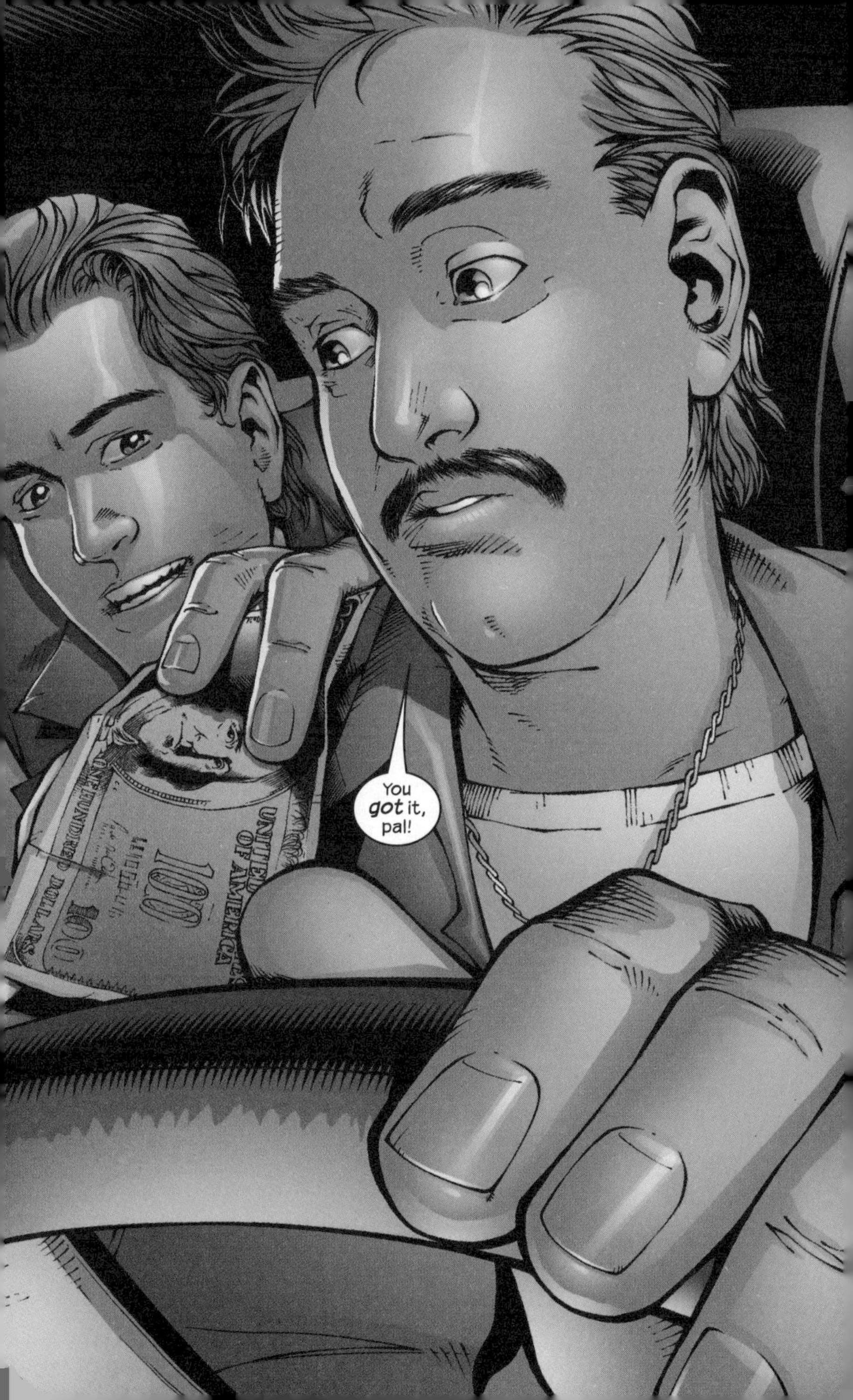
You got it, pal!

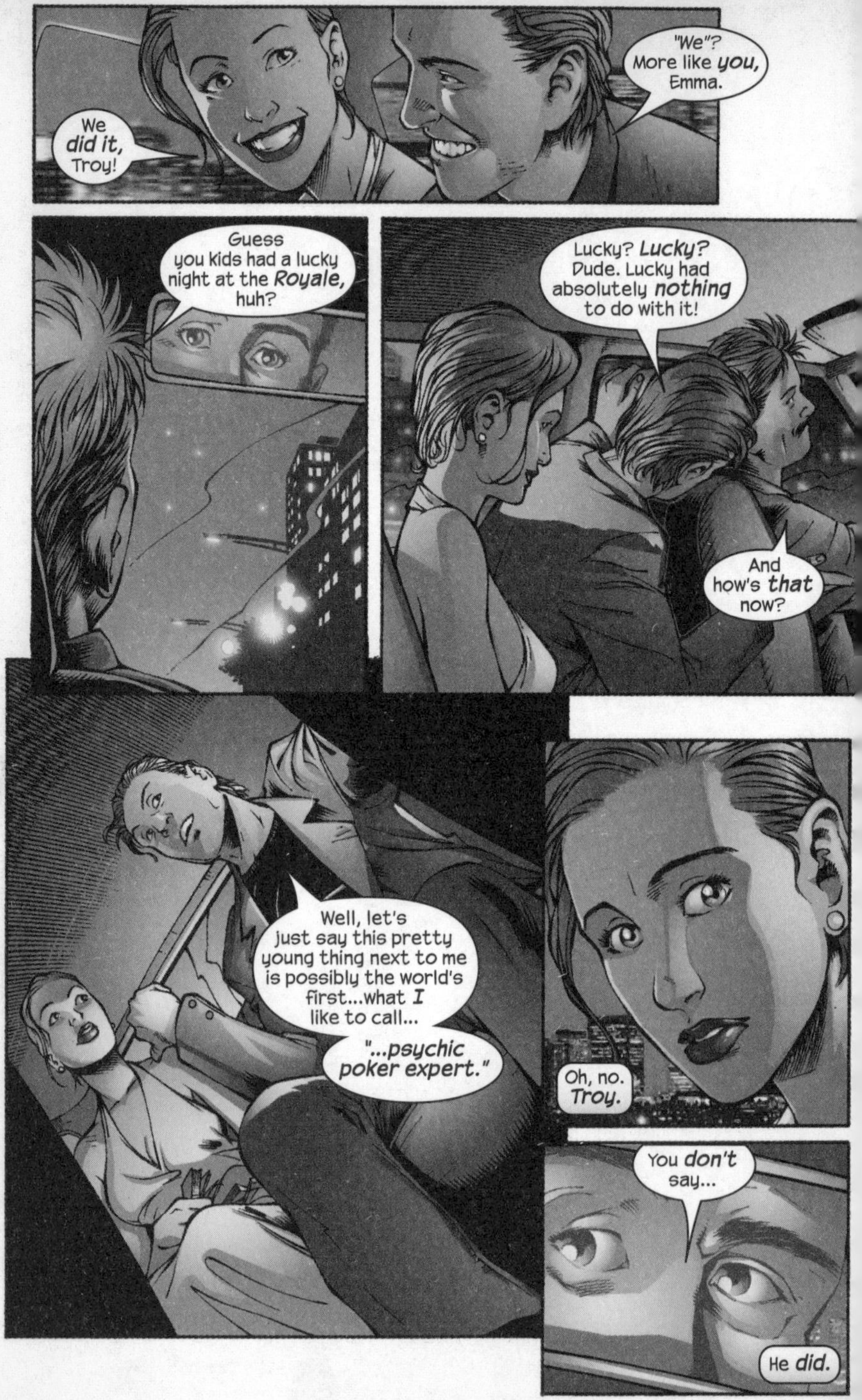

We did it, Troy!
"We"? More like you, Emma.
Guess you kids had a lucky night at the Royale, huh?
Lucky? Lucky? Dude. Lucky had absolutely nothing to do with it!
And how's that now?
Well, let's just say this pretty young thing next to me is possibly the world's first...what I like to call...
"...psychic poker expert."
Oh, no. Troy.
You don't say...
He did.

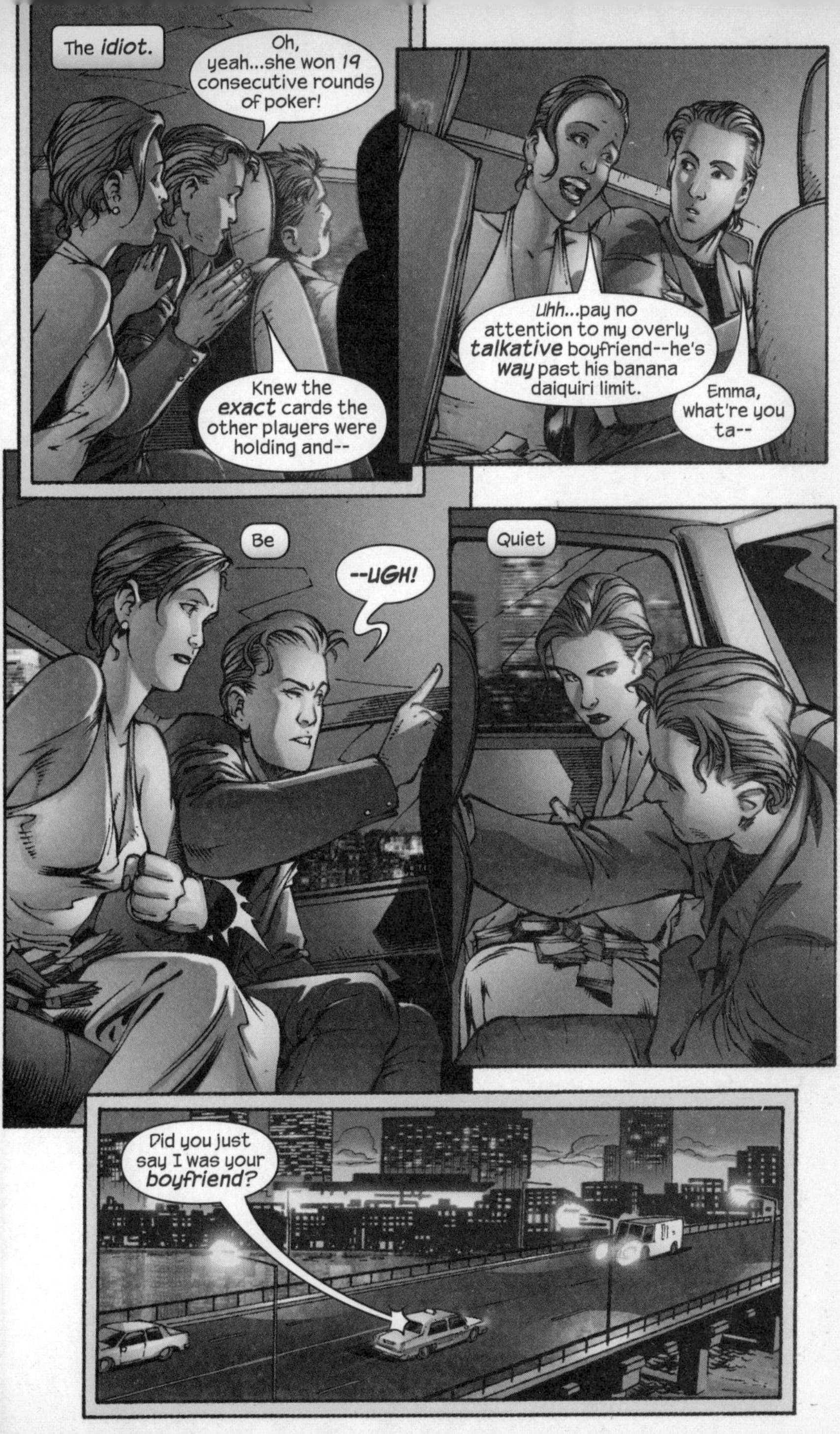
The idiot.
Oh, yeah...she won 19 consecutive rounds of poker!
Knew the exact cards the other players were holding and--
Uhh...pay no attention to my overly talkative boyfriend--he's way past his banana daiquiri limit.
Emma, what're you ta--
Be
--UGH!
Quiet
Did you just say I was your boyfriend?

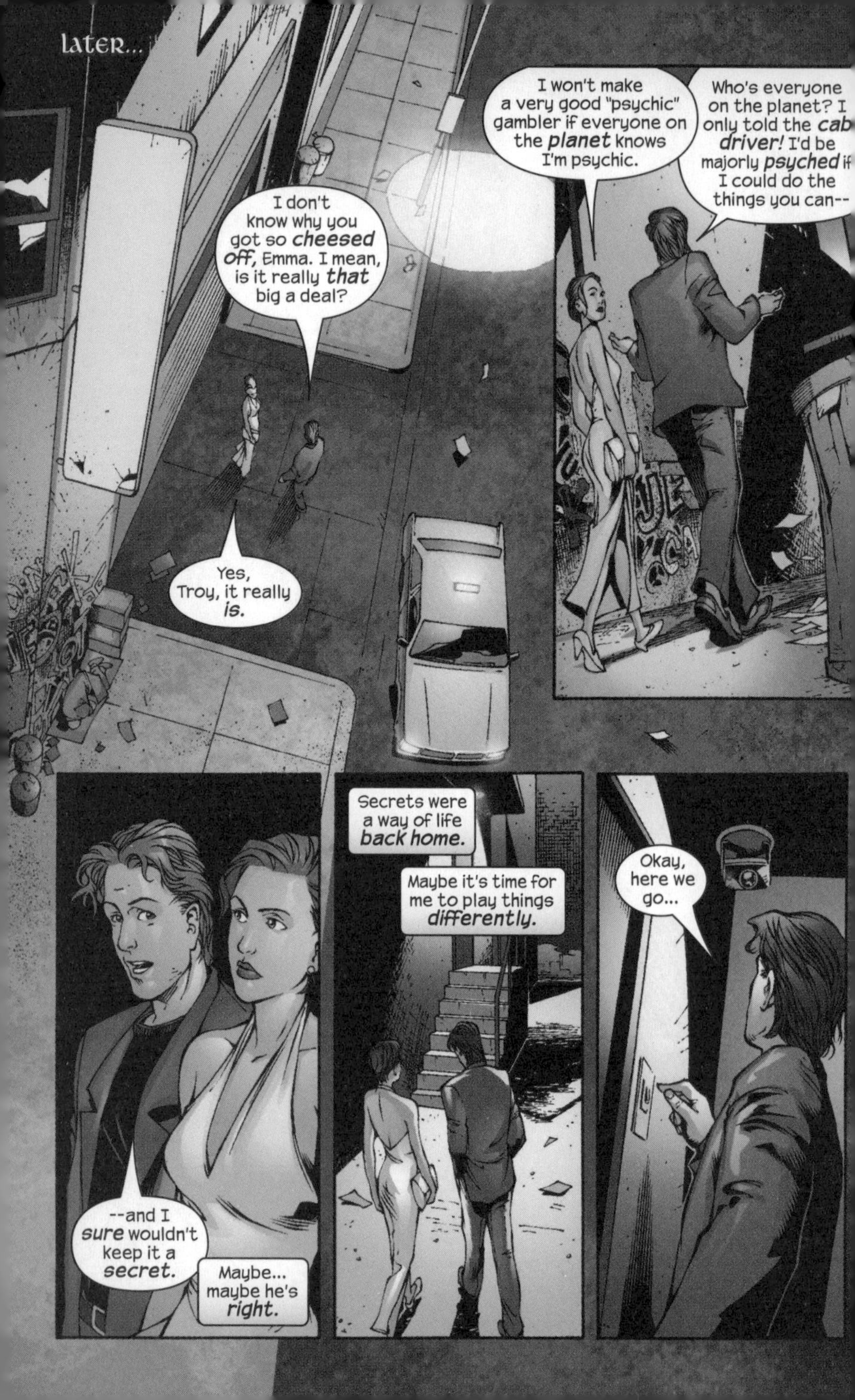
later...
I don't know why you got so cheesed off, Emma. I mean, is it really that big a deal?
Yes, Troy, it really is.
I won't make a very good "psychic" gambler if everyone on the planet knows I'm psychic.
Who's everyone on the planet? I only told the cab driver! I'd be majorly psyched if I could do the things you can--
--and I sure wouldn't keep it a secret.
Maybe... maybe he's right.
Secrets were a way of life back home.
Maybe it's time for me to play things differently.
Okay, here we go...

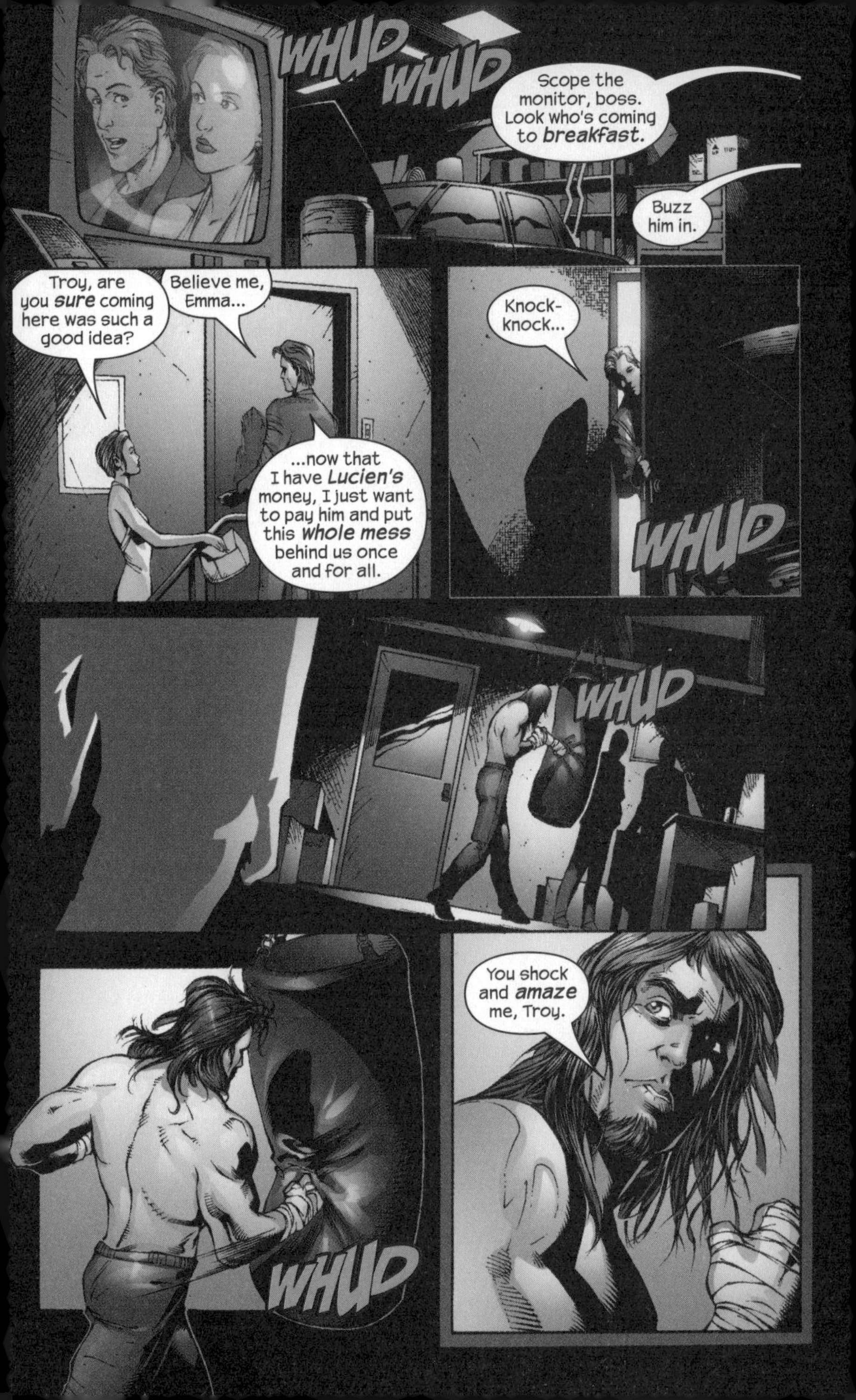
WHUD
WHUD
Scope the monitor, boss. Look who's coming to *breakfast.*
Buzz him in.
Troy, are you *sure* coming here was such a good idea?
Believe me, Emma...
...now that I have *Lucien's* money, I just want to pay him and put this *whole mess* behind us once and for all.
Knock-knock...
WHUD
WHUD
WHUD
You shock and *amaze* me, Troy.

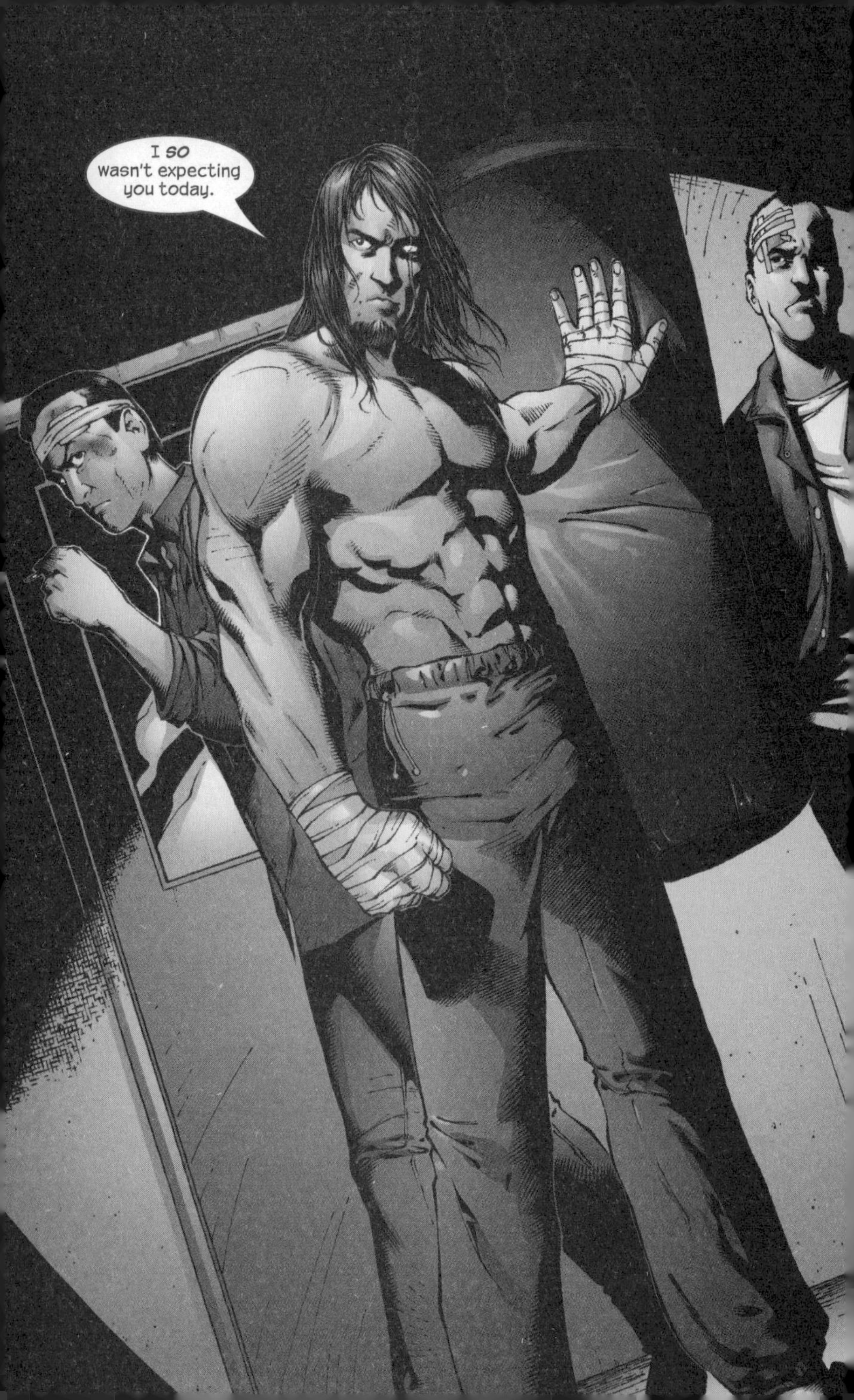
I SO wasn't expecting you today.

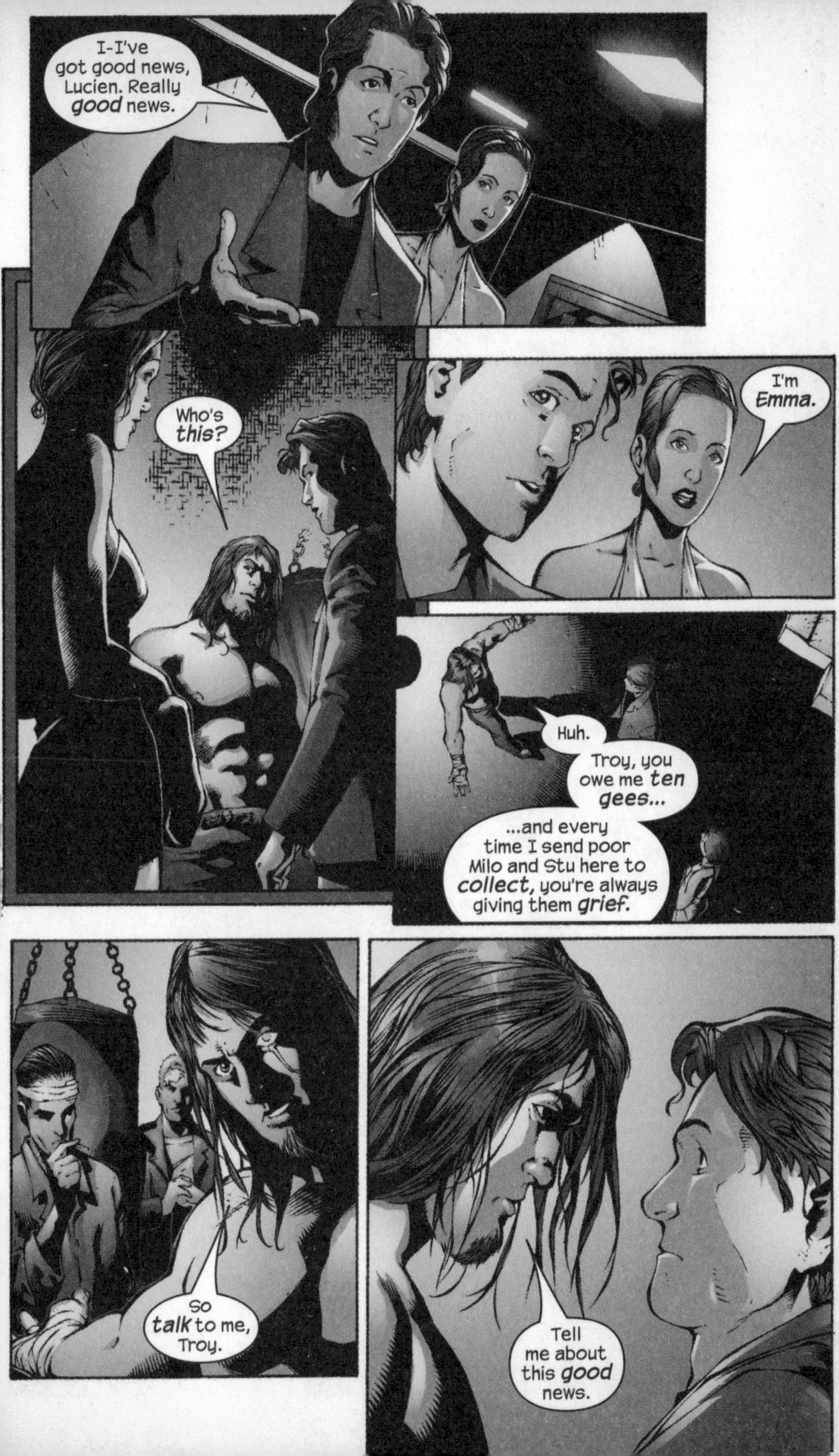
I-I've got good news, Lucien. Really good news.
Who's this?
I'm Emma.
Huh.
Troy, you owe me ten gees...
...and every time I send poor Milo and Stu here to collect, you're always giving them grief.
So talk to me, Troy.
Tell me about this good news.

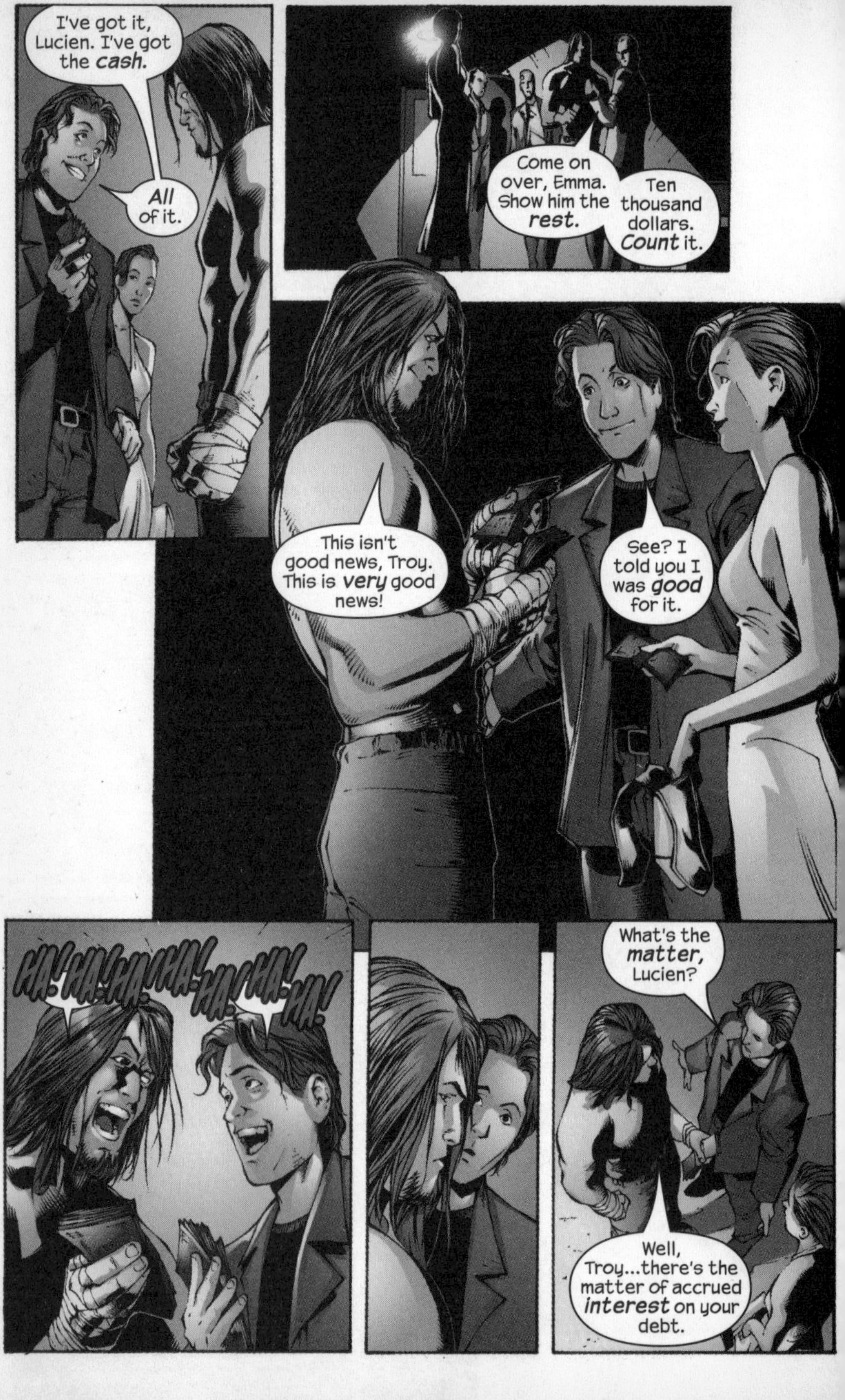
I've got it, Lucien. I've got the cash.
All of it.
Come on over, Emma. Show him the rest.
Ten thousand dollars. Count it.
This isn't good news, Troy. This is very good news!
See? I told you I was good for it.
HA! HA! HA! HA! HA! HA! HA!
What's the matter, Lucien?
Well, Troy...there's the matter of accrued interest on your debt.

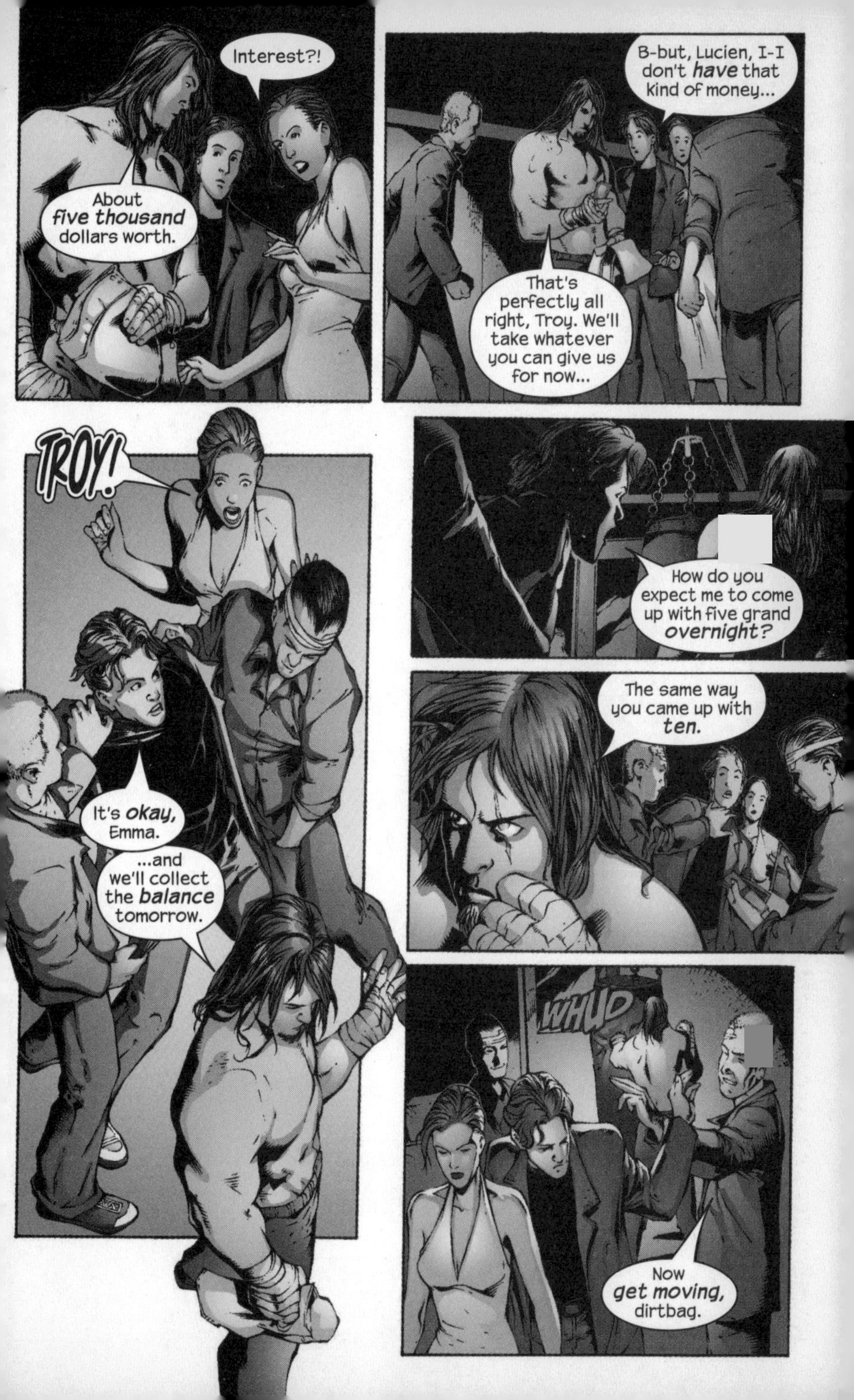
Interest?!
About five thousand dollars worth.
B-but, Lucien, I-I don't have that kind of money...
That's perfectly all right, Troy. We'll take whatever you can give us for now...
TROY!
It's okay, Emma.
...and we'll collect the balance tomorrow.
How do you expect me to come up with five grand overnight?
The same way you came up with ten.
WHUD
Now get moving, dirtbag.

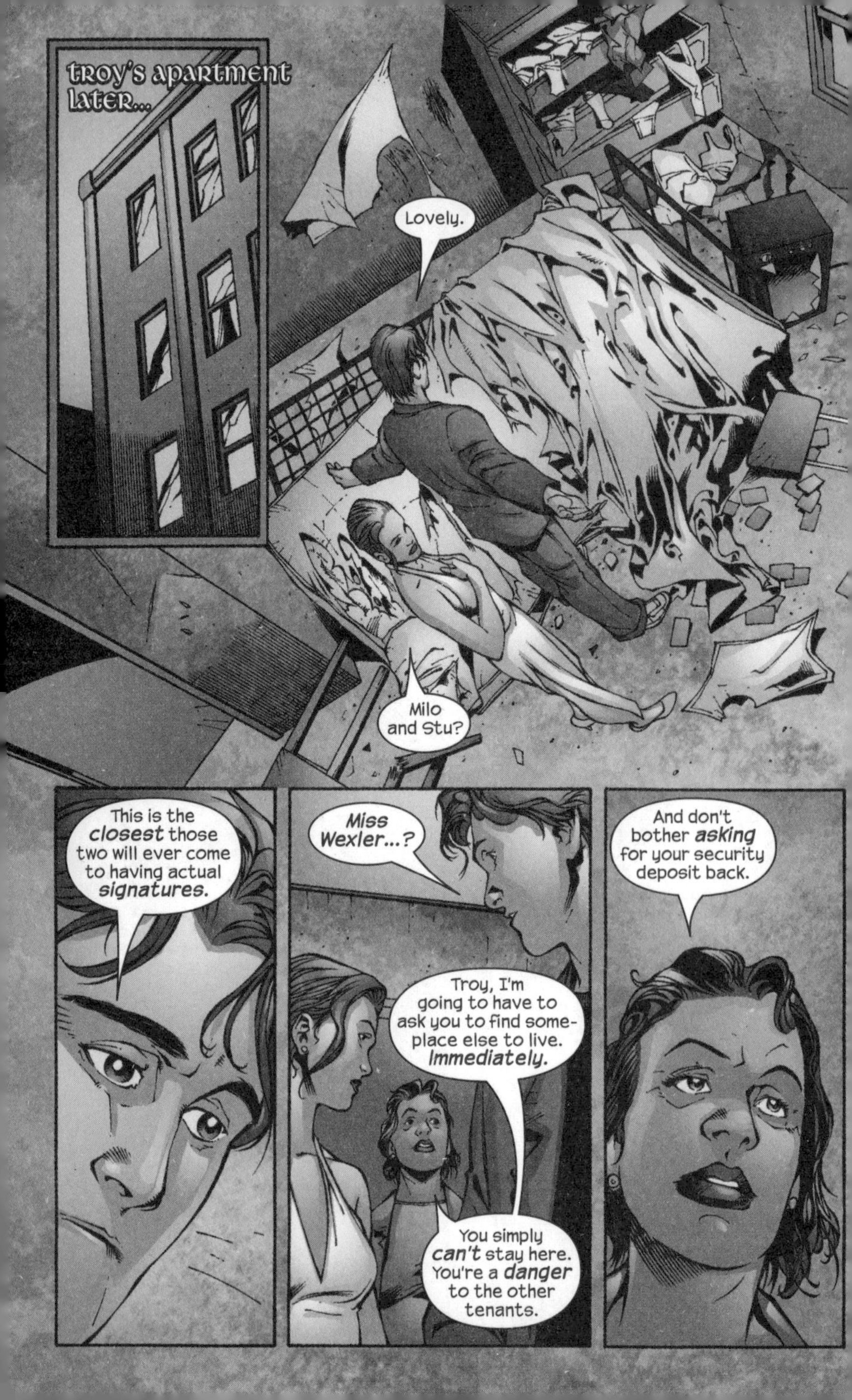
troy's apartment
later...
Lovely.
Milo and Stu?
This is the closest those two will ever come to having actual signatures.
Miss Wexler...?
Troy, I'm going to have to ask you to find some-place else to live. Immediately.
You simply can't stay here. You're a danger to the other tenants.
And don't bother asking for your security deposit back.

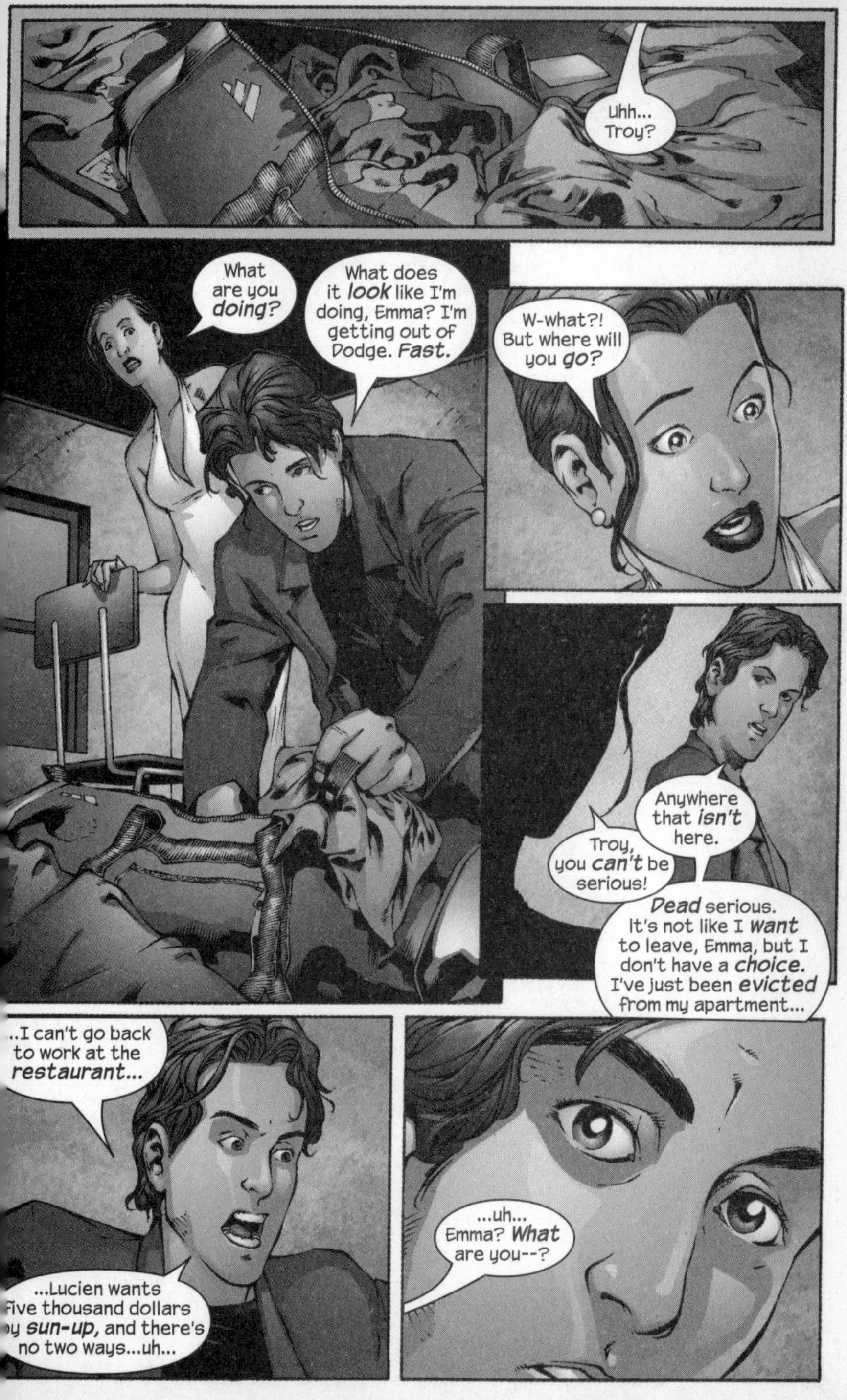
Uhh... Troy?
What are you doing?
What does it look like I'm doing, Emma? I'm getting out of Dodge. Fast.
W-what?! But where will you go?
Anywhere that isn't here.
Troy, you can't be serious!
Dead serious. It's not like I want to leave, Emma, but I don't have a choice. I've just been evicted from my apartment...
..I can't go back to work at the restaurant...
...Lucien wants five thousand dollars by sun-up, and there's no two ways...uh...
...uh... Emma? What are you--?

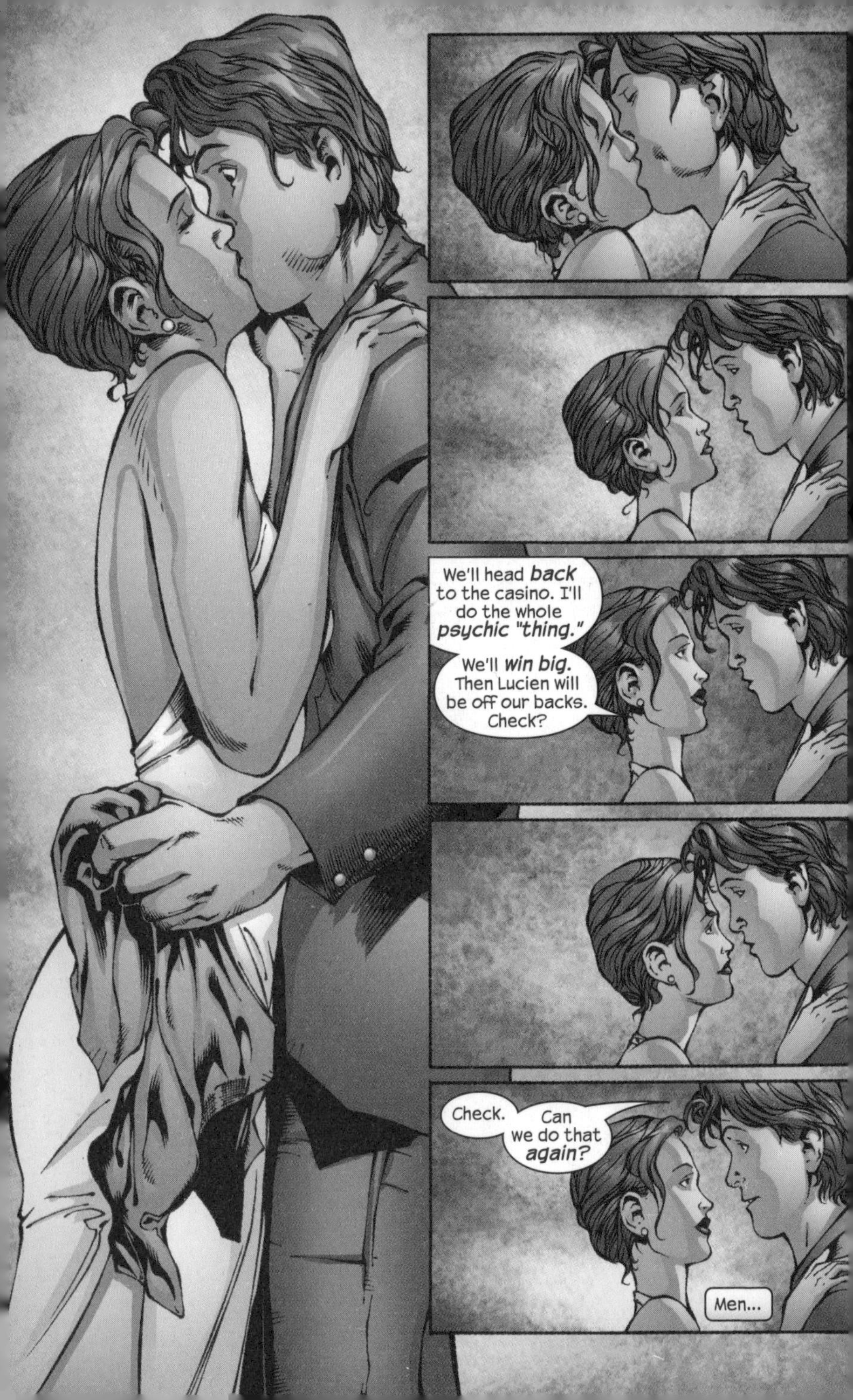

We'll head *back* to the casino. I'll do the whole *psychic "thing."*
We'll *win big.* Then Lucien will be off our backs. Check?
Check.
Can we do that *again?*
Men...

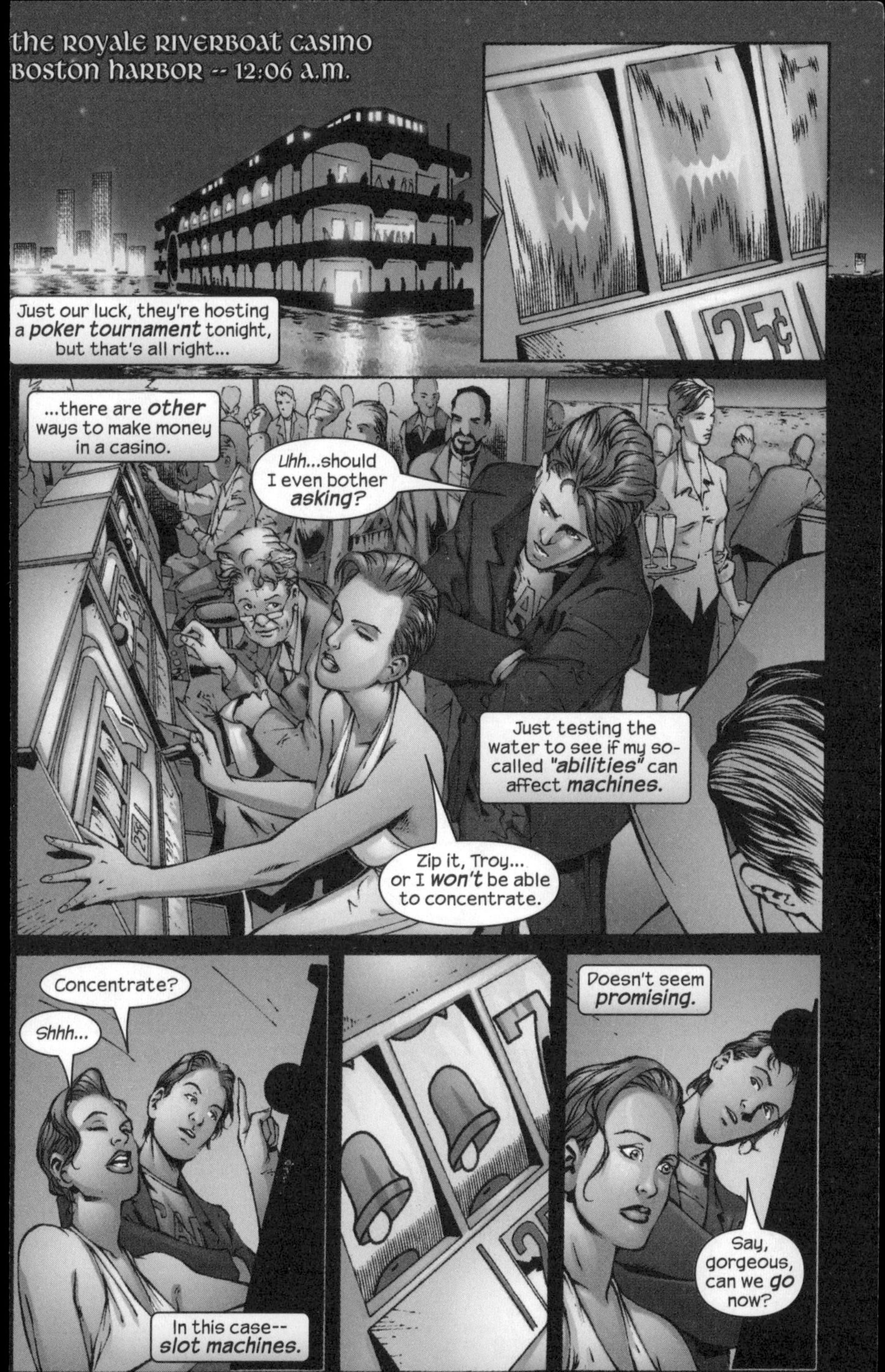

THE ROYALE RIVERBOAT CASINO
BOSTON HARBOR -- 12:06 A.M.
Just our luck, they're hosting a *poker tournament* tonight, but that's all right...
25¢
...there are *other* ways to make money in a casino.
Uhh...should I even bother *asking?*
Just testing the water to see if my so-called *"abilities"* can affect *machines.*
Zip it, Troy... or I *won't* be able to concentrate.
Concentrate?
Shhh...
In this case-- *slot machines.*
Doesn't seem *promising.*
Say, gorgeous, can we *go* now?

Not *yet*, "handsome." I'm *going* to make this work.

Come on, Emma. Picture it in your *mind*.

Focus.

Cherries

Cherries

Cherries

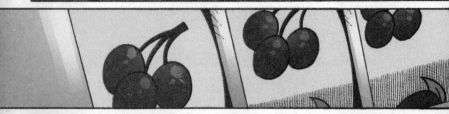

Emma! It worked! We *won*!

Um...

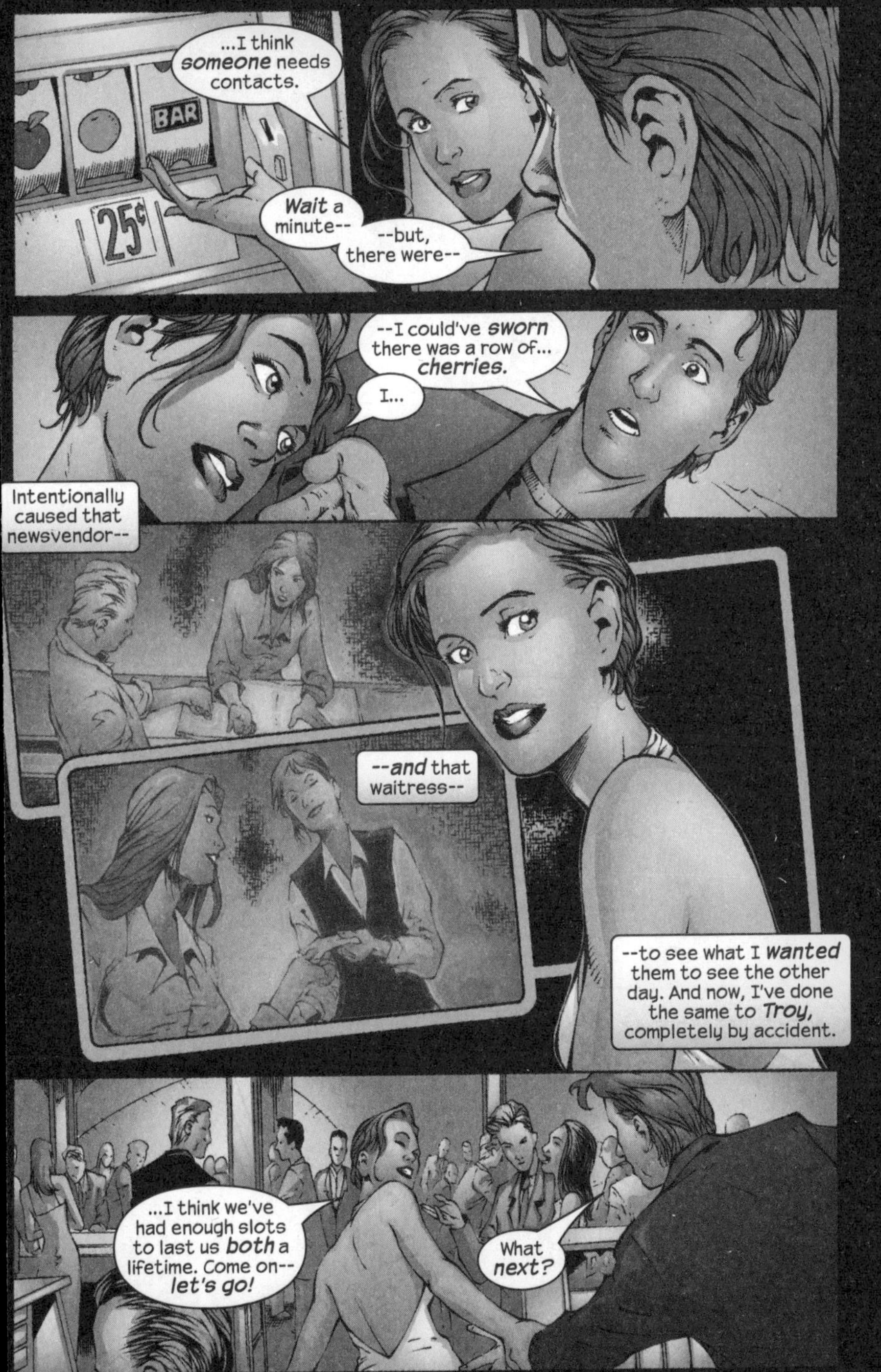

...I think someone needs contacts.
Wait a minute--
--but, there were--
I...
--I could've sworn there was a row of... cherries.
Intentionally caused that newsvendor--
--and that waitress--
--to see what I wanted them to see the other day. And now, I've done the same to Troy, completely by accident.
...I think we've had enough slots to last us both a lifetime. Come on-- let's go!
What next?

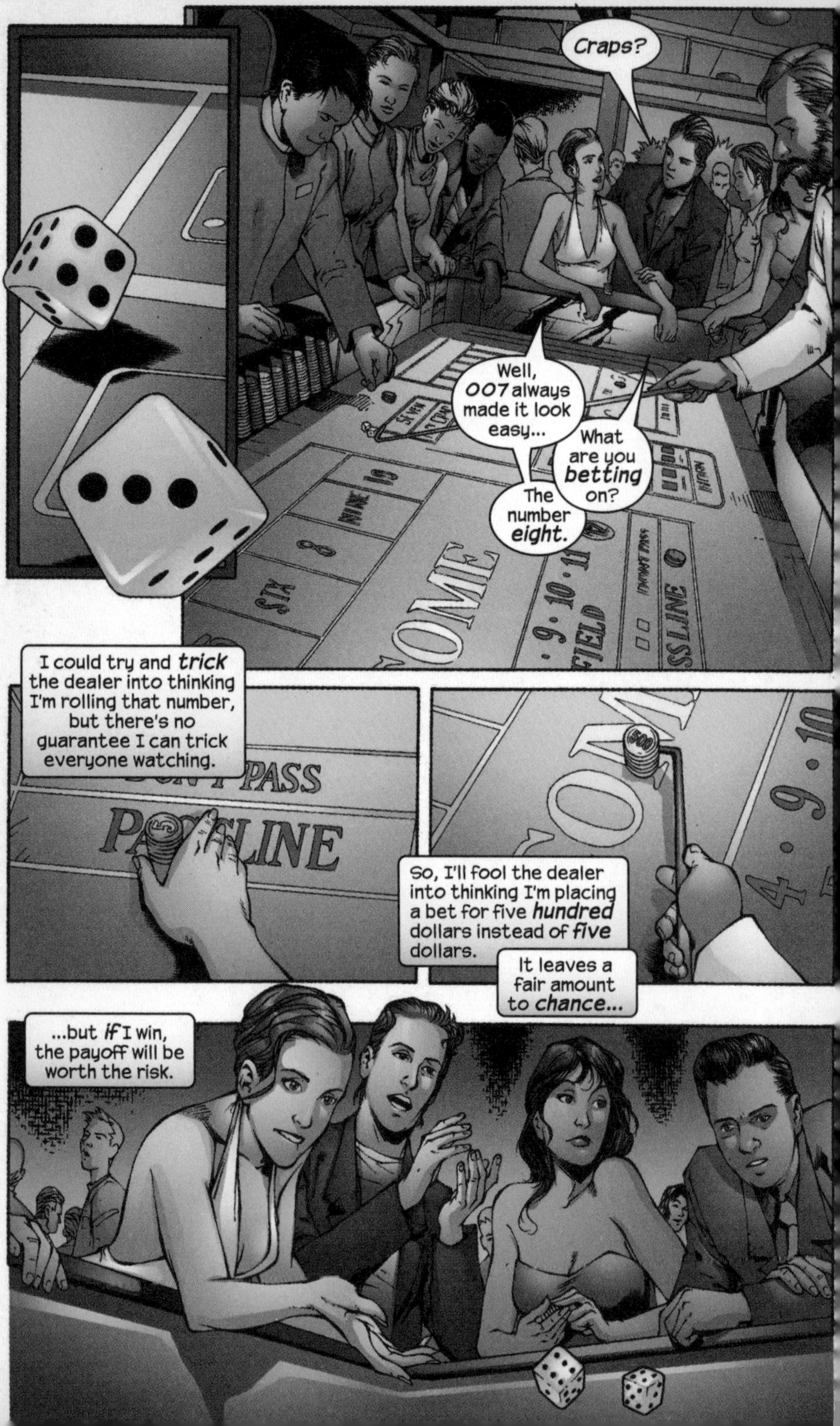
Craps?
Well, 007 always made it look easy...
What are you betting on?
The number eight.
I could try and trick the dealer into thinking I'm rolling that number, but there's no guarantee I can trick everyone watching.
So, I'll fool the dealer into thinking I'm placing a bet for five hundred dollars instead of five dollars.
It leaves a fair amount to chance...
...but if I win, the payoff will be worth the risk.

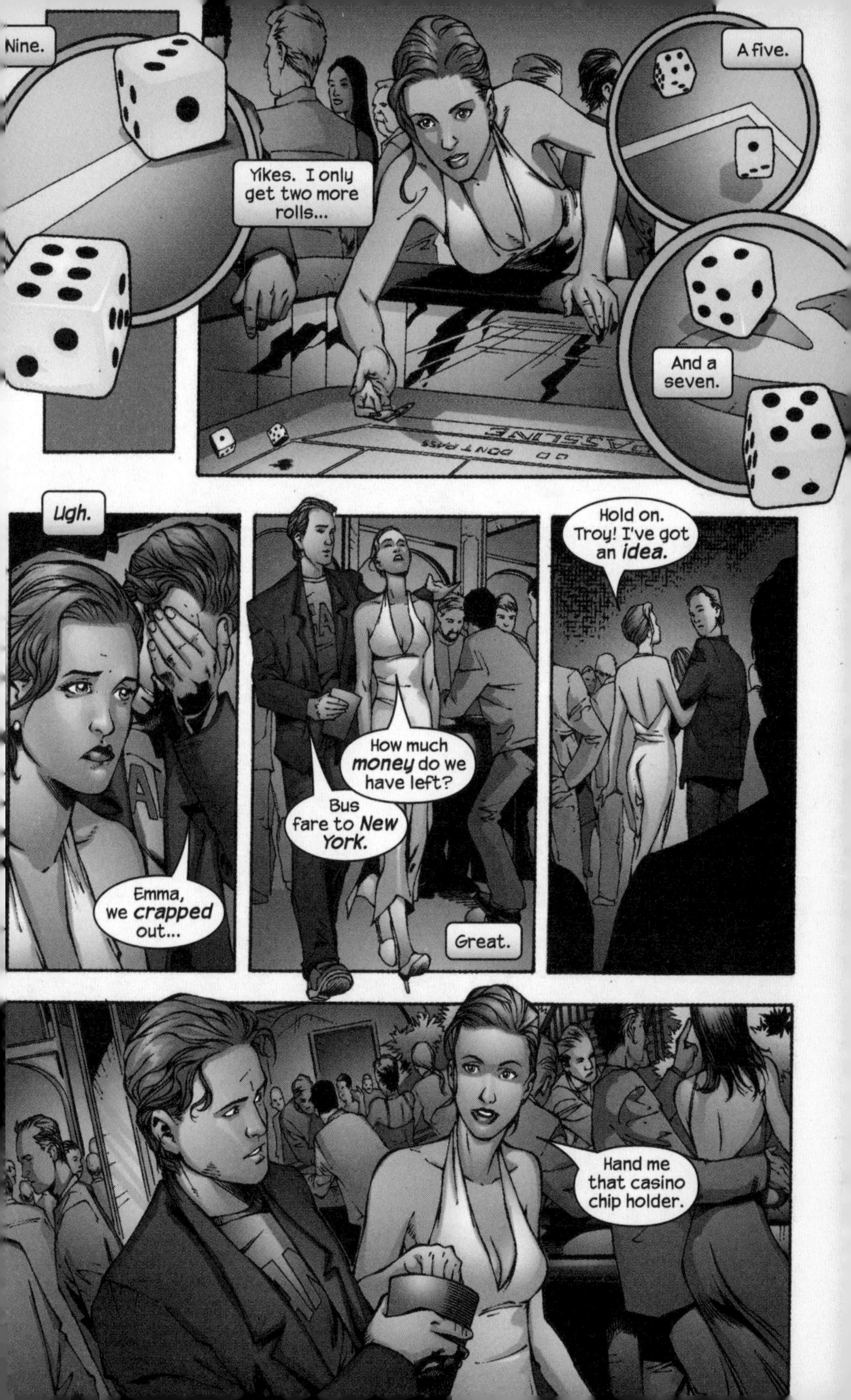
Nine.
Yikes. I only get two more rolls...
A five.
And a seven.
Ugh.
Emma, we crapped out...
How much money do we have left?
Bus fare to New York.
Great.
Hold on. Troy! I've got an idea.
Hand me that casino chip holder.

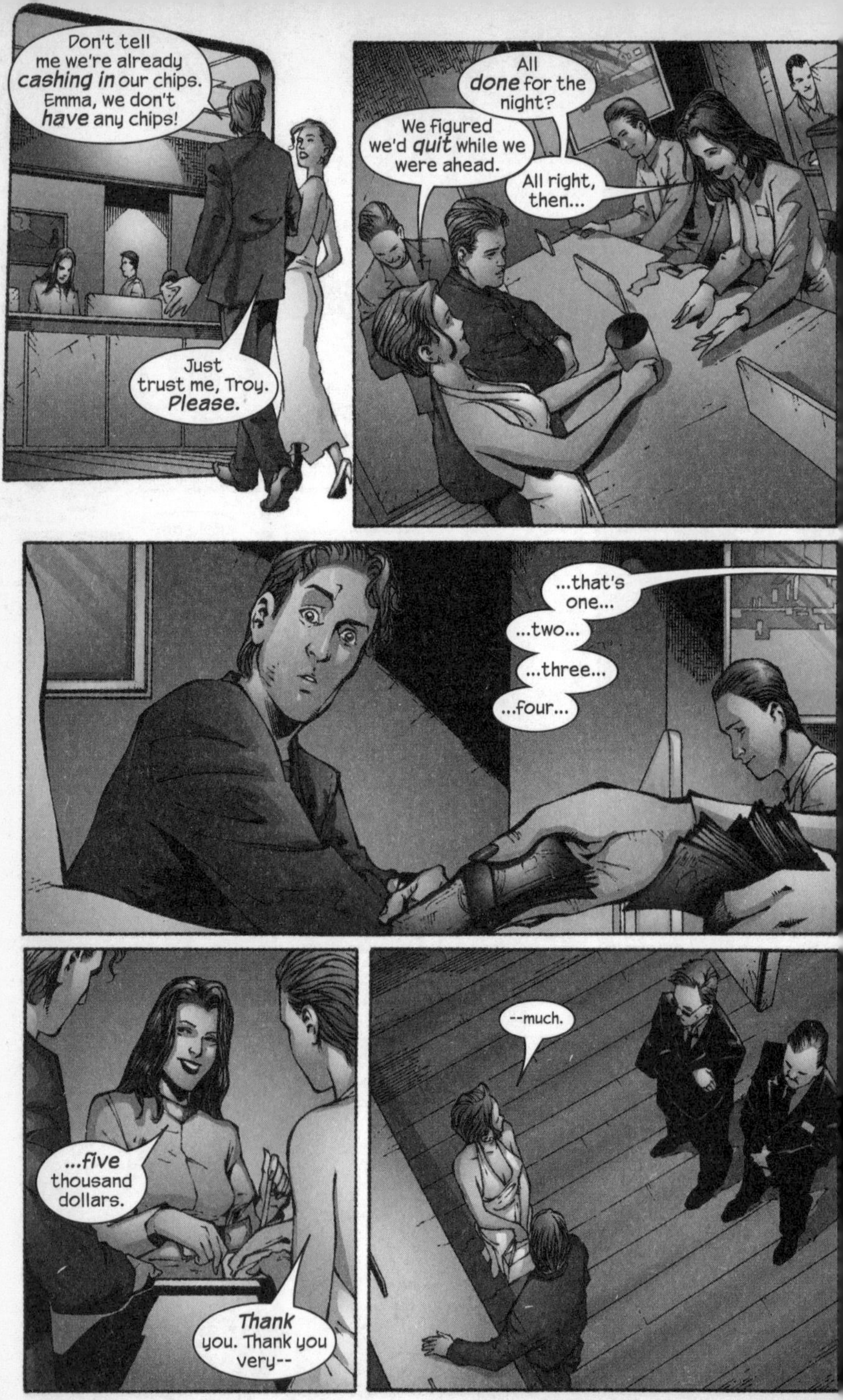
Don't tell me we're already cashing in our chips. Emma, we don't have any chips!
Just trust me, Troy. Please.
All done for the night?
We figured we'd quit while we were ahead.
All right, then...
...that's one...
...two...
...three...
...four...
...five thousand dollars.
Thank you. Thank you very--
--much.

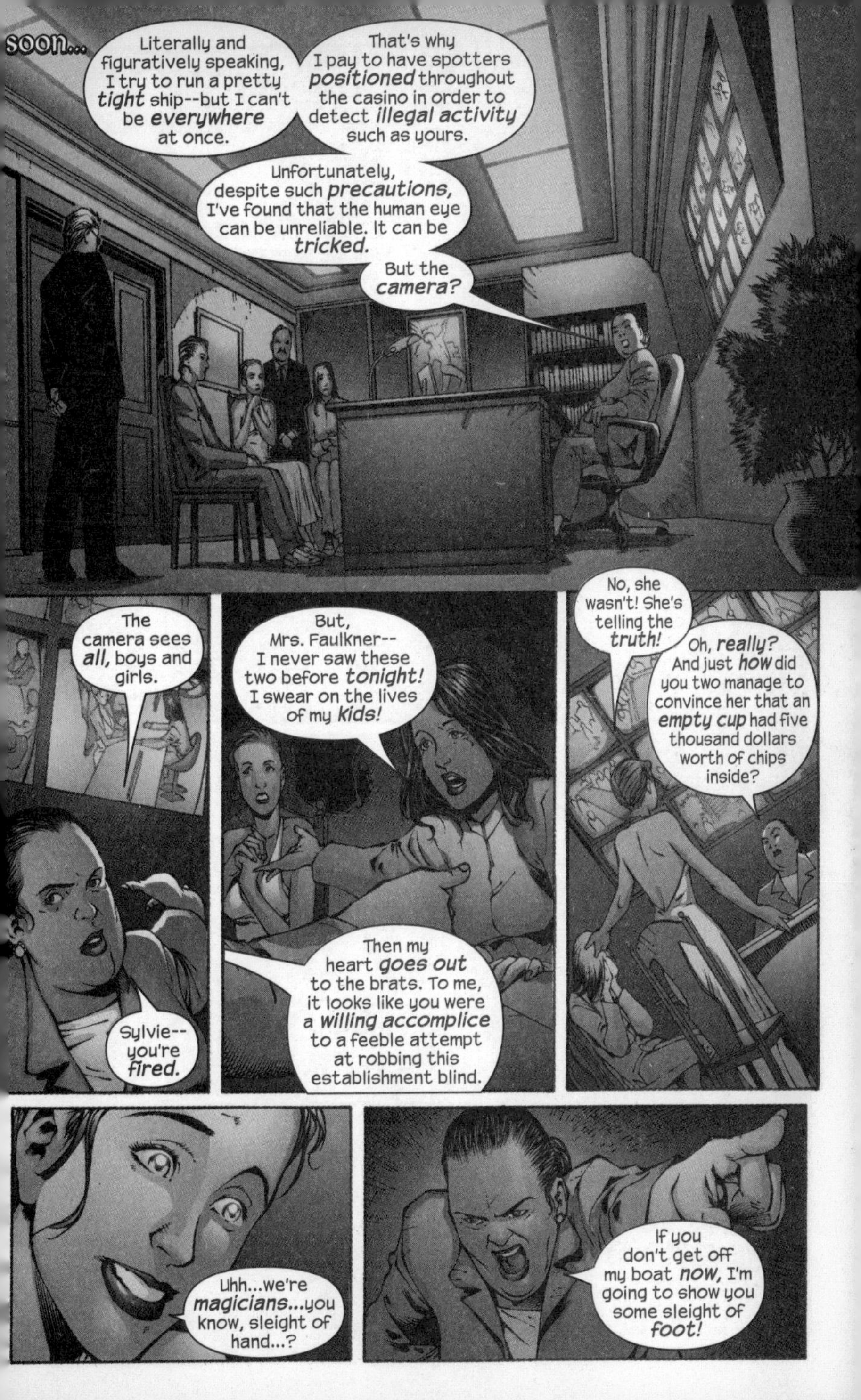
SOON...
Literally and figuratively speaking, I try to run a pretty tight ship--but I can't be everywhere at once.
That's why I pay to have spotters positioned throughout the casino in order to detect illegal activity such as yours.
Unfortunately, despite such precautions, I've found that the human eye can be unreliable. It can be tricked.
But the camera?
The camera sees all, boys and girls.
Sylvie--you're fired.
But, Mrs. Faulkner--I never saw these two before tonight! I swear on the lives of my kids!
Then my heart goes out to the brats. To me, it looks like you were a willing accomplice to a feeble attempt at robbing this establishment blind.
No, she wasn't! She's telling the truth!
Oh, really? And just how did you two manage to convince her that an empty cup had five thousand dollars worth of chips inside?
Uhh...we're magicians...you know, sleight of hand...?
If you don't get off my boat now, I'm going to show you some sleight of foot!

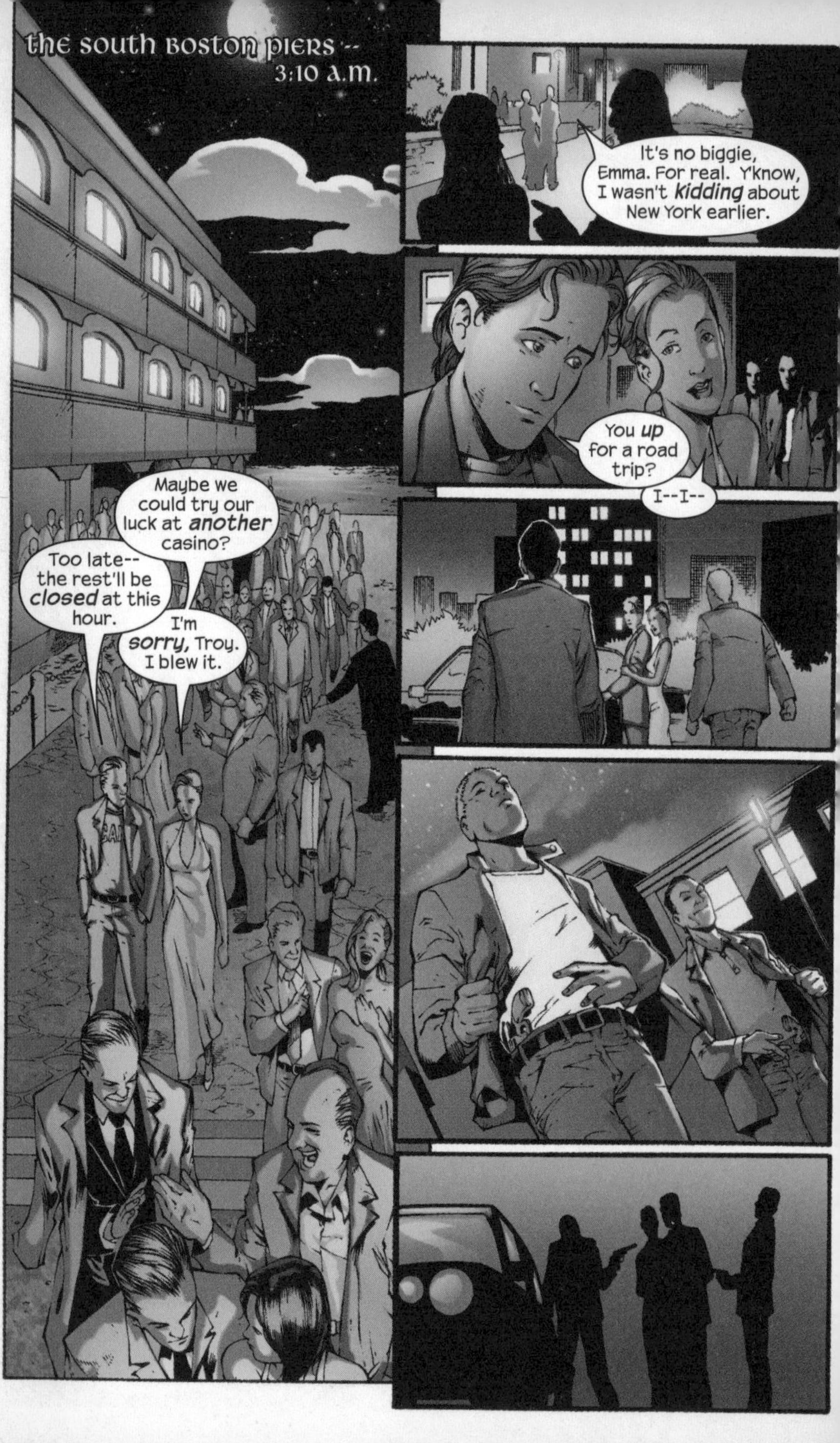
the south boston piers --
3:10 a.m.
Maybe we could try our luck at another casino?
Too late-- the rest'll be closed at this hour.
I'm sorry, Troy. I blew it.
It's no biggie, Emma. For real. Y'know, I wasn't kidding about New York earlier.
You up for a road trip?
I--I--

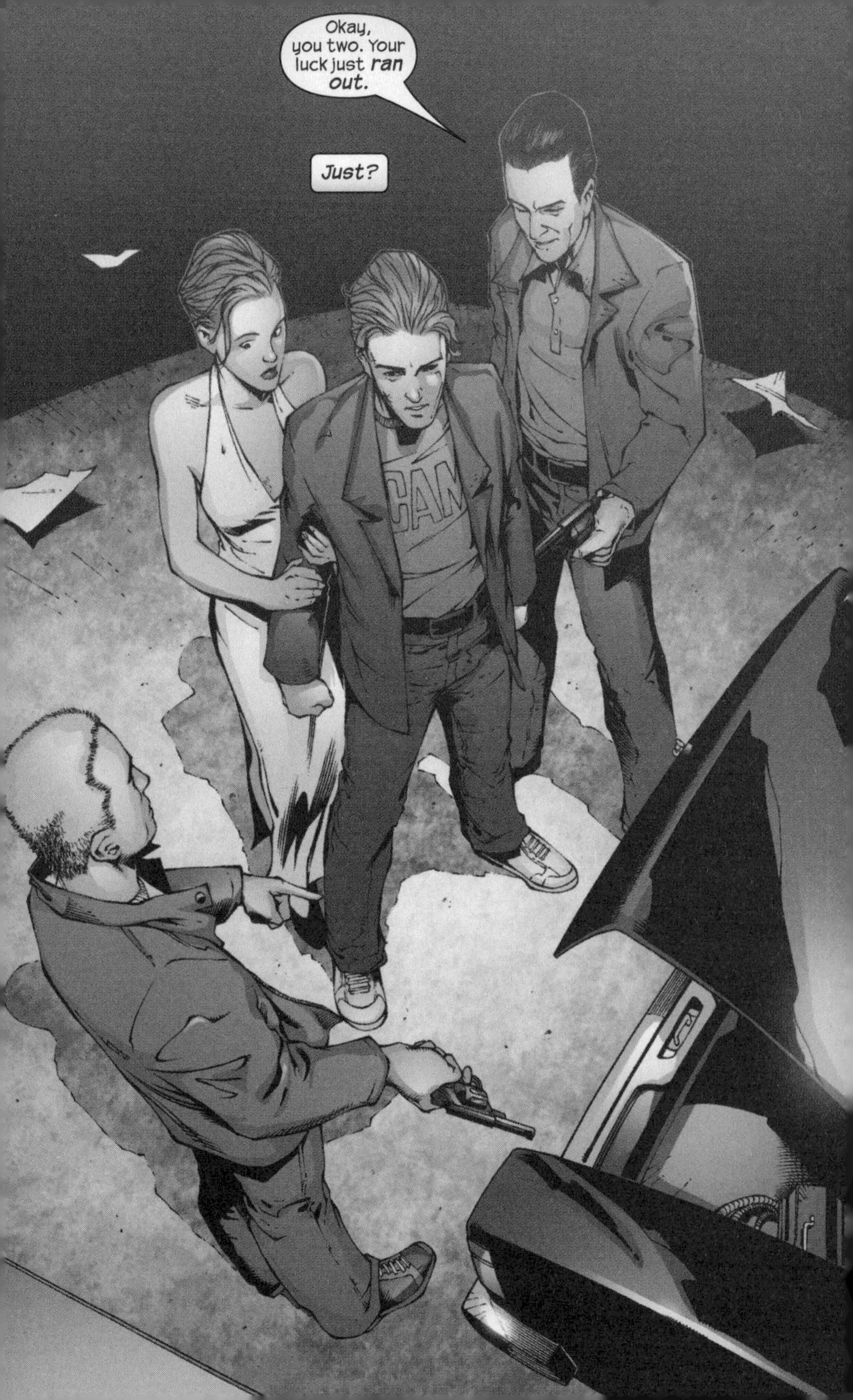
Okay, you two. Your luck just **ran** **out**.
Just?

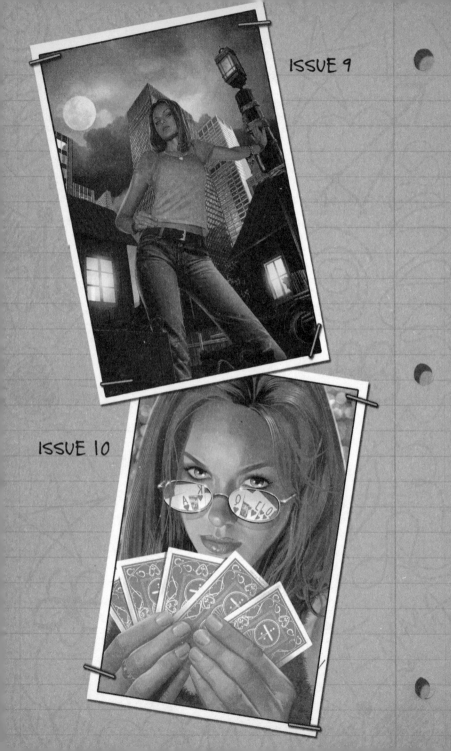

ISSUE 9

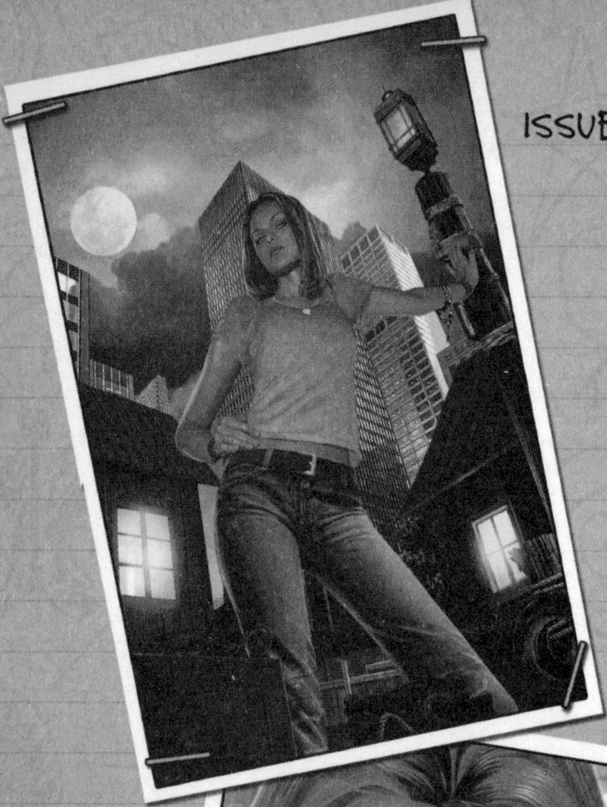

ISSUE 10

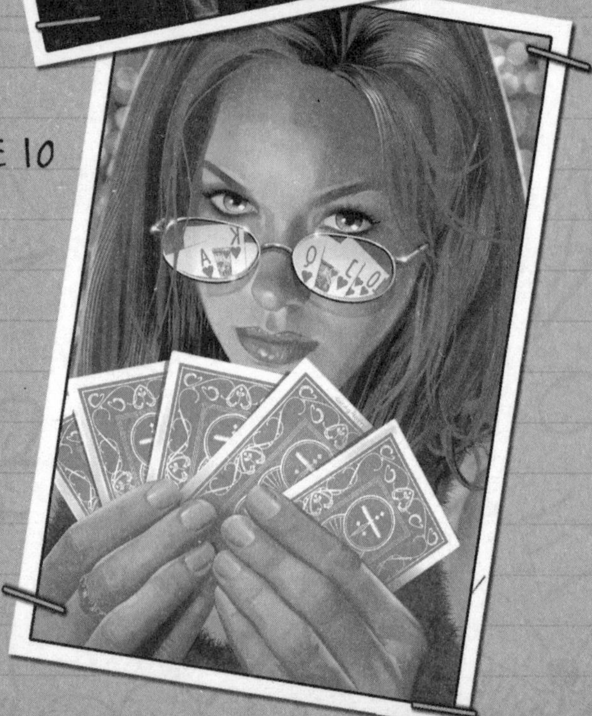

MIND GAMES 4 OF 6

A SIMPLE PLAN

Want to know the *best* thing about a box of *Cracker Jacks?*

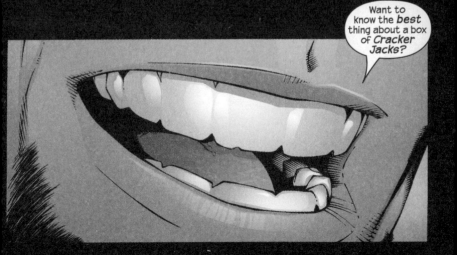

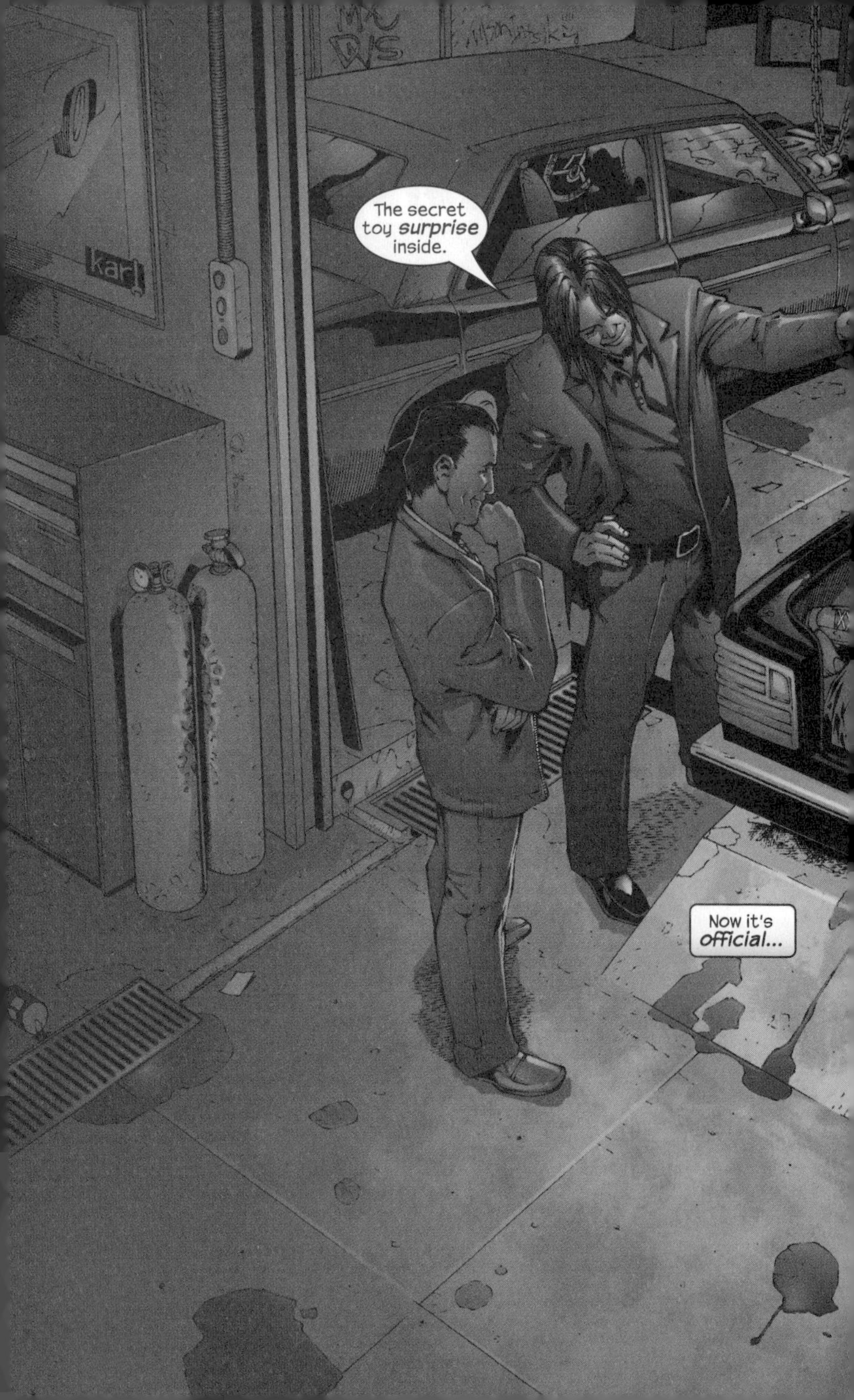
karl
The secret toy *surprise* inside.
Now it's *official...*

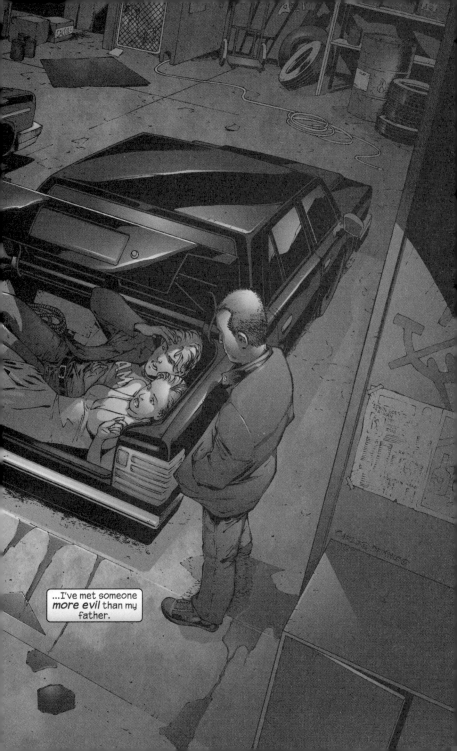

...I've met someone *more evil* than my father.

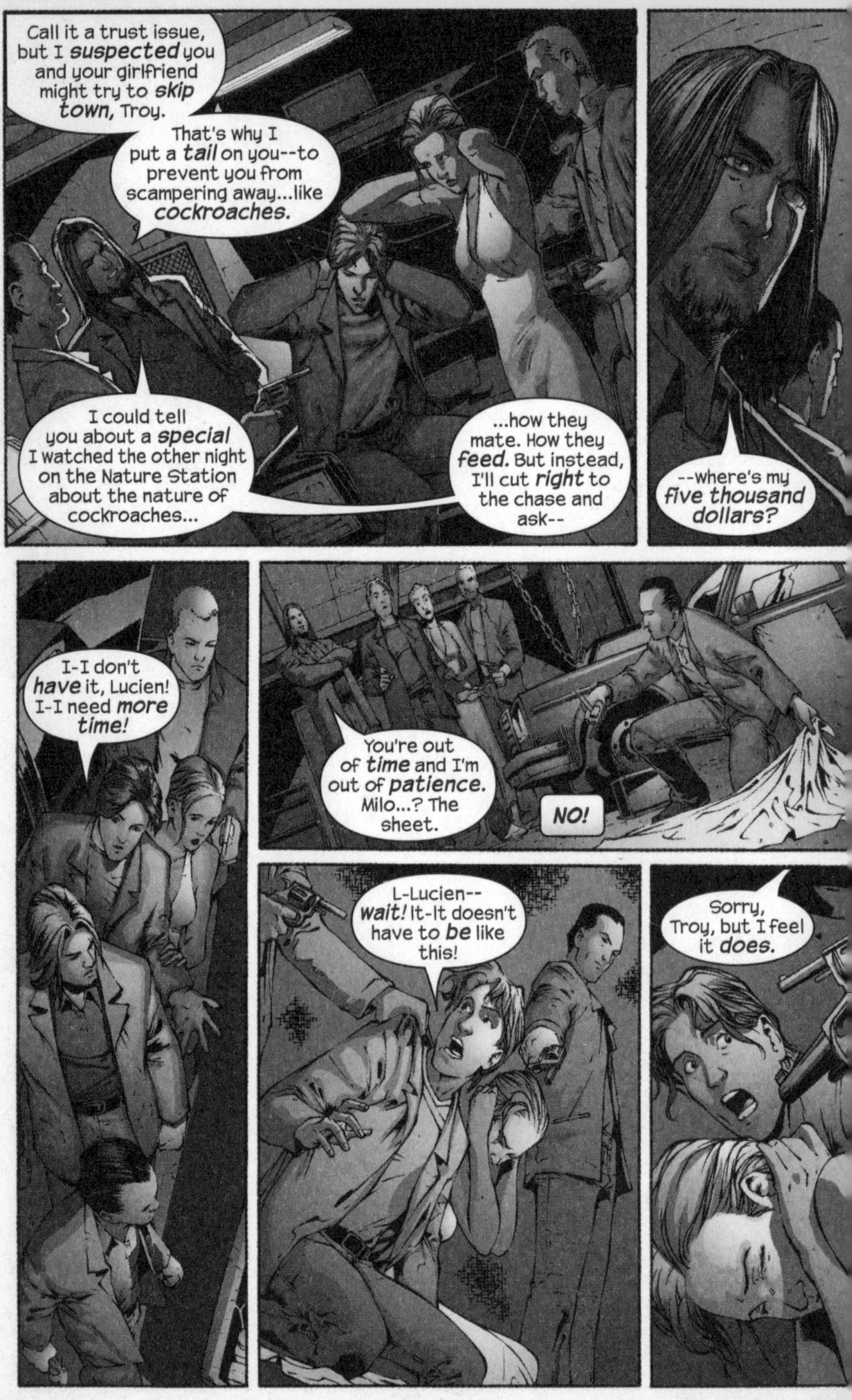
Call it a trust issue, but I suspected you and your girlfriend might try to skip town, Troy.
That's why I put a tail on you--to prevent you from scampering away...like cockroaches.
I could tell you about a special I watched the other night on the Nature Station about the nature of cockroaches...
...how they mate. How they feed. But instead, I'll cut right to the chase and ask--
--where's my five thousand dollars?
I-I don't have it, Lucien! I-I need more time!
You're out of time and I'm out of patience. Milo...? The sheet.
NO!
L-Lucien-- wait! It-It doesn't have to be like this!
Sorry, Troy, but I feel it does.

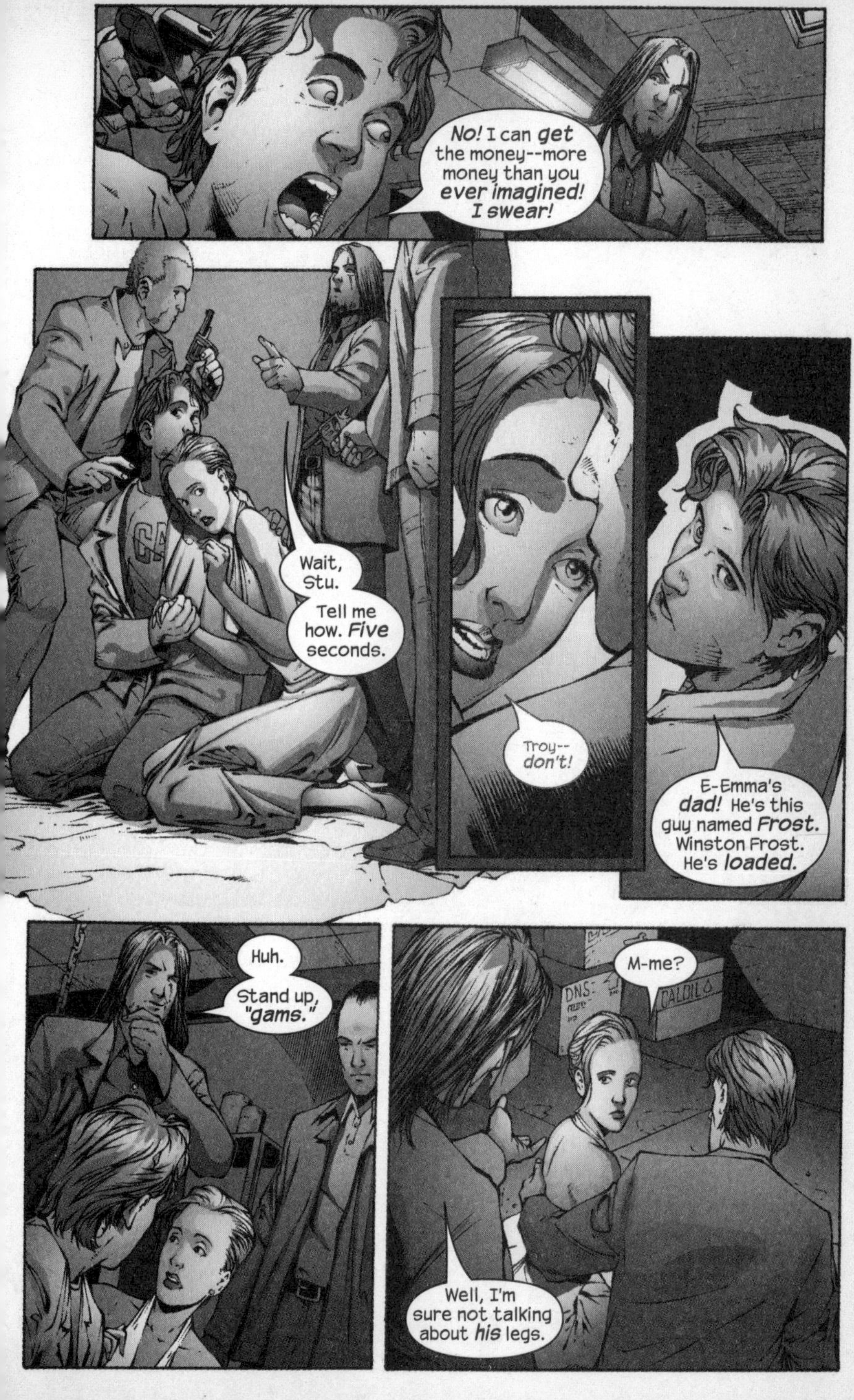
No! I can get the money--more money than you ever imagined! I swear!
Wait, Stu.
Tell me how. Five seconds.
Troy--don't!
E-Emma's dad! He's this guy named Frost. Winston Frost. He's loaded.
Huh.
Stand up, "gams."
M-me?
Well, I'm sure not talking about his legs.

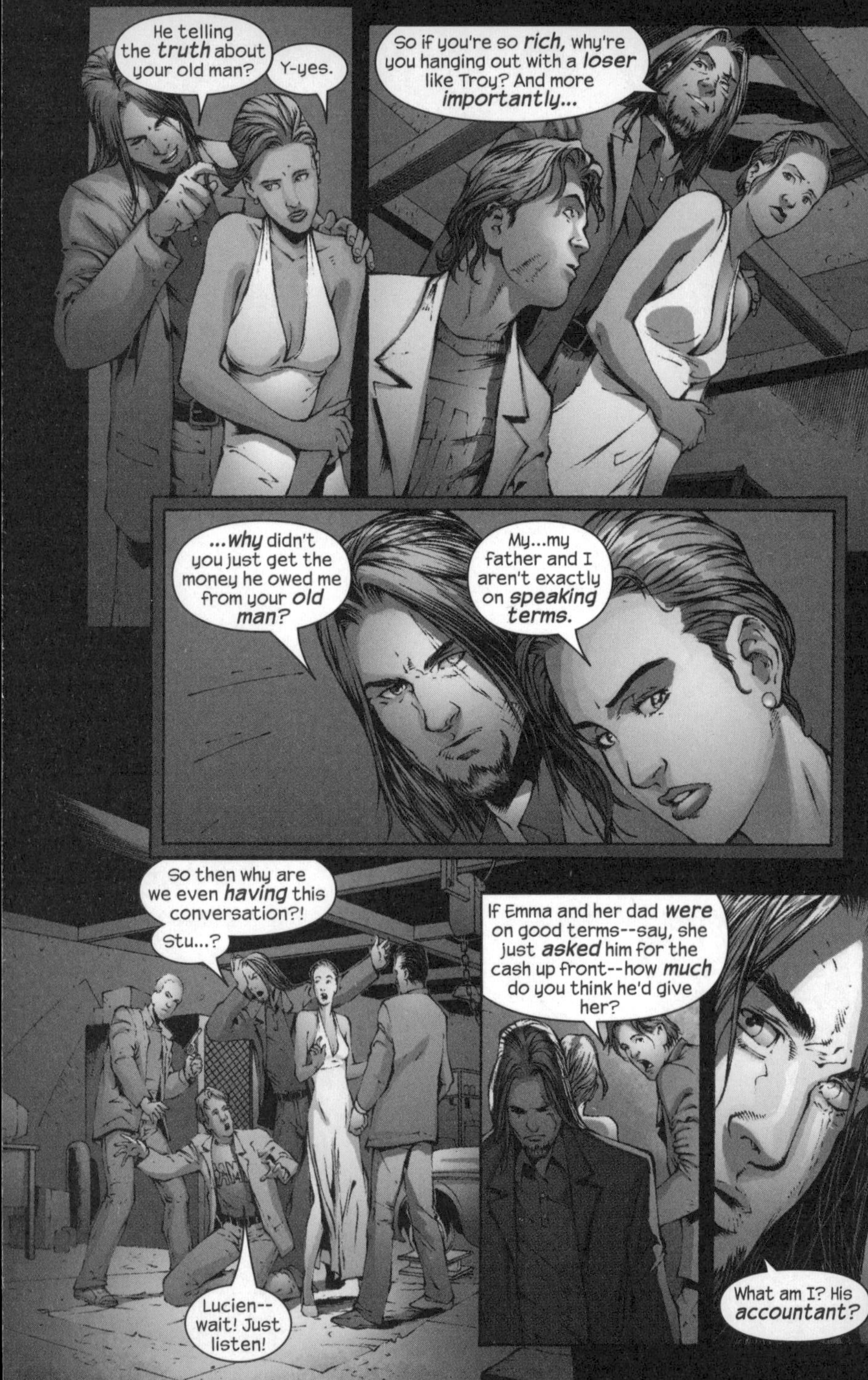
He telling the truth about your old man?
Y-yes.
So if you're so rich, why're you hanging out with a loser like Troy? And more importantly...
...why didn't you just get the money he owed me from your old man?
My...my father and I aren't exactly on speaking terms.
So then why are we even having this conversation?!
Stu...?
Lucien--wait! Just listen!
If Emma and her dad were on good terms--say, she just asked him for the cash up front--how much do you think he'd give her?
What am I? His accountant?

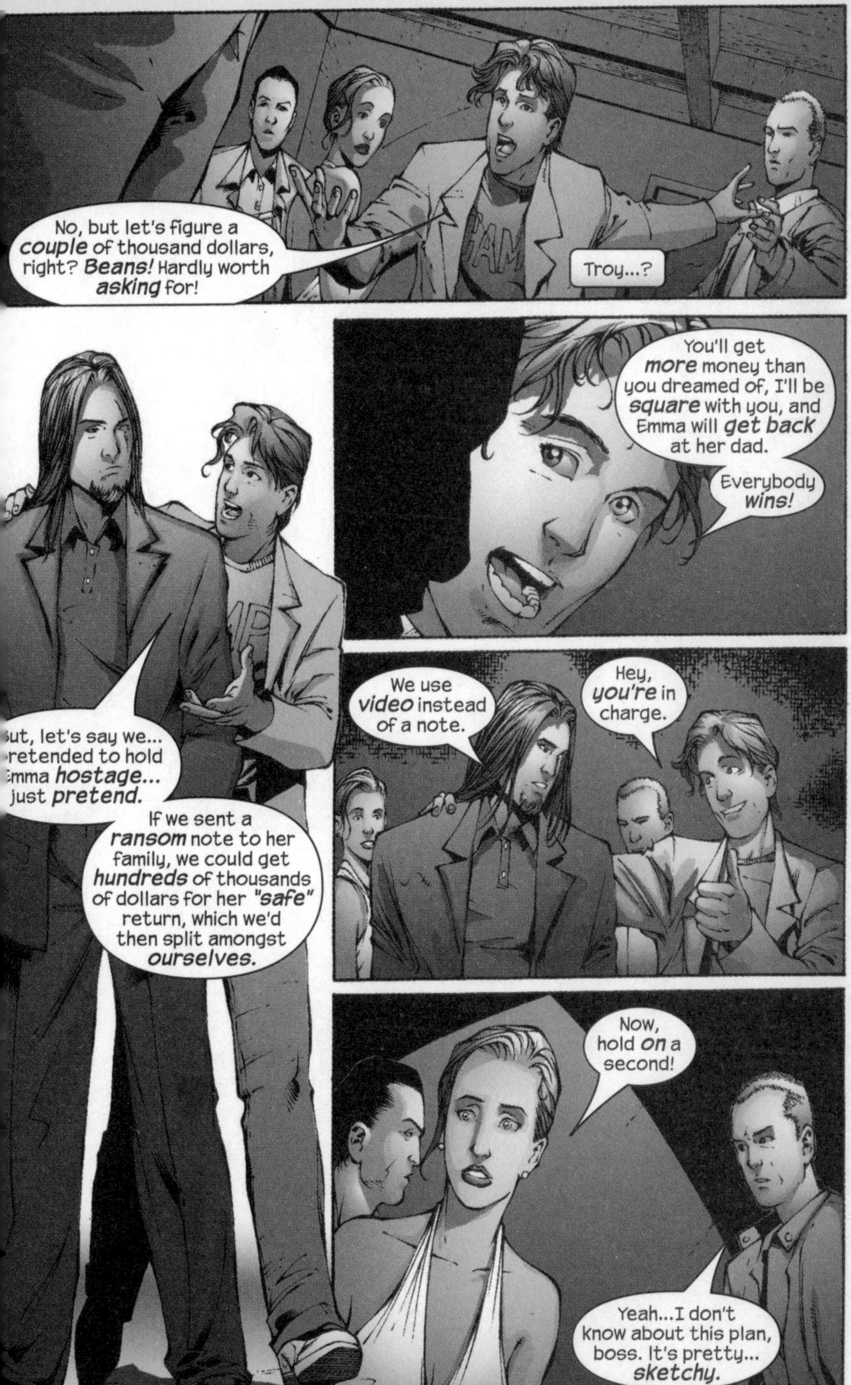
No, but let's figure a couple of thousand dollars, right? Beans! Hardly worth asking for!
Troy...?
ut, let's say we... retended to hold mma hostage... just pretend.
If we sent a ransom note to her family, we could get hundreds of thousands of dollars for her "safe" return, which we'd then split amongst ourselves.
You'll get more money than you dreamed of, I'll be square with you, and Emma will get back at her dad.
Everybody wins!
We use video instead of a note.
Hey, you're in charge.
Now, hold on a second!
Yeah...I don't know about this plan, boss. It's pretty... sketchy.

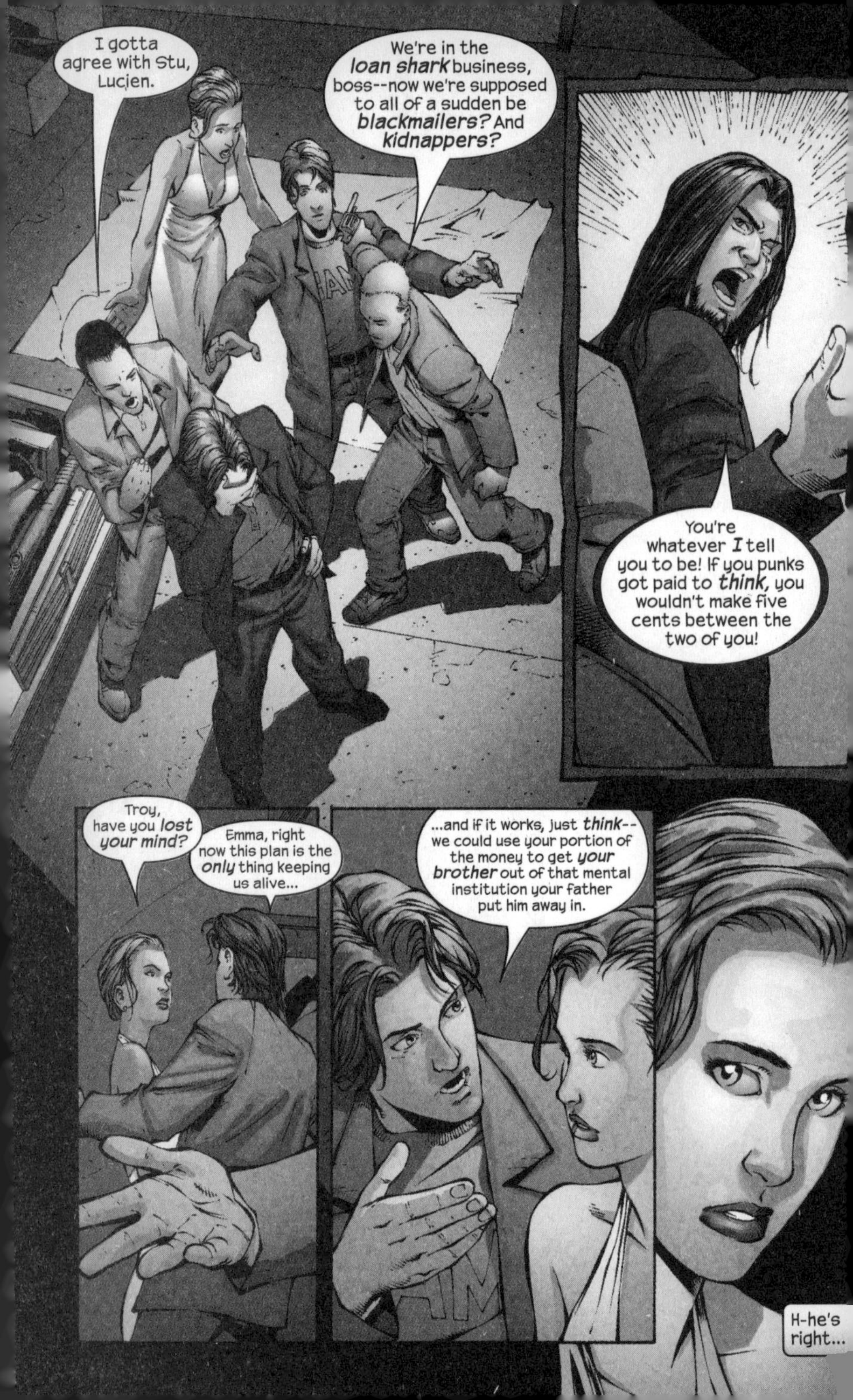
I gotta agree with Stu, Lucien.
We're in the loan shark business, boss--now we're supposed to all of a sudden be blackmailers? And kidnappers?
You're whatever I tell you to be! If you punks got paid to think, you wouldn't make five cents between the two of you!
Troy, have you lost your mind?
Emma, right now this plan is the only thing keeping us alive...
...and if it works, just think--we could use your portion of the money to get your brother out of that mental institution your father put him away in.
H-he's right...

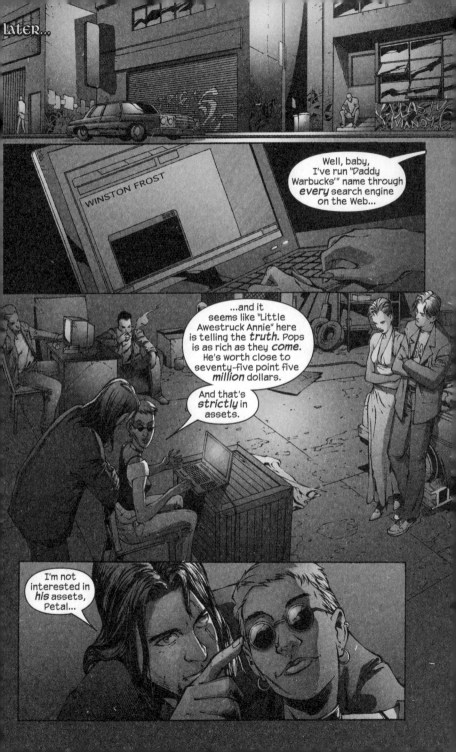

LATER...

WINSTON FROST

Well, baby, I've run "Daddy Warbucks'" name through *every* search engine on the Web...

...and it seems like "Little Awestruck Annie" here is telling the *truth*. Pops is as rich as they *come*. He's worth close to seventy-five point five *million* dollars.

And that's *strictly* in assets.

I'm not interested in *his* assets, Petal...

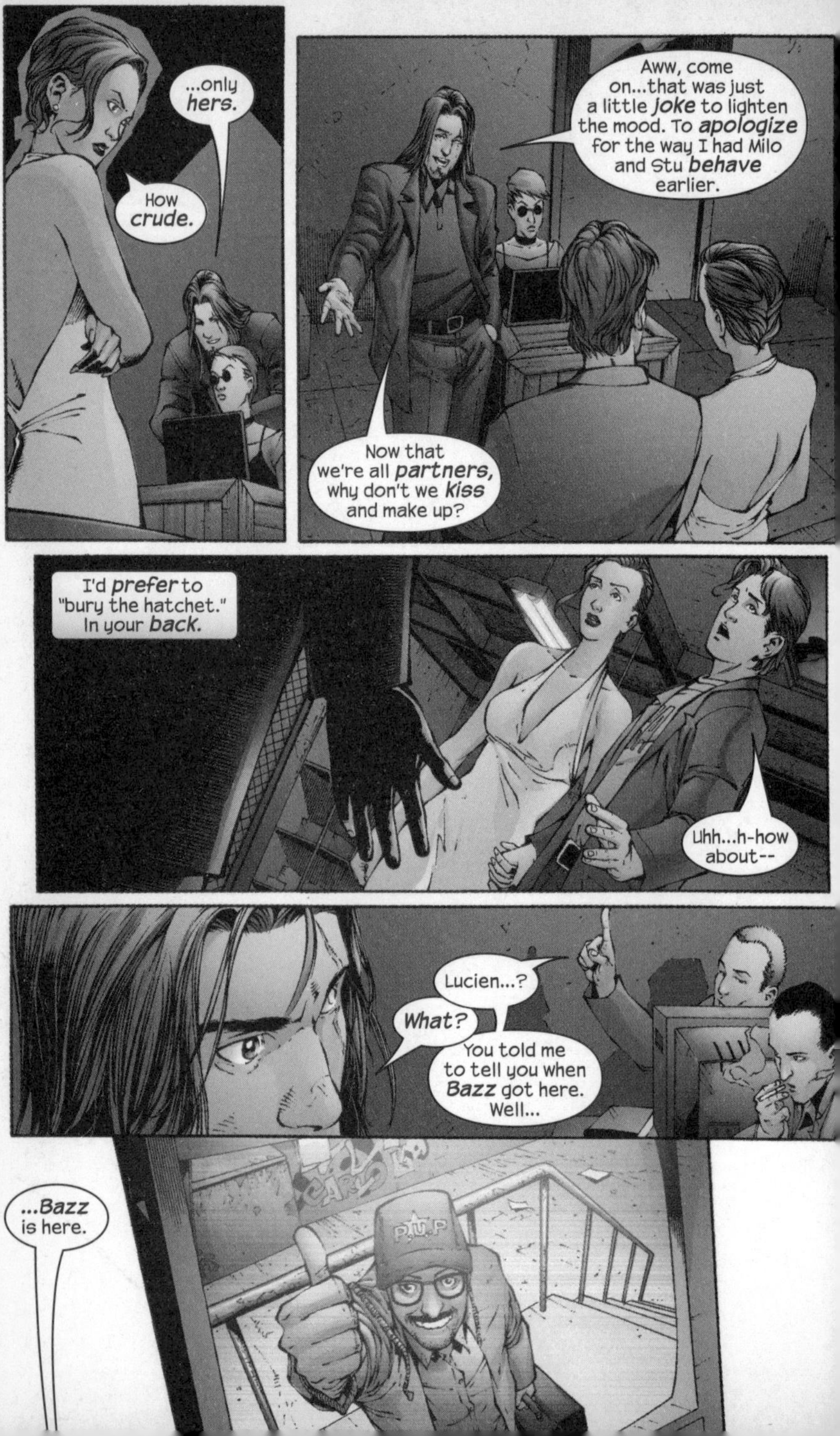
...only hers.
How crude.
Aww, come on...that was just a little joke to lighten the mood. To apologize for the way I had Milo and Stu behave earlier.
Now that we're all partners, why don't we kiss and make up?
I'd prefer to "bury the hatchet." In your back.
Uhh...h-how about--
Lucien...?
What?
You told me to tell you when Bazz got here. Well...
...Bazz is here.
P.U.P

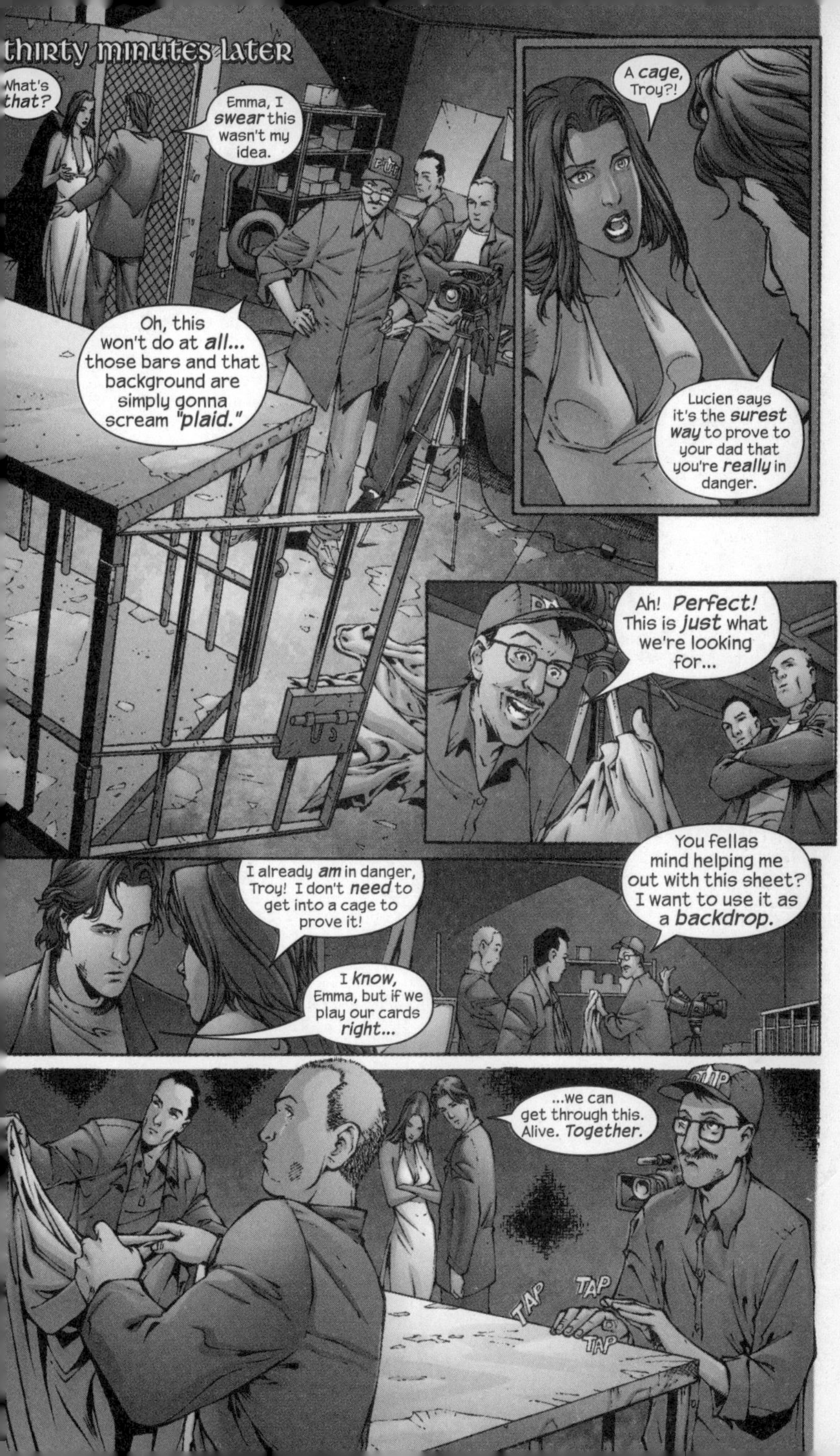
thirty minutes later
What's that?
Emma, I swear this wasn't my idea.
A cage, Troy?!
Oh, this won't do at all... those bars and that background are simply gonna scream "plaid."
Lucien says it's the surest way to prove to your dad that you're really in danger.
Ah! Perfect! This is just what we're looking for...
I already am in danger, Troy! I don't need to get into a cage to prove it!
You fellas mind helping me out with this sheet? I want to use it as a backdrop.
I know, Emma, but if we play our cards right...
...we can get through this. Alive. Together.
TAP
TAP
TAP

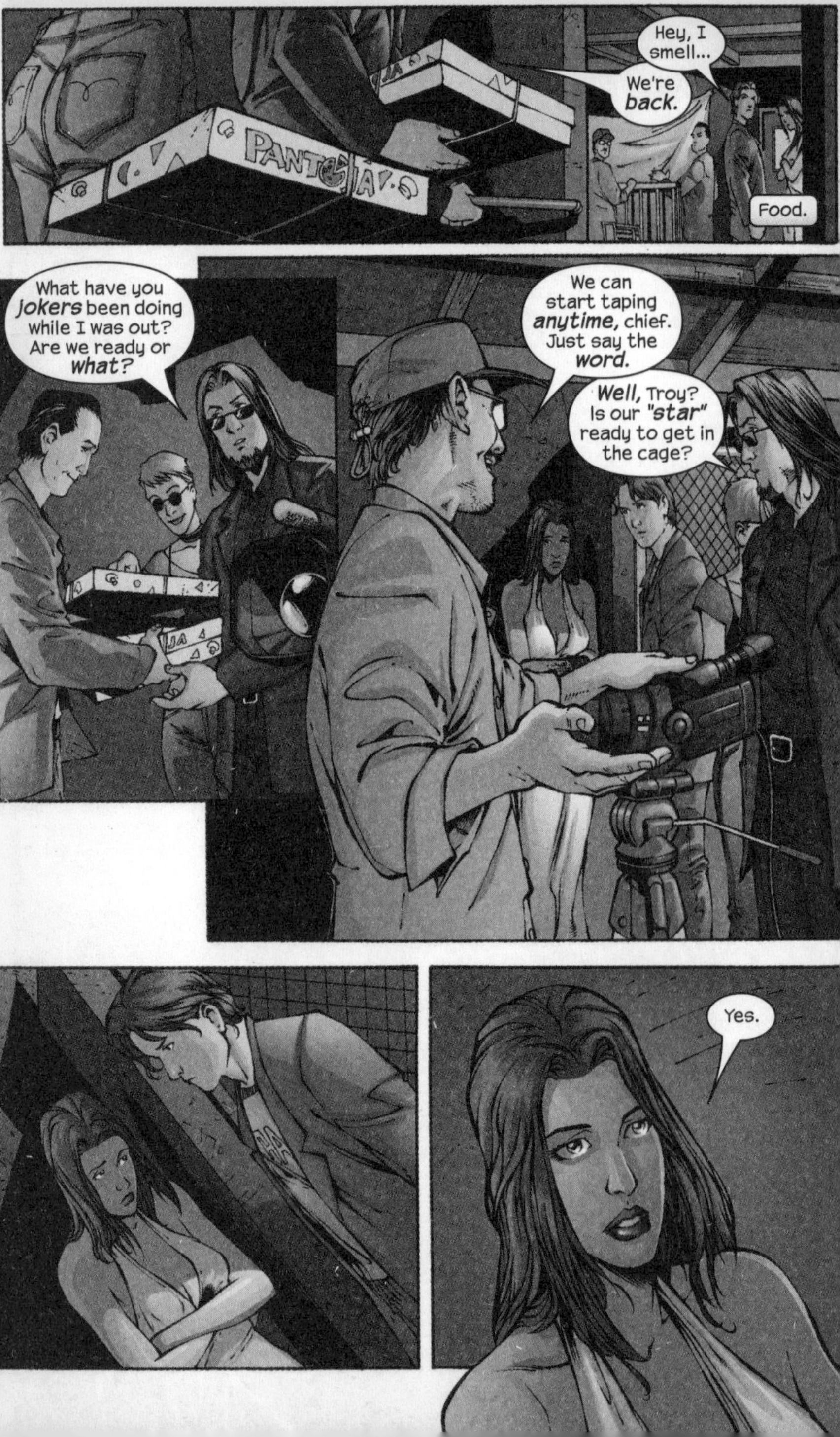
We're back.
Hey, I smell...
Food.
What have you jokers been doing while I was out? Are we ready or what?
We can start taping anytime, chief. Just say the word.
Well, Troy? Is our "star" ready to get in the cage?
Yes.

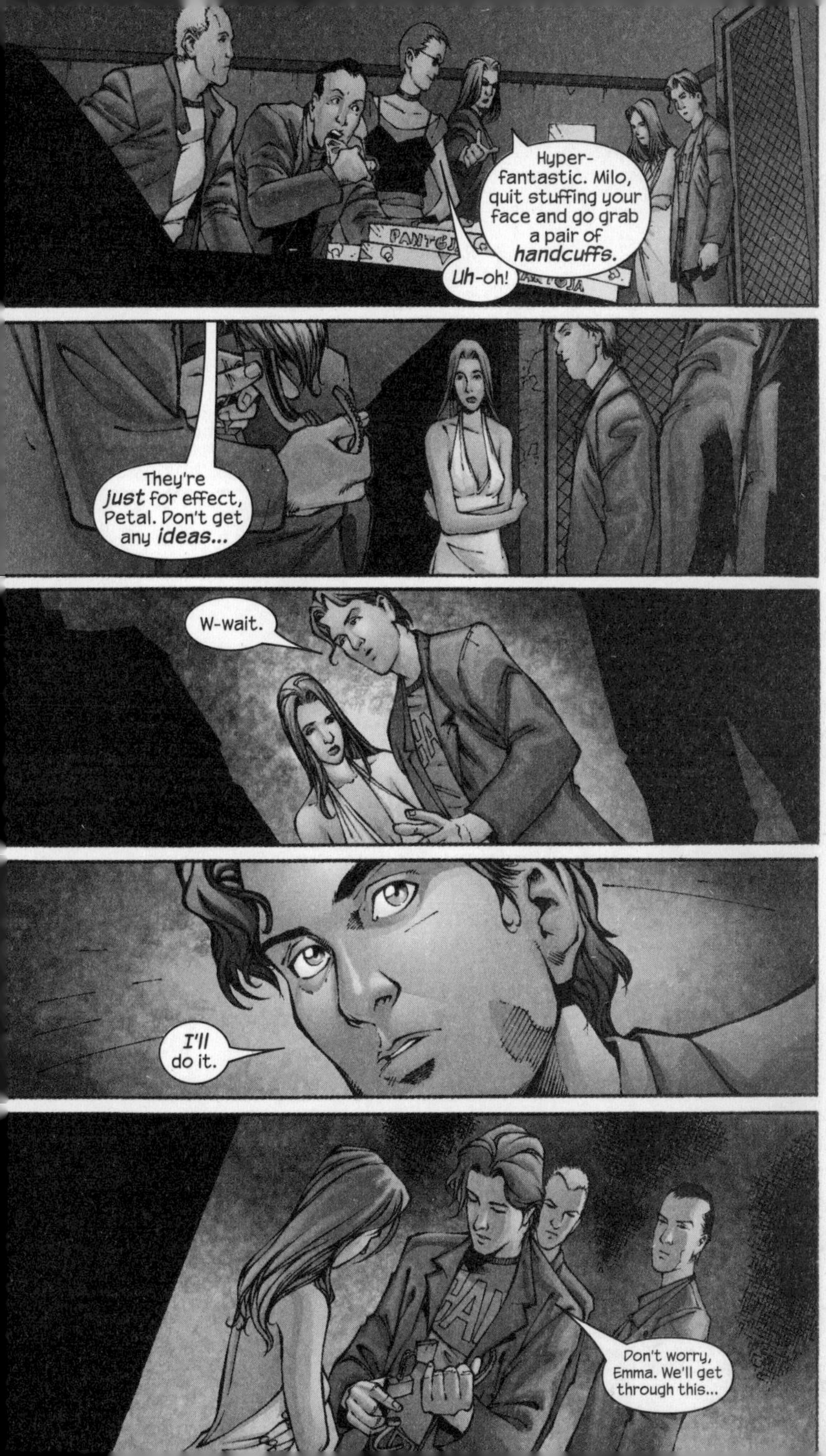
Hyper-fantastic. Milo, quit stuffing your face and go grab a pair of handcuffs.
Uh-oh!
They're just for effect, Petal. Don't get any ideas...
W-wait.
I'll do it.
Don't worry, Emma. We'll get through this...

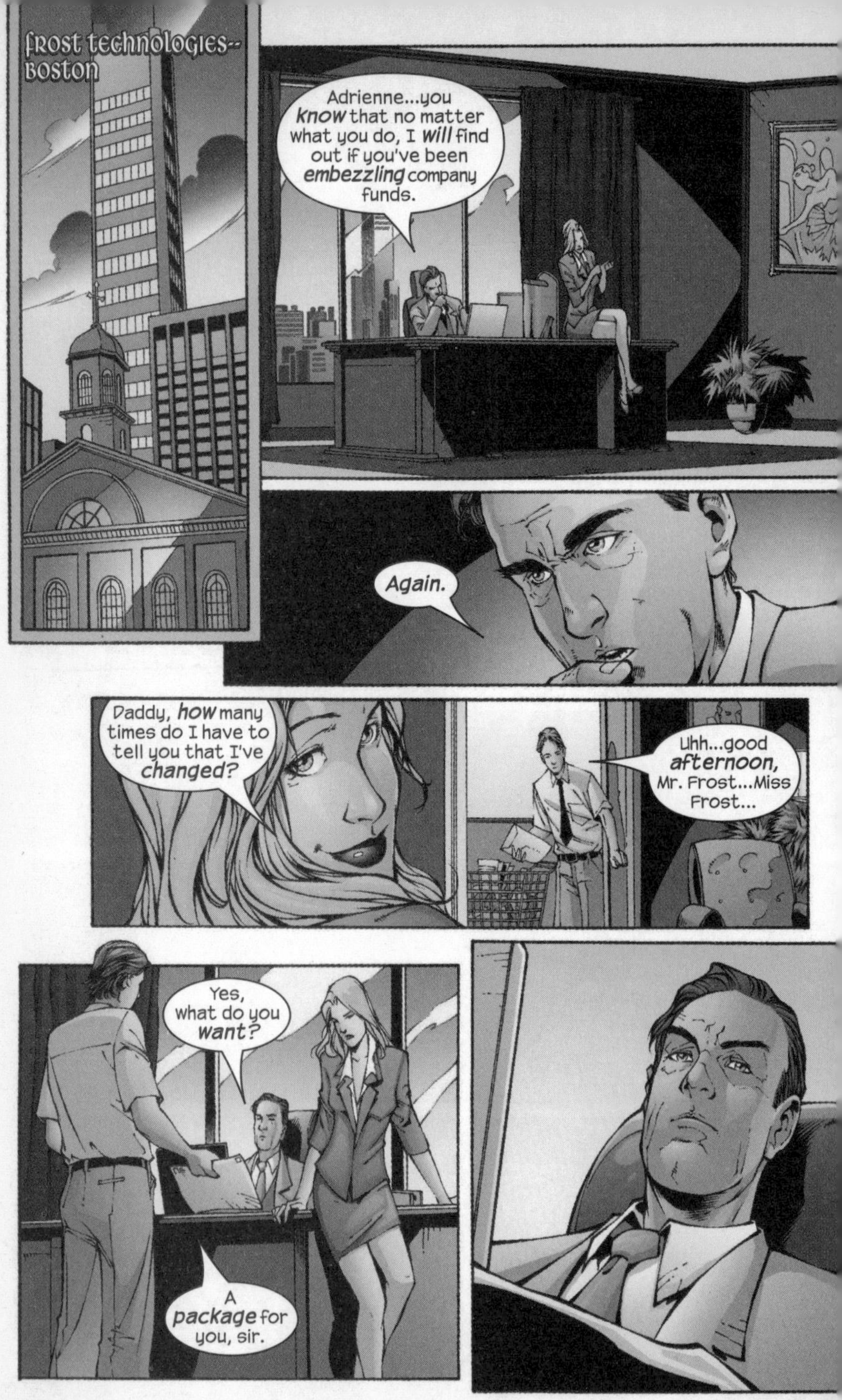
Frost Technologies--
Boston
Adrienne...you know that no matter what you do, I will find out if you've been embezzling company funds.
Again.
Daddy, how many times do I have to tell you that I've changed?
Uhh...good afternoon, Mr. Frost...Miss Frost...
Yes, what do you want?
A package for you, sir.

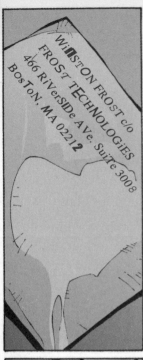

WiNSTON FROST c/o
FROST TECHNOLOGiES
466 RiVerSiDe AVe. SuiTe 3008
BoSToN, MA 02212

What is it, Daddy...?

I don't **care**.

Very creative packaging, **that's** for sure...

It's a... **videocassette.** And it...it's marked...

FWUMP

... "DIL-EMMA".

W-**what** did you say...?

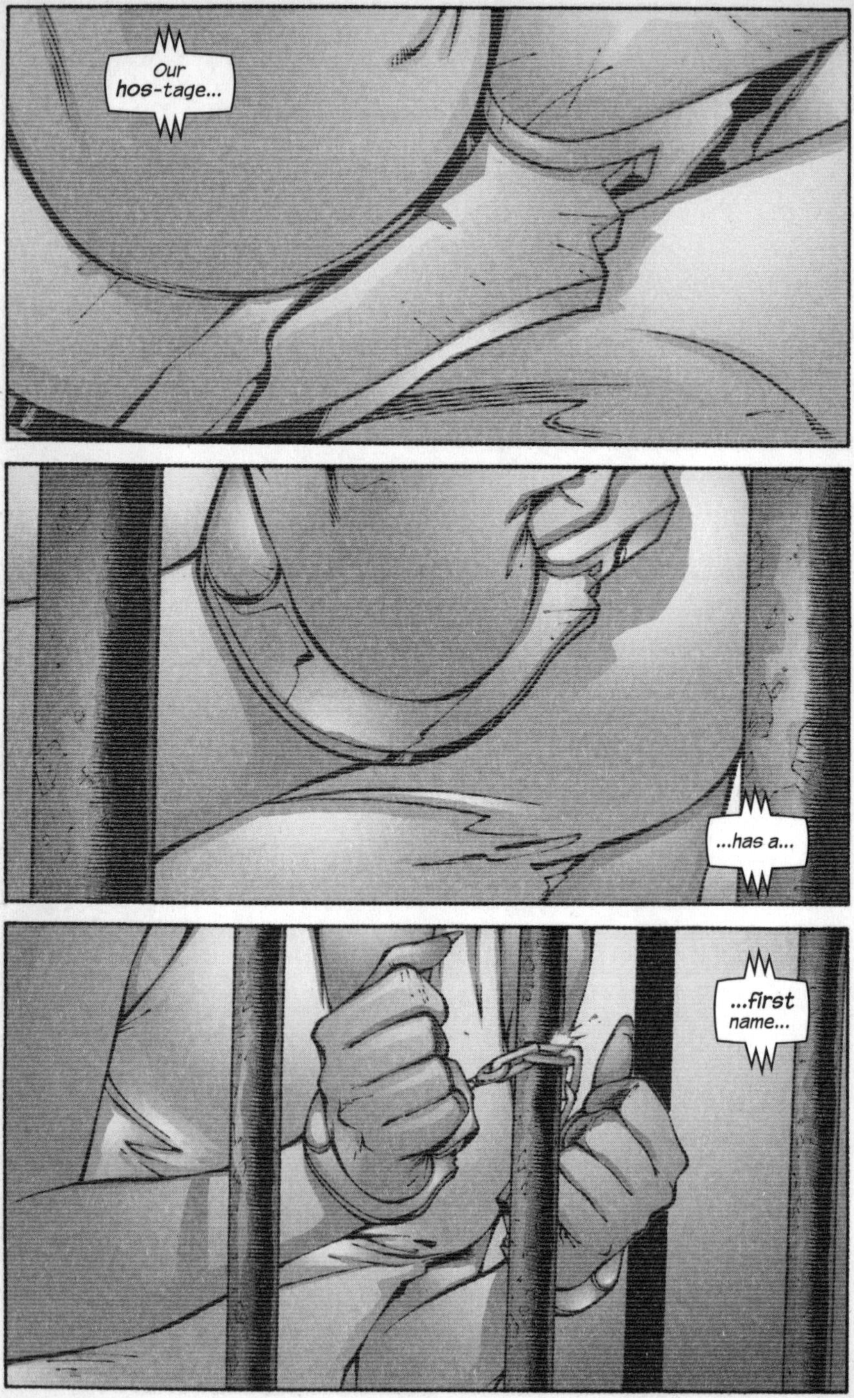

Our hos-tage...
...has a...
...first name...

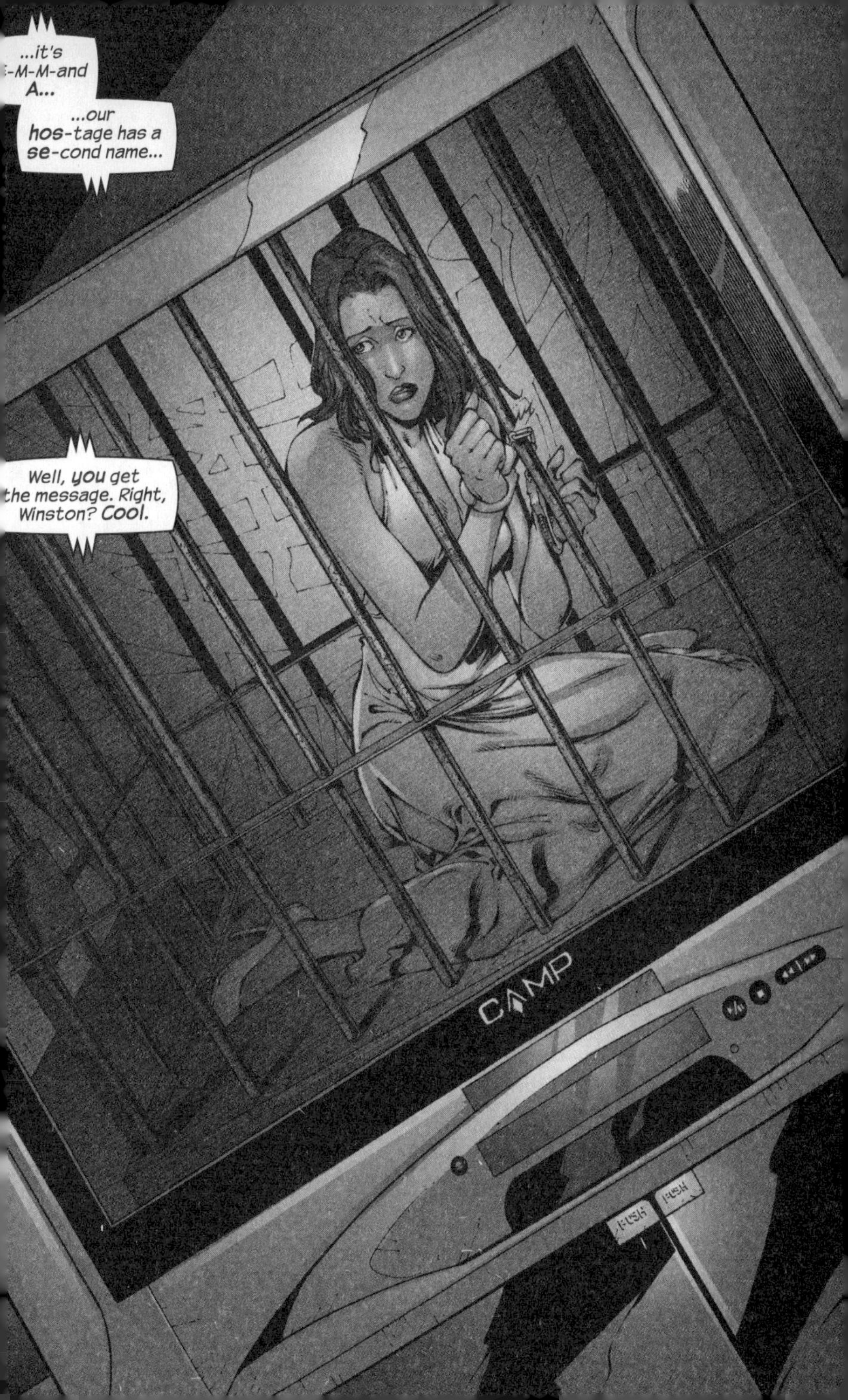
...it's
E-M-M-and
A...
...our
hos-tage has a
se-cond name...
Well, you get
the message. Right,
Winston? Cool.
CAMP
PUSH
PUSH

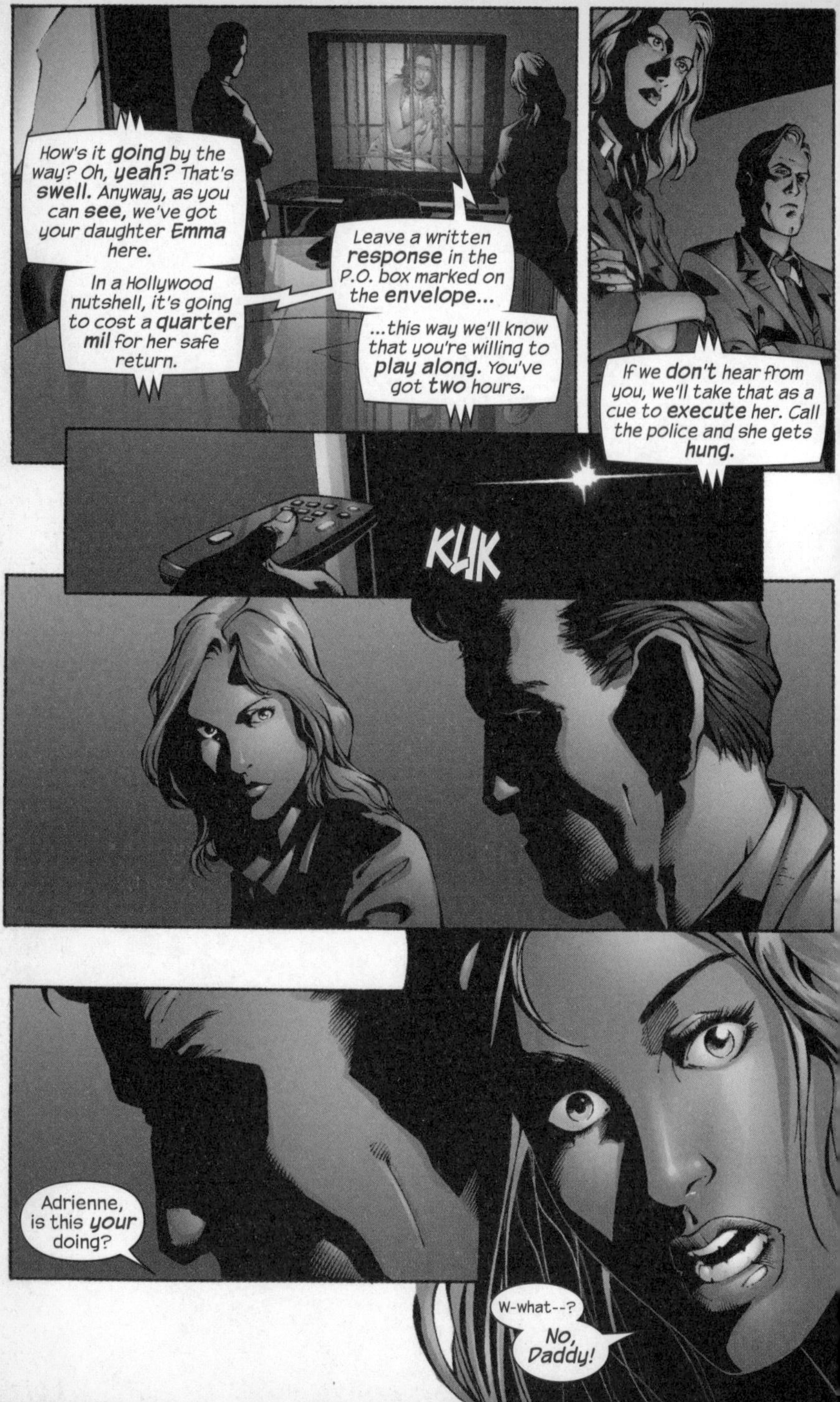
How's it going by the way? Oh, yeah? That's swell. Anyway, as you can see, we've got your daughter Emma here.
In a Hollywood nutshell, it's going to cost a quarter mil for her safe return.
Leave a written response in the P.O. box marked on the envelope...
...this way we'll know that you're willing to play along. You've got two hours.
If we don't hear from you, we'll take that as a cue to execute her. Call the police and she gets hung.
KLIK
Adrienne, is this your doing?
W-what--?
No, Daddy!

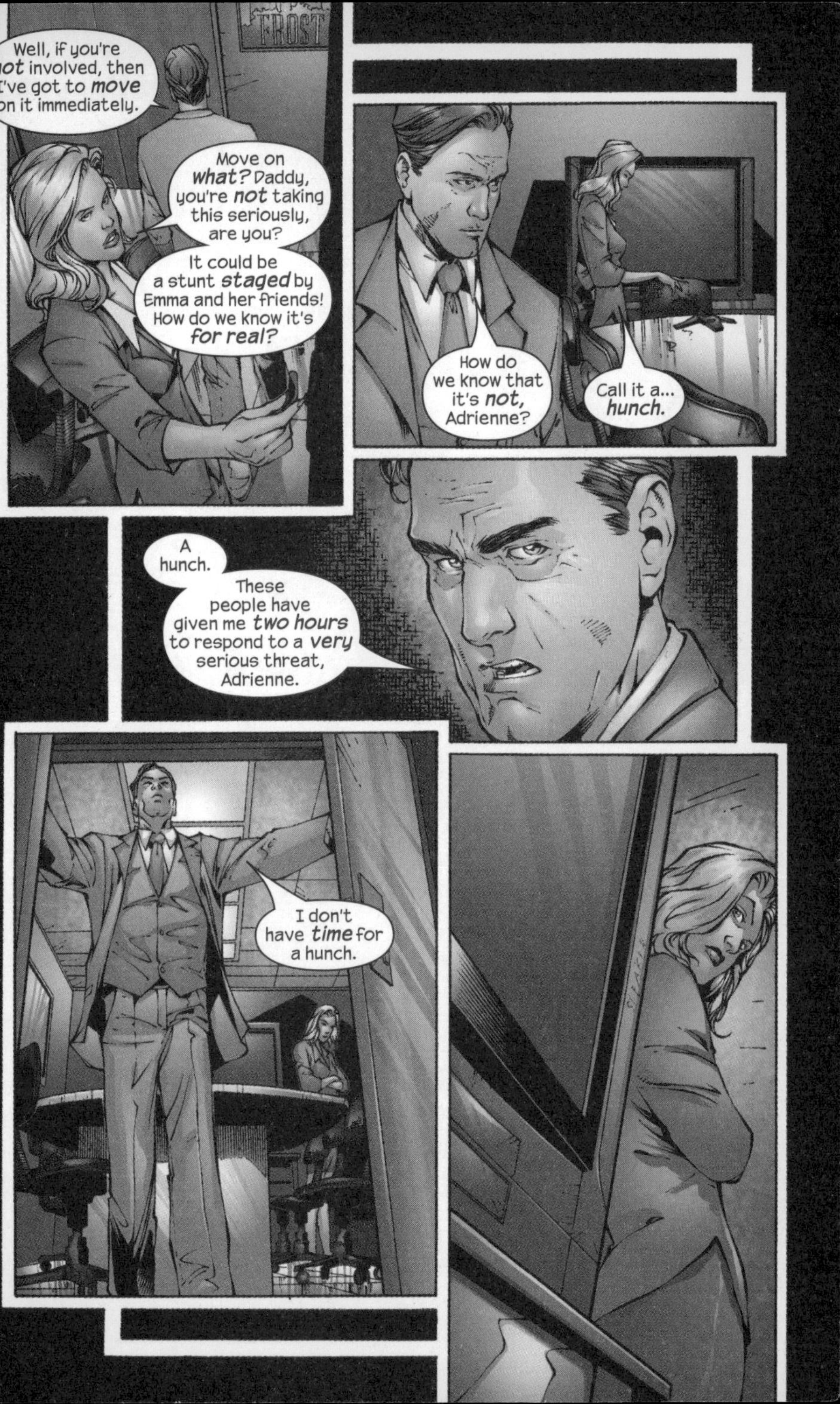

Well, if you're ot involved, then 've got to move on it immediately.
Move on what? Daddy, you're not taking this seriously, are you?
It could be a stunt staged by Emma and her friends! How do we know it's for real?
How do we know that it's not, Adrienne?
Call it a... hunch.
A hunch.
These people have given me two hours to respond to a very serious threat, Adrienne.
I don't have time for a hunch.

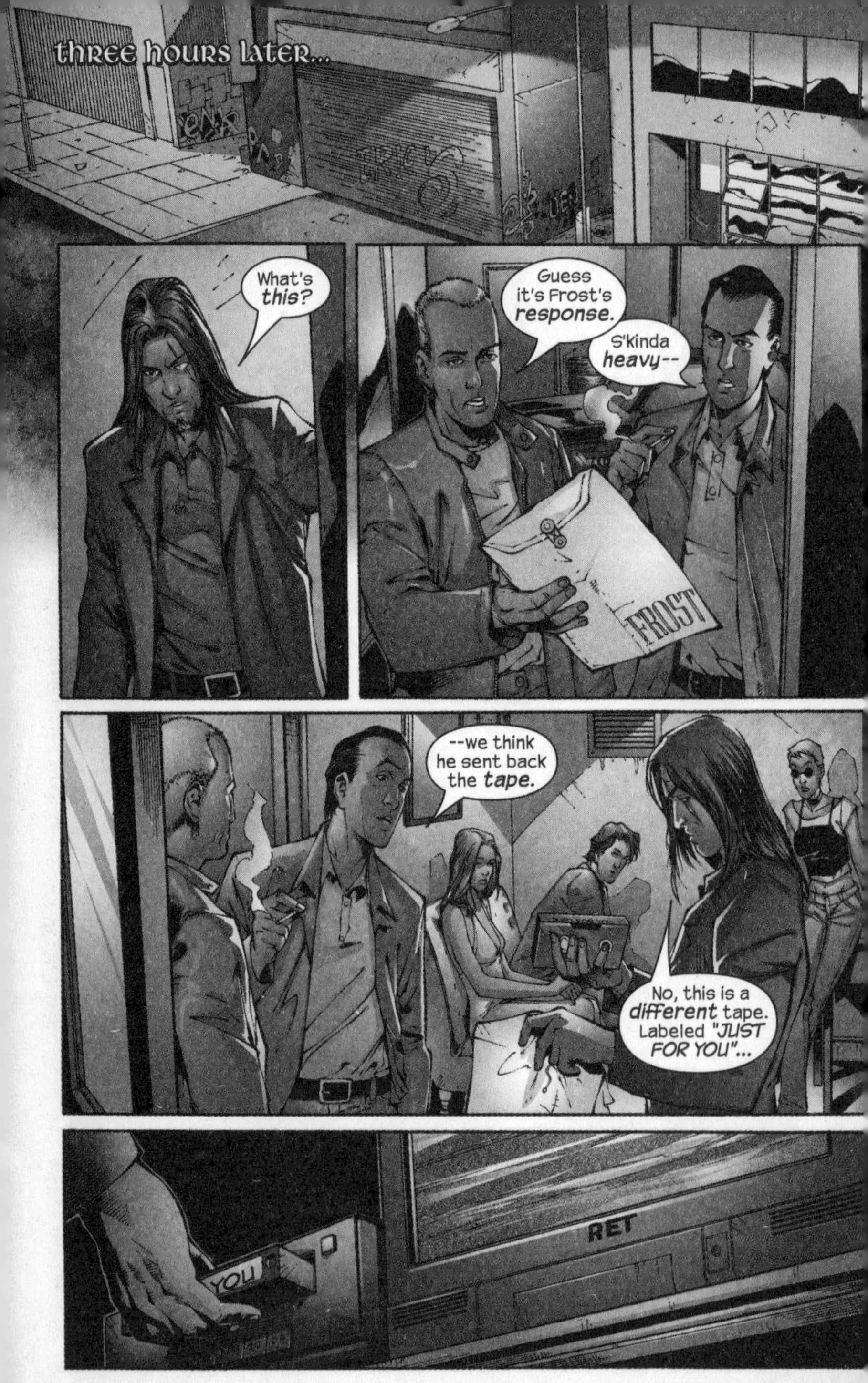
THREE HOURS LATER...
What's this?
Guess it's Frost's response.
S'kinda heavy--
FROST
--we think he sent back the tape.
No, this is a different tape. Labeled "JUST FOR YOU"...
YOU
RET

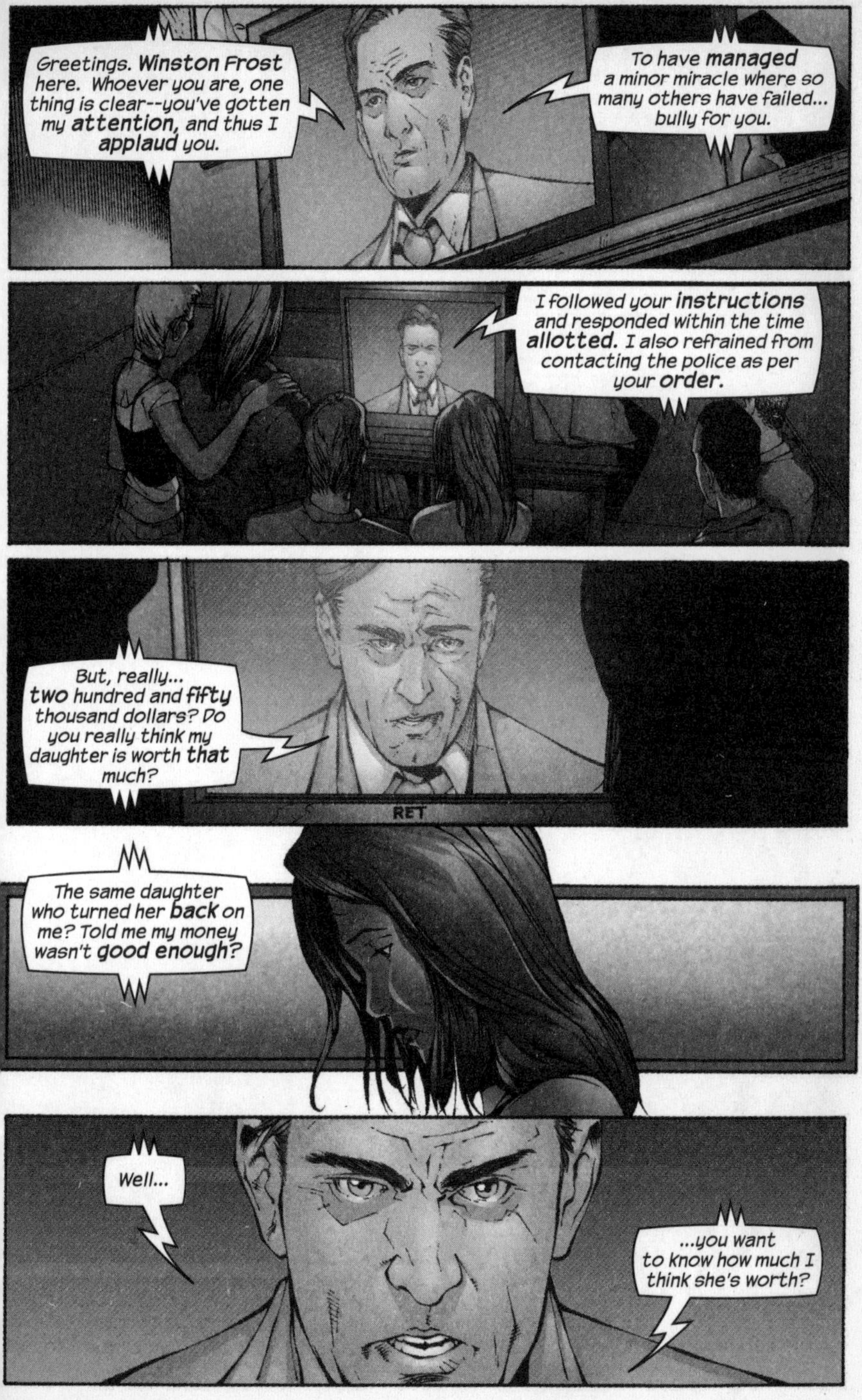

Greetings. Winston Frost here. Whoever you are, one thing is clear--you've gotten my attention, and thus I applaud you.
To have managed a minor miracle where so many others have failed... bully for you.
I followed your instructions and responded within the time allotted. I also refrained from contacting the police as per your order.
But, really... two hundred and fifty thousand dollars? Do you really think my daughter is worth that much?
RET
The same daughter who turned her back on me? Told me my money wasn't good enough?
Well...
...you want to know how much I think she's worth?

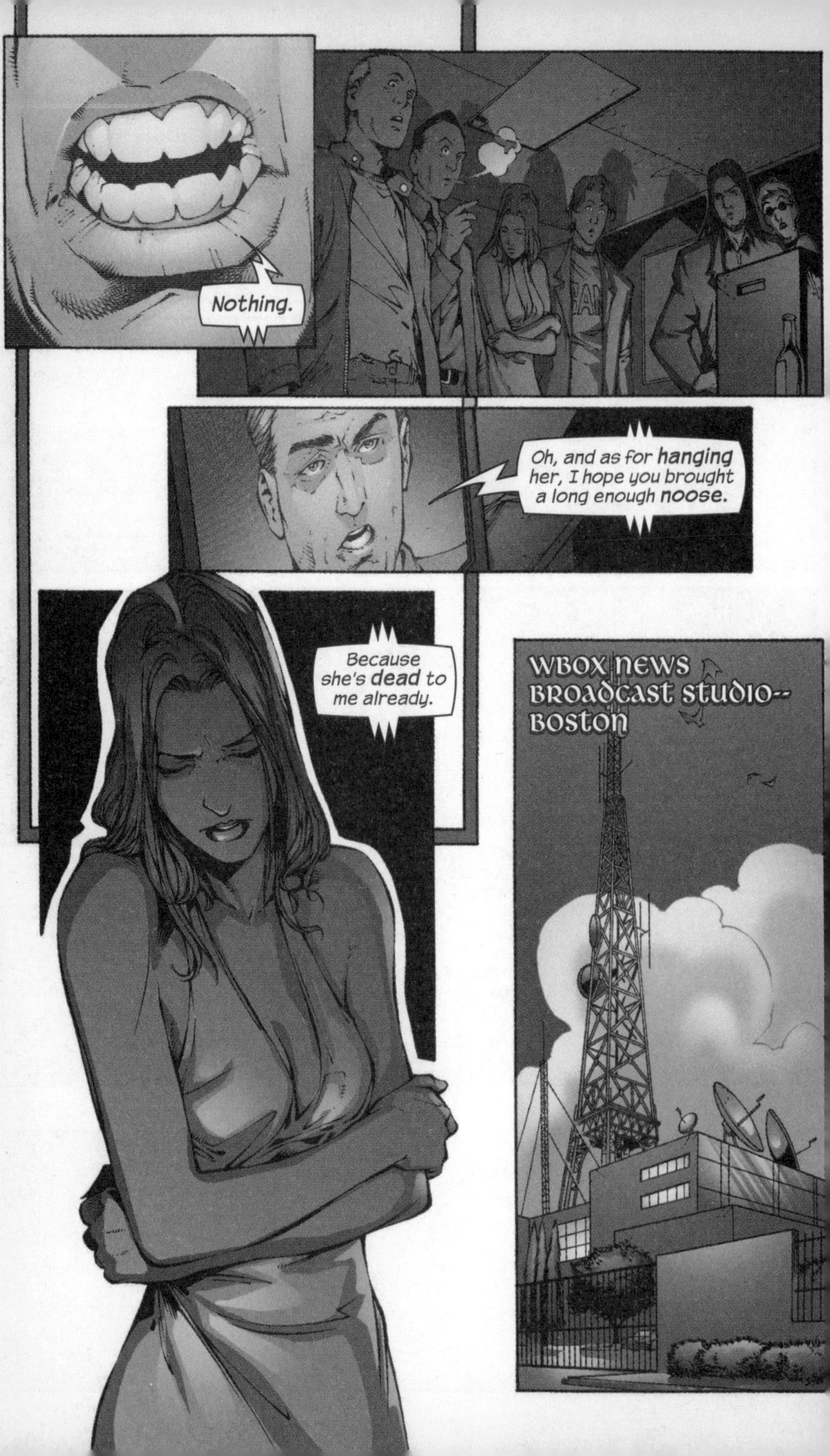
Nothing.
Oh, and as for hanging her, I hope you brought a long enough noose.
Because she's dead to me already.
WBOX NEWS BROADCAST STUDIO-- BOSTON

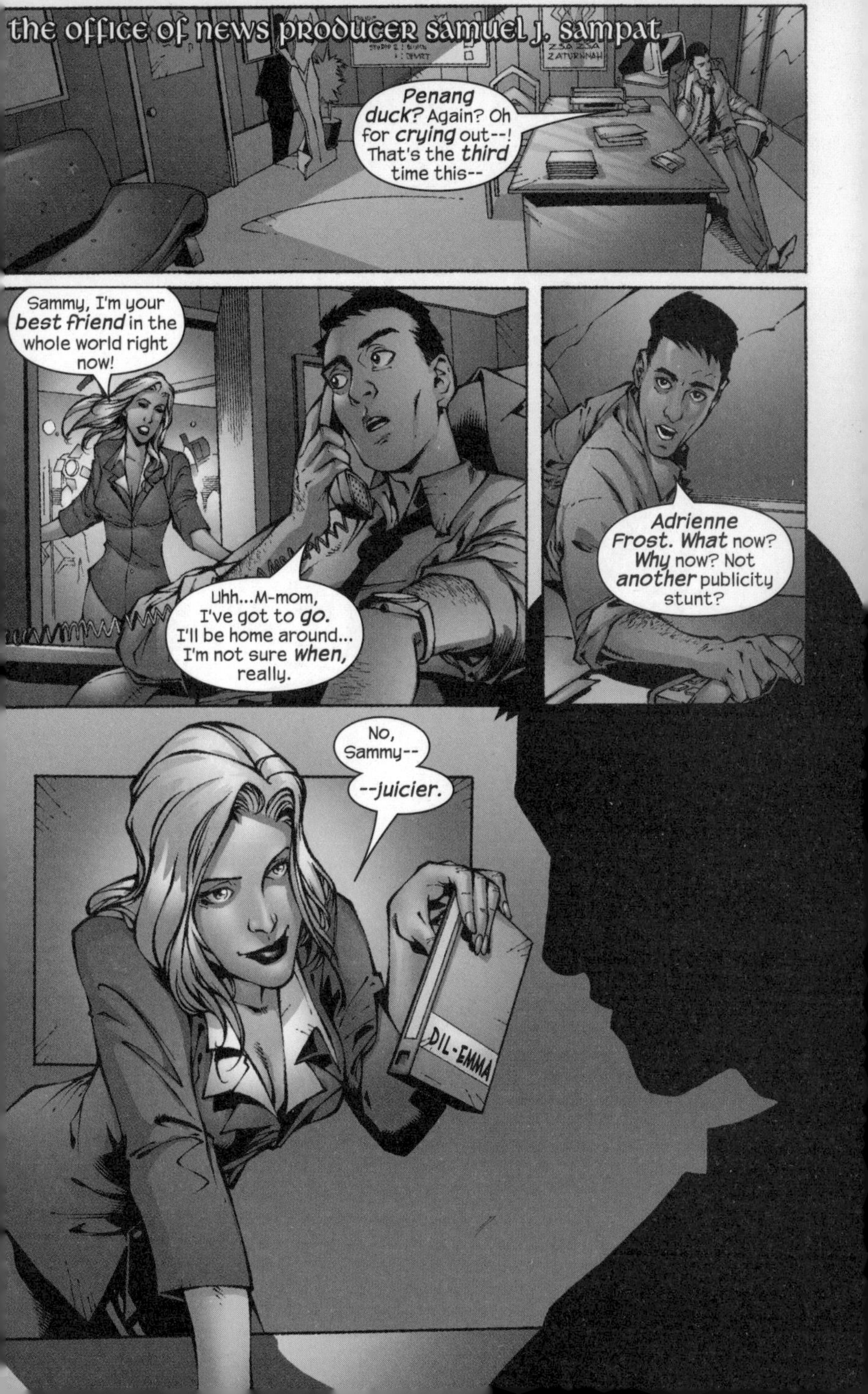
the office of news producer samuel j. sampat
Penang duck? Again? Oh for crying out--! That's the third time this--
Sammy, I'm your best friend in the whole world right now!
Uhh...M-mom, I've got to go. I'll be home around... I'm not sure when, really.
Adrienne Frost. What now? Why now? Not another publicity stunt?
No, Sammy--
--juicier.
DIL-EMMA

ISSUE 11

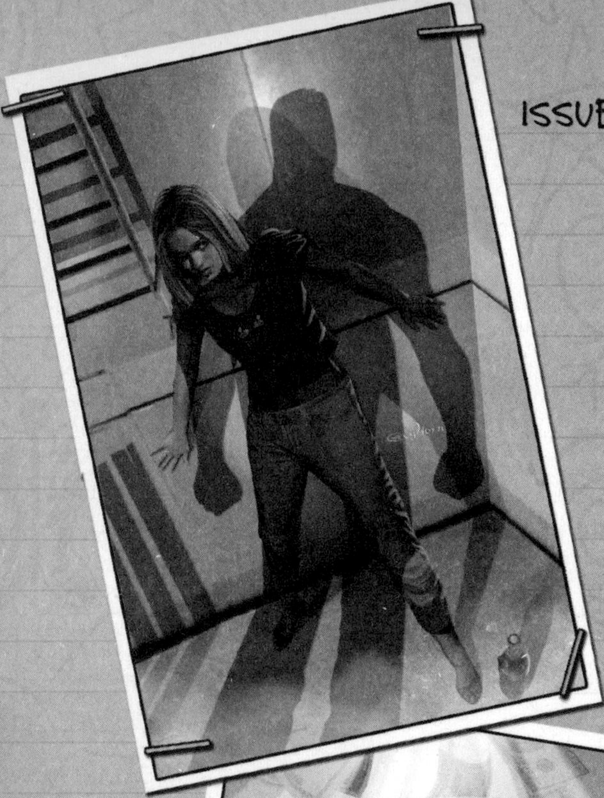

ISSUE 12

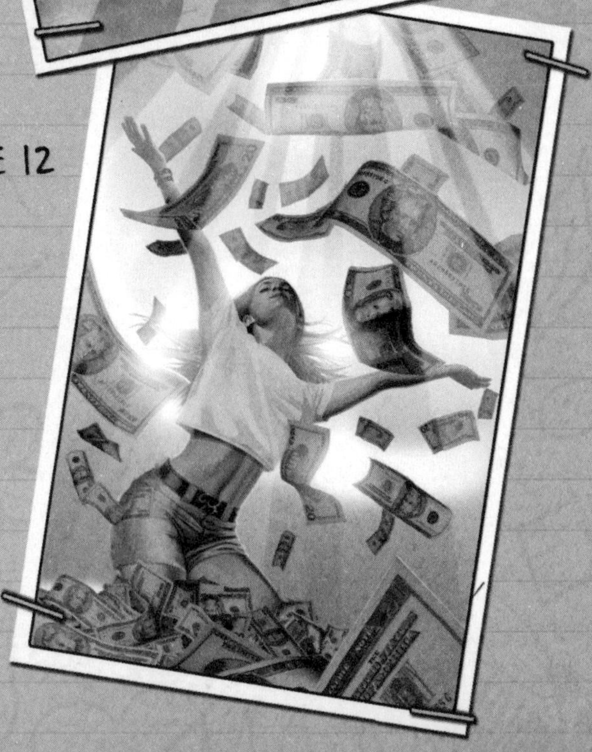

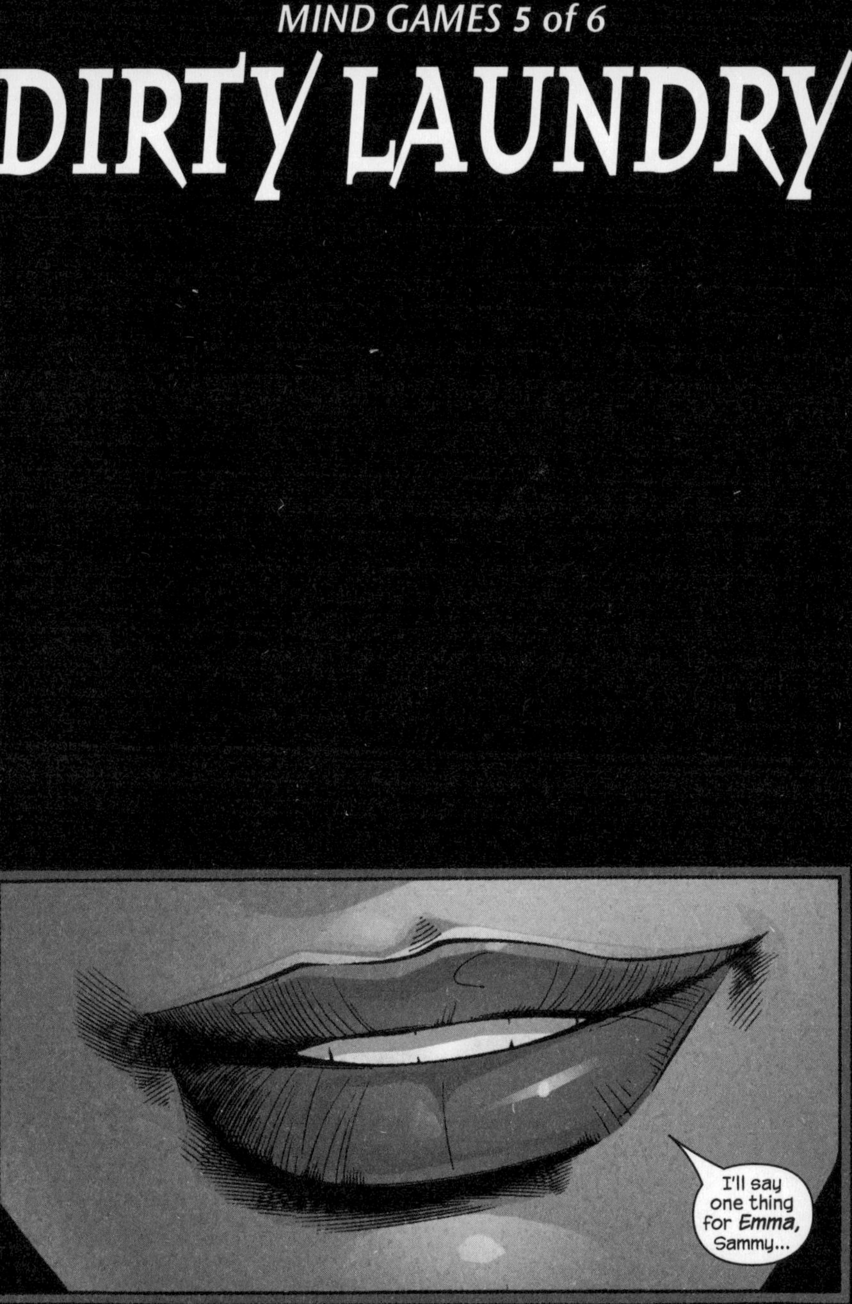
MIND GAMES 5 of 6
DIRTY LAUNDRY
I'll say one thing for *Emma,* Sammy...

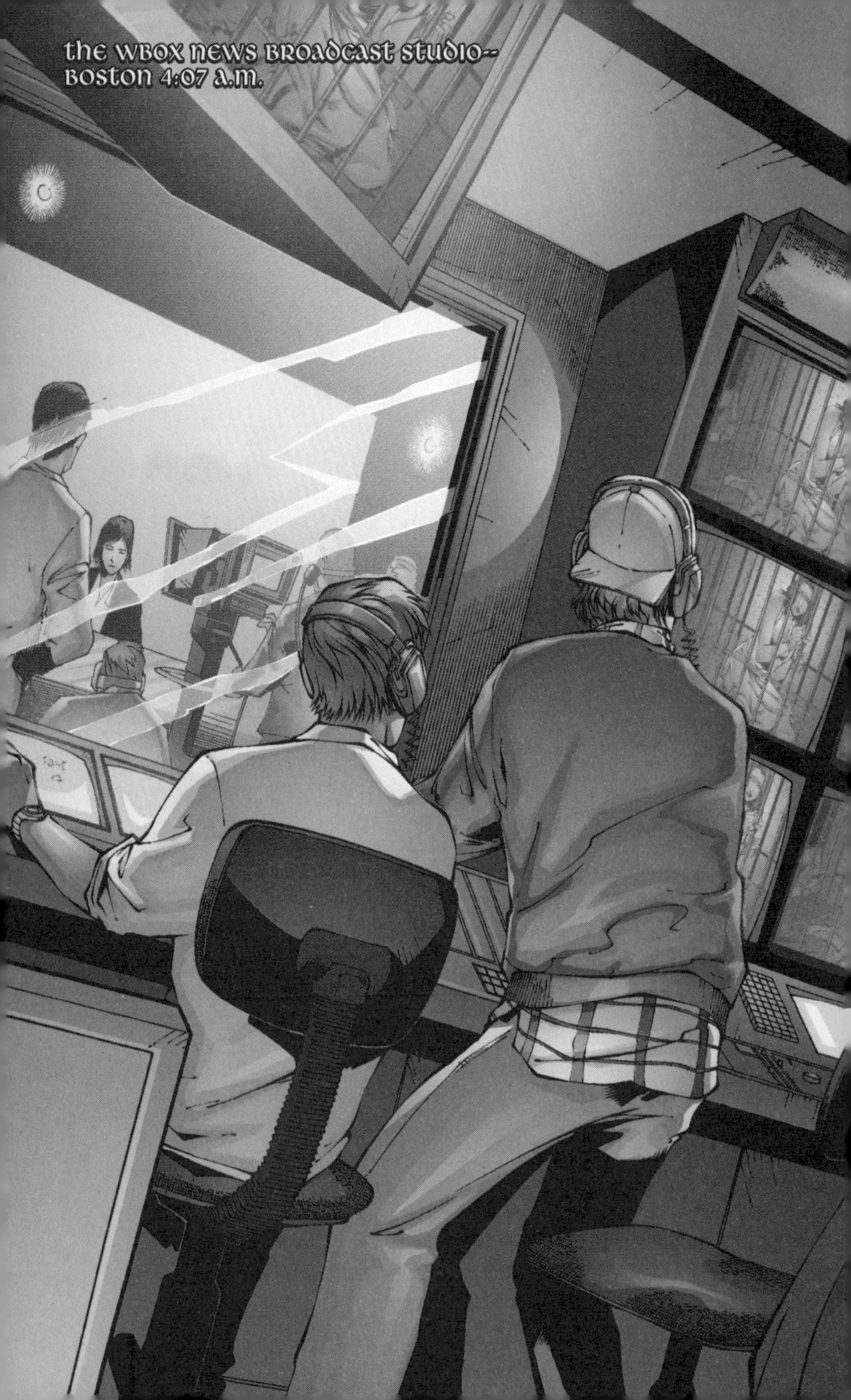
THE WBOX NEWS BROADCAST STUDIO--
BOSTON 4:07 A.M.

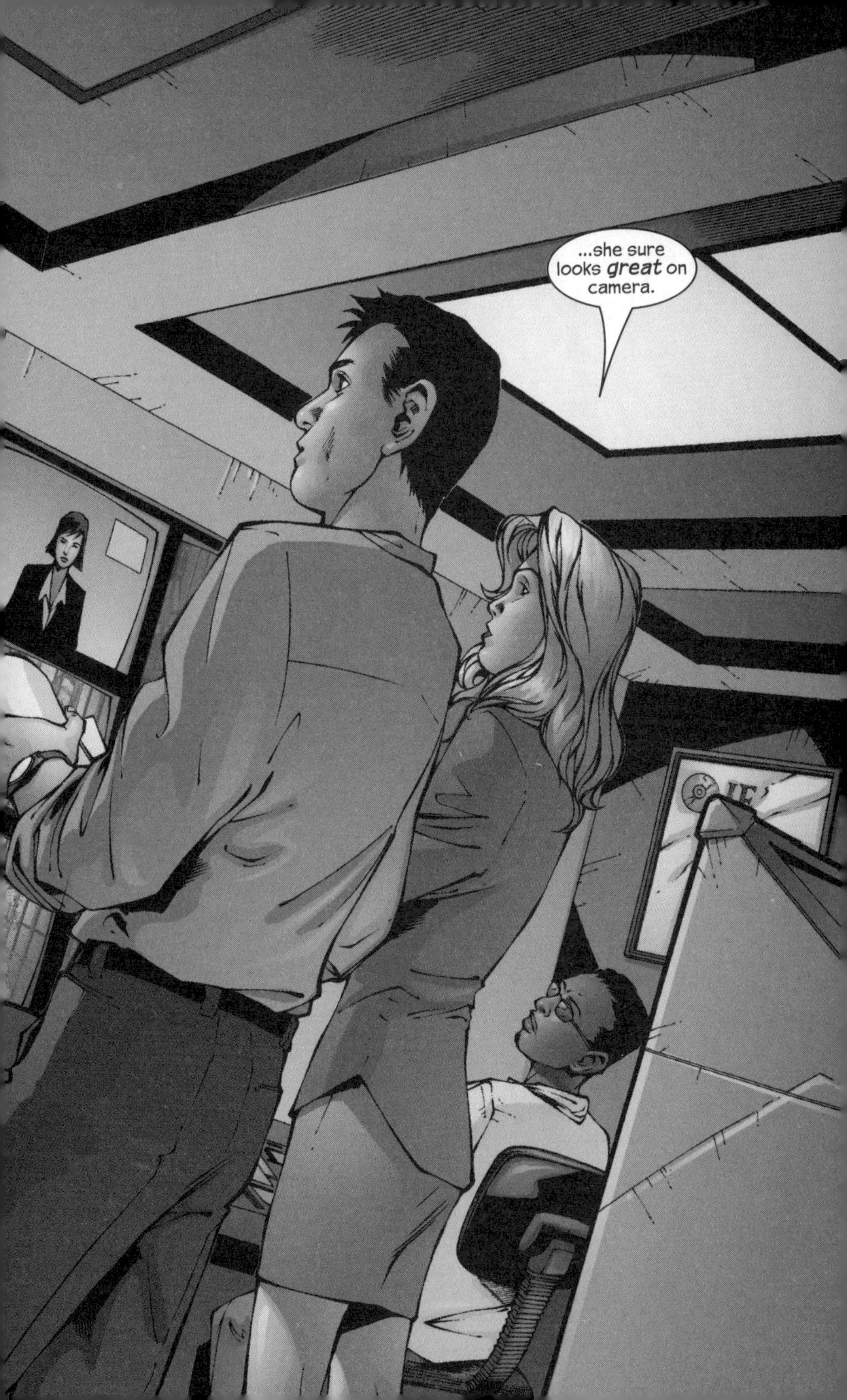
...she sure looks great on camera.

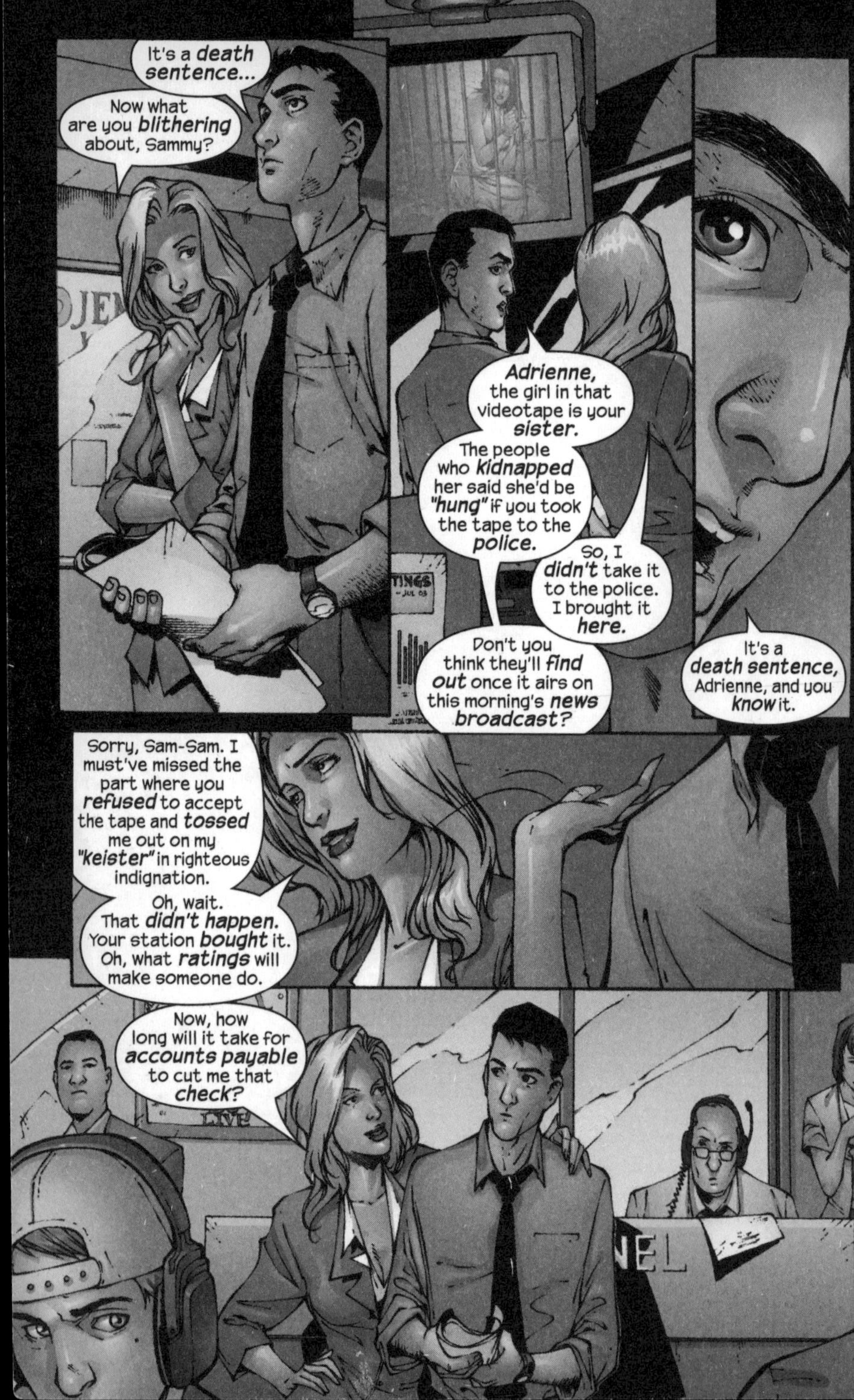
It's a death sentence...
Now what are you blithering about, Sammy?
Adrienne, the girl in that videotape is your sister.
The people who kidnapped her said she'd be "hung" if you took the tape to the police.
So, I didn't take it to the police. I brought it here.
Don't you think they'll find out once it airs on this morning's news broadcast?
It's a death sentence, Adrienne, and you know it.
Sorry, Sam-Sam. I must've missed the part where you refused to accept the tape and tossed me out on my "keister" in righteous indignation.
Oh, wait. That didn't happen. Your station bought it. Oh, what ratings will make someone do.
Now, how long will it take for accounts payable to cut me that check?

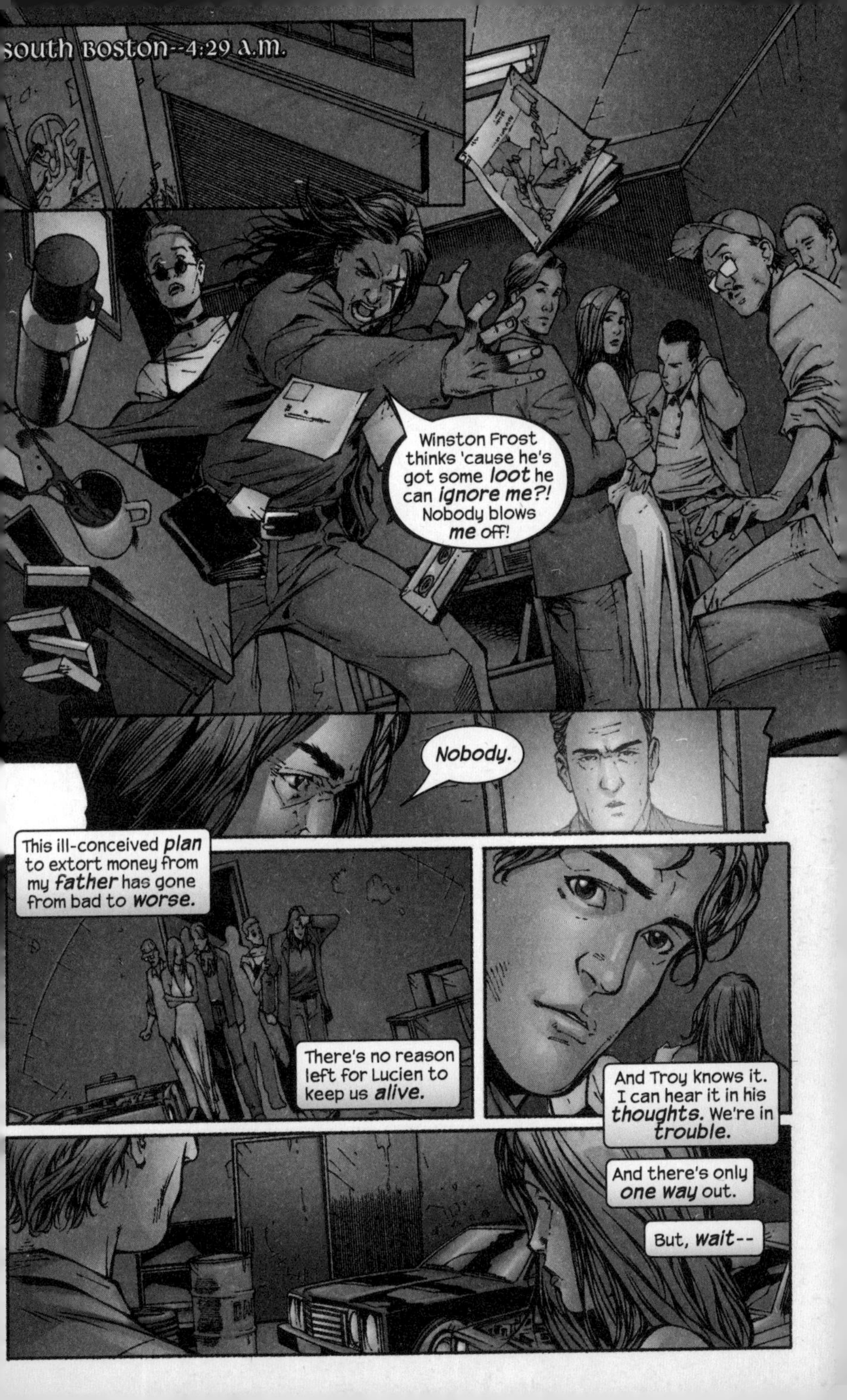
South Boston--4:29 A.M.
Winston Frost thinks 'cause he's got some loot he can ignore me?! Nobody blows me off!
Nobody.
This ill-conceived plan to extort money from my father has gone from bad to worse.
There's no reason left for Lucien to keep us alive.
And Troy knows it. I can hear it in his thoughts. We're in trouble.
And there's only one way out.
But, wait--

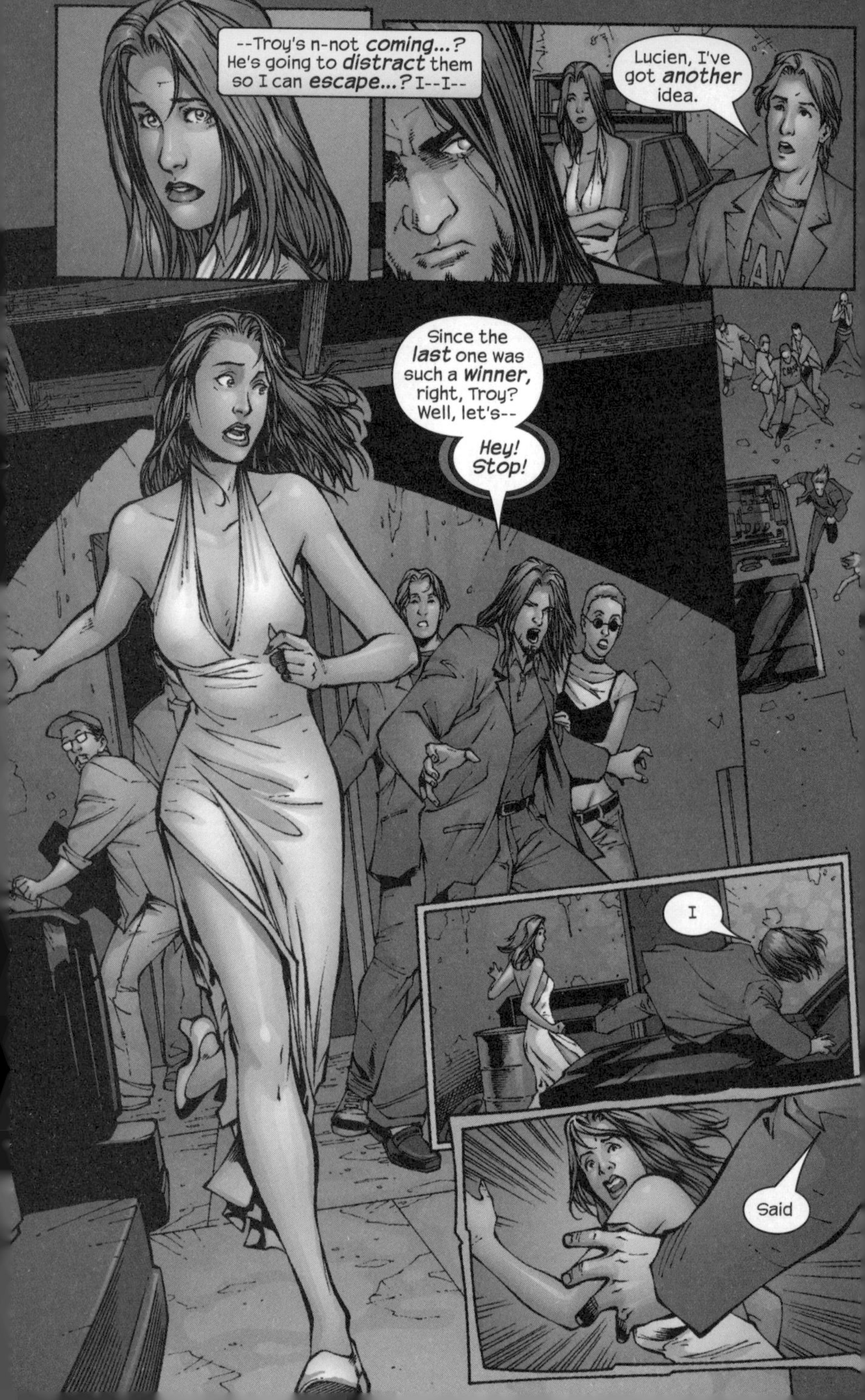
--Troy's n-not *coming...?* He's going to *distract* them so I can *escape...?* I--I--
Lucien, I've got *another* idea.
Since the *last* one was such a *winner,* right, Troy? Well, let's--
Hey! Stop!
I
Said

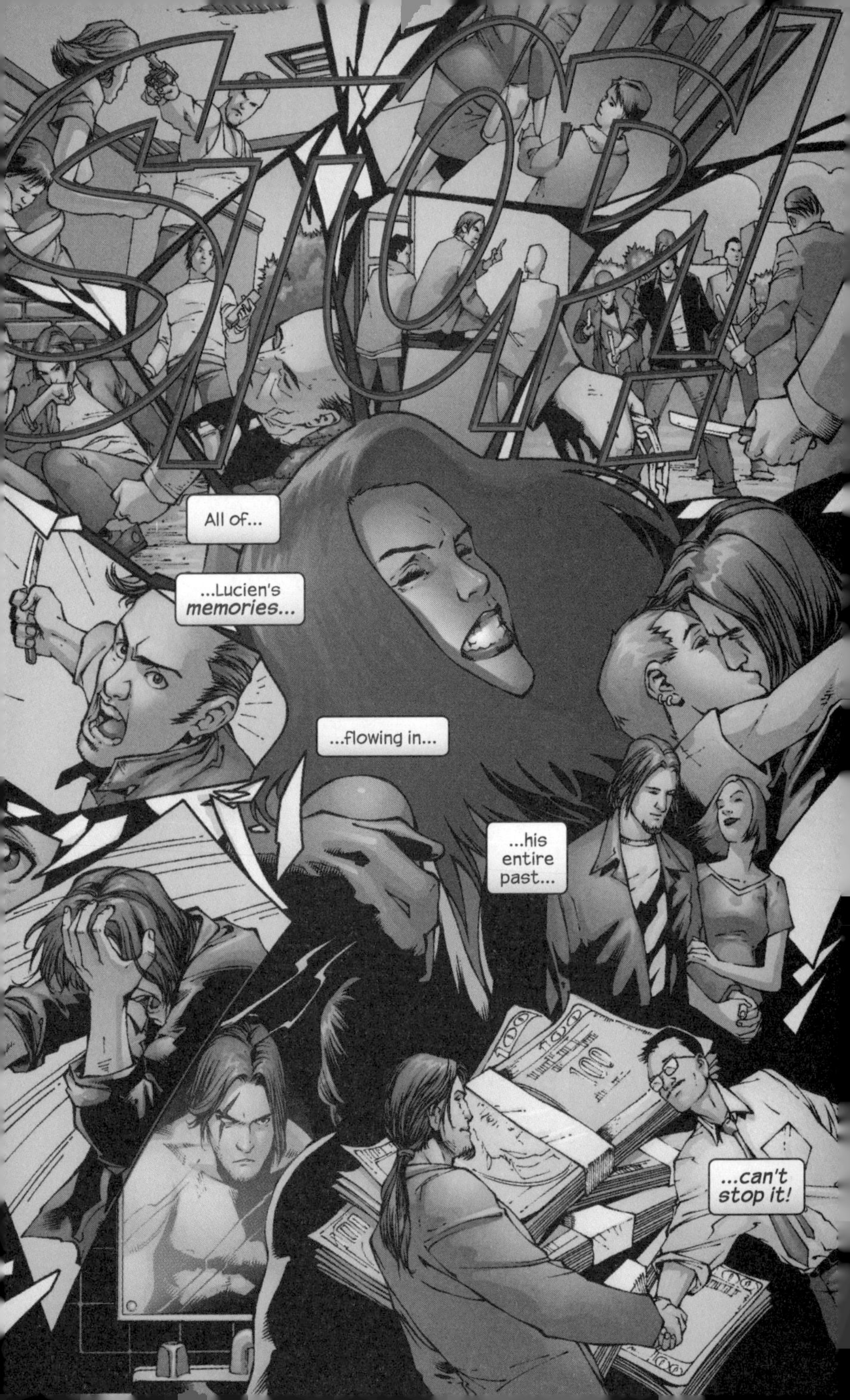
All of...
...Lucien's *memories*...
...flowing in...
...his entire past...
...can't stop it!

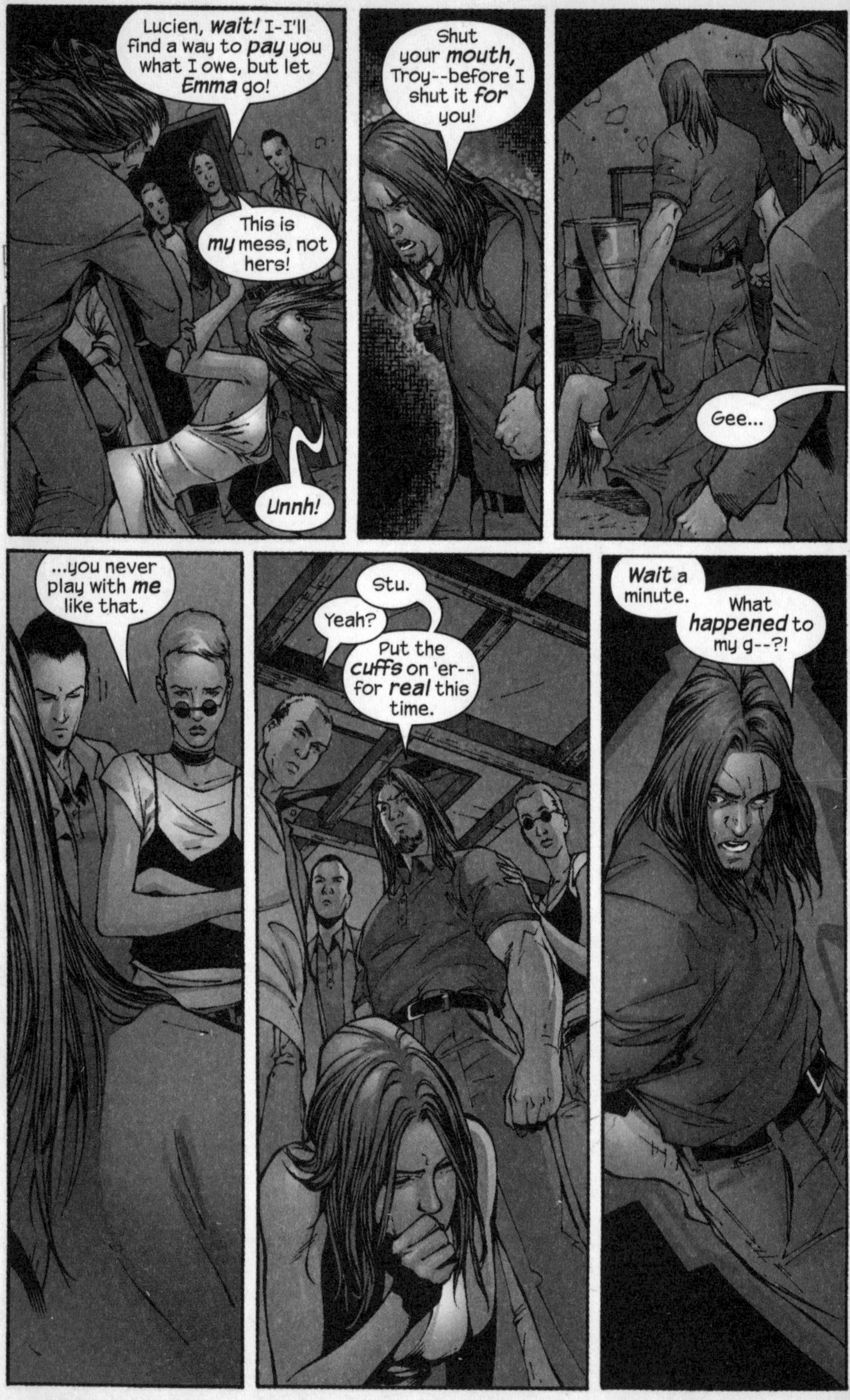
Lucien, wait! I-I'll find a way to pay you what I owe, but let Emma go!
This is my mess, not hers!
Unnh!
Shut your mouth, Troy--before I shut it for you!
Gee...
...you never play with me like that.
Stu.
Yeah?
Put the cuffs on 'er--for real this time.
Wait a minute.
What happened to my g--?!

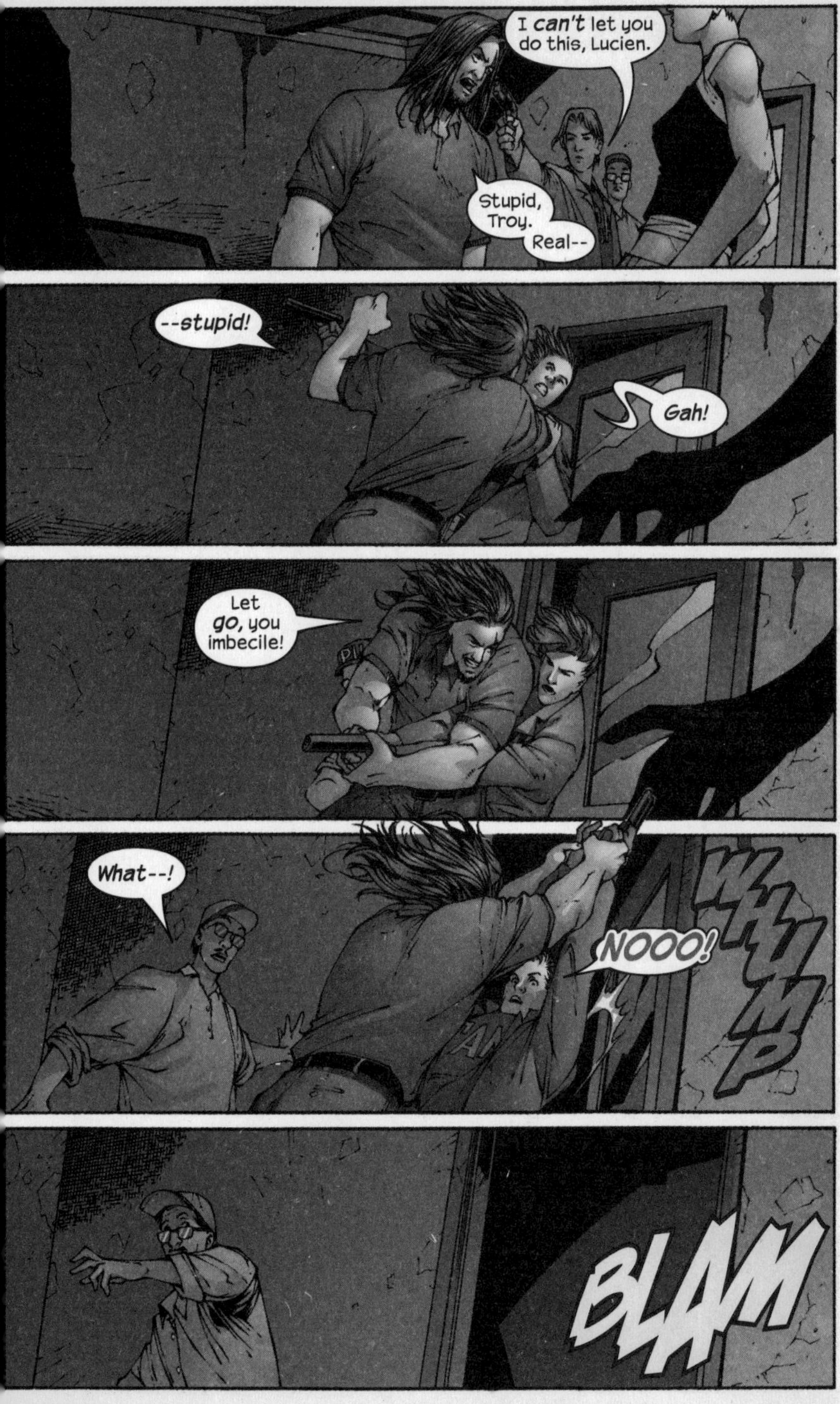
I can't let you do this, Lucien.
Stupid, Troy.
Real--
--stupid!
Gah!
Let go, you imbecile!
What--!
NOOO!
WHUMP
BLAM

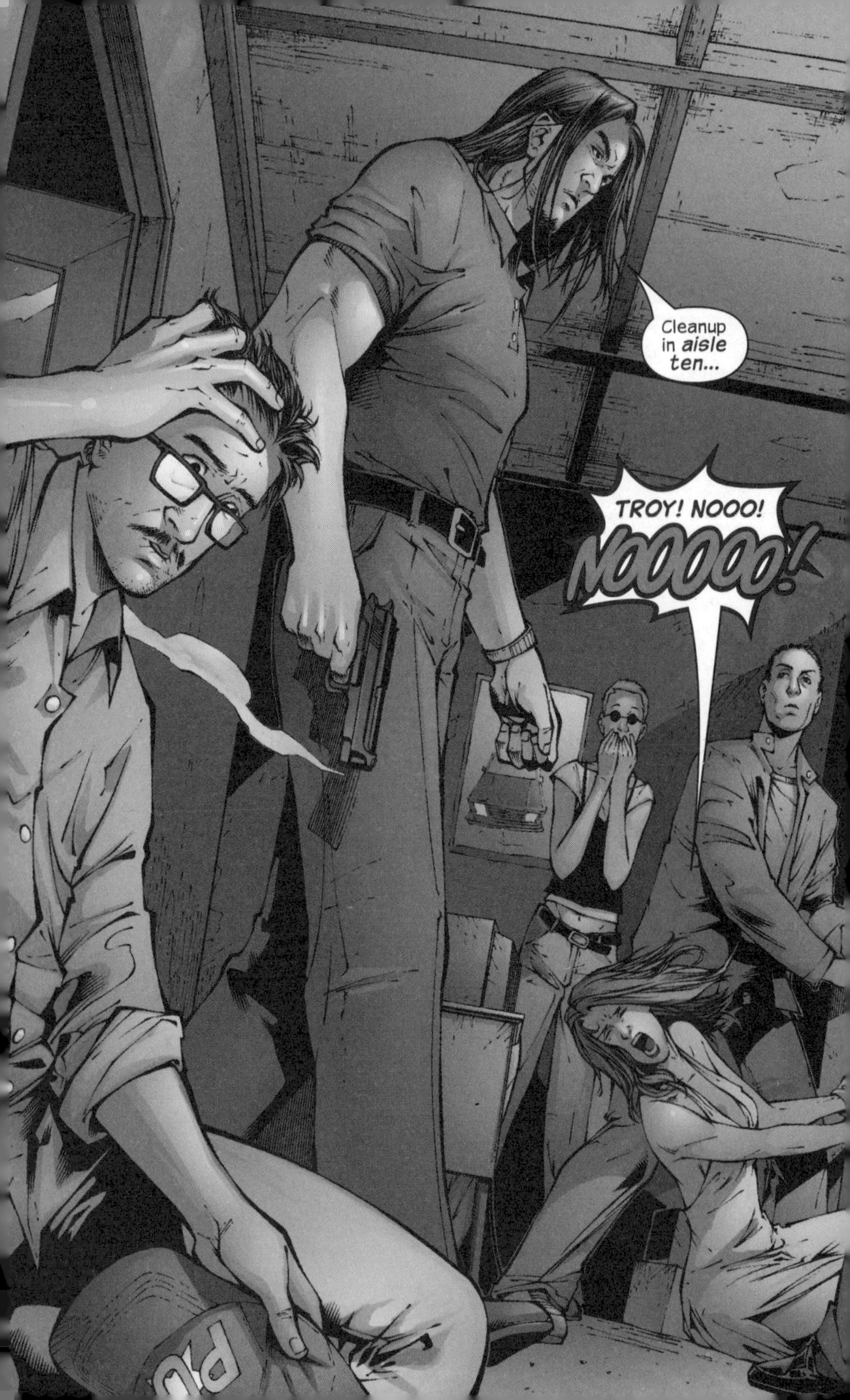
Cleanup in *aisle* ten...
TROY! NOOO!
NOOOOO!

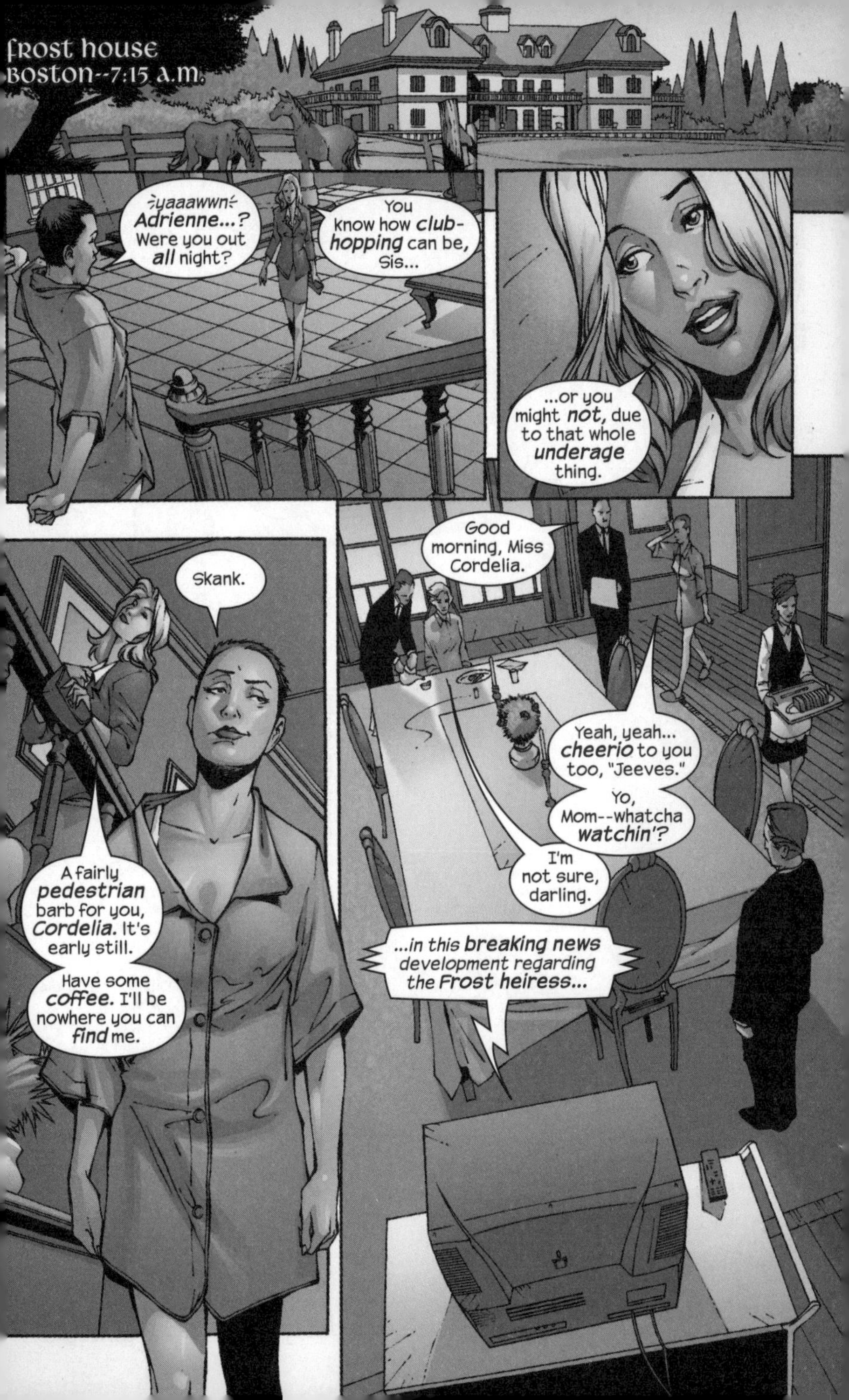
Frost House
Boston--7:15 A.M.
~yaaawwn~ Adrienne...? Were you out all night?
You know how club-hopping can be, Sis...
...or you might not, due to that whole underage thing.
Skank.
A fairly pedestrian barb for you, Cordelia. It's early still.
Have some coffee. I'll be nowhere you can find me.
Good morning, Miss Cordelia.
Yeah, yeah... cheerio to you too, "Jeeves."
Yo, Mom--whatcha watchin'?
I'm not sure, darling.
...in this breaking news development regarding the Frost heiress...

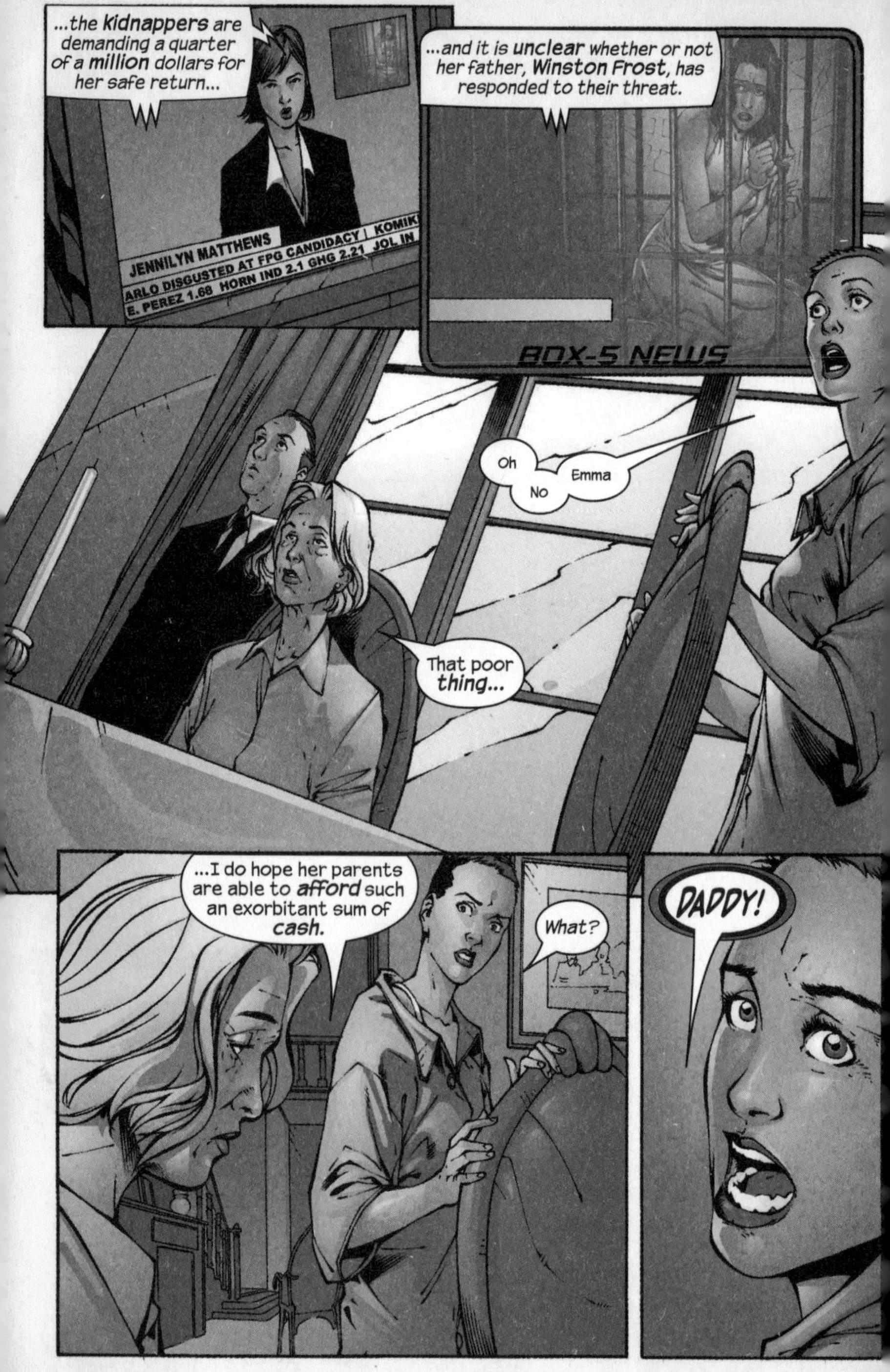
...the kidnappers are demanding a quarter of a million dollars for her safe return...
JENNILYN MATTHEWS
ARLO DISGUSTED AT FPG CANDIDACY | KOMIK
E. PEREZ 1.68 HORN IND 2.1 GHG 2.21 JOL IN
...and it is unclear whether or not her father, Winston Frost, has responded to their threat.
BDX-5 NEWS
Oh
No
Emma
That poor thing...
...I do hope her parents are able to afford such an exorbitant sum of cash.
What?
DADDY!

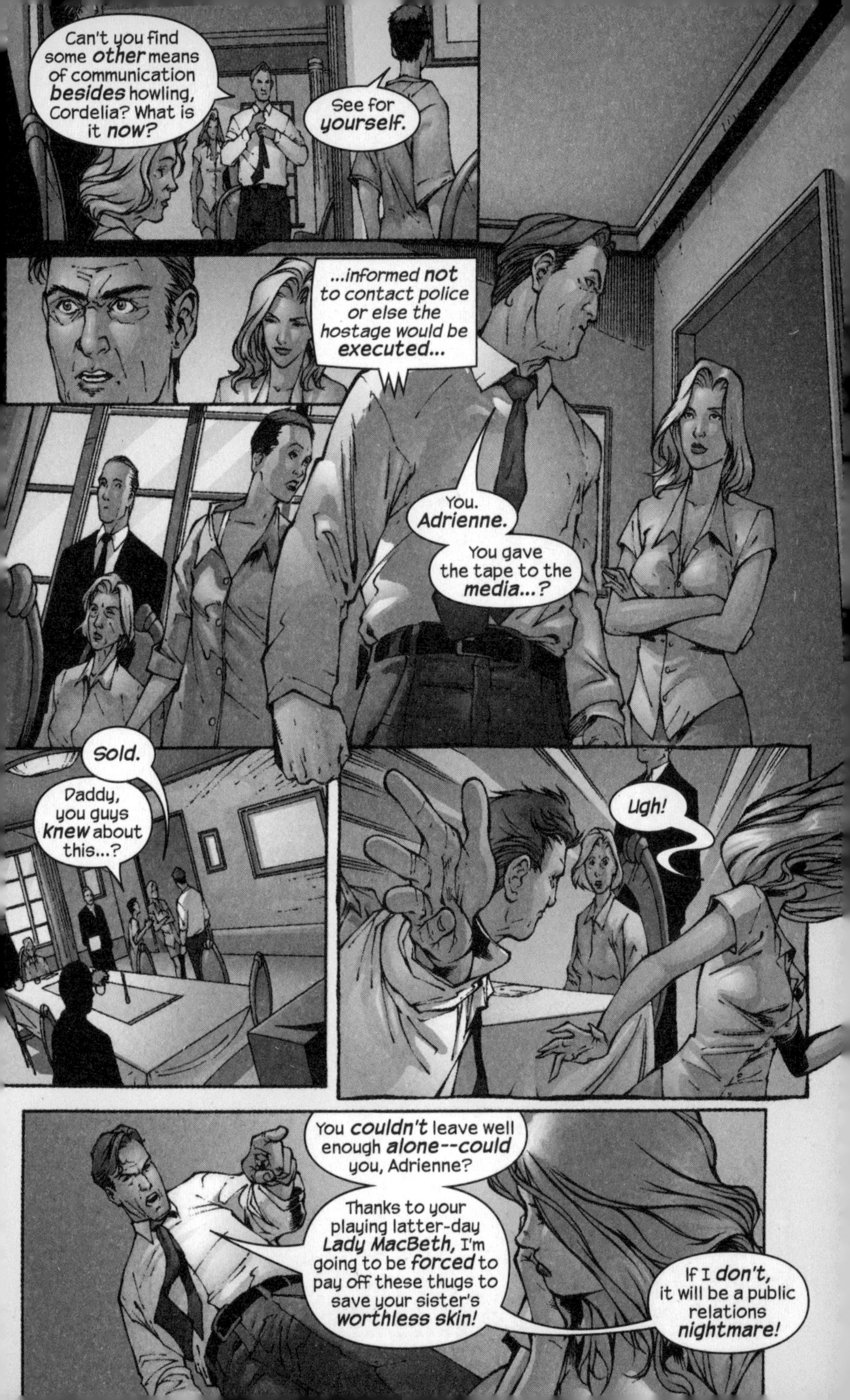
Can't you find some other means of communication besides howling, Cordelia? What is it now?
See for yourself.
...informed not to contact police or else the hostage would be executed...
You. Adrienne.
You gave the tape to the media...?
Sold.
Daddy, you guys knew about this...?
Ugh!
You couldn't leave well enough alone--could you, Adrienne?
Thanks to your playing latter-day Lady MacBeth, I'm going to be forced to pay off these thugs to save your sister's worthless skin!
If I don't, it will be a public relations nightmare!

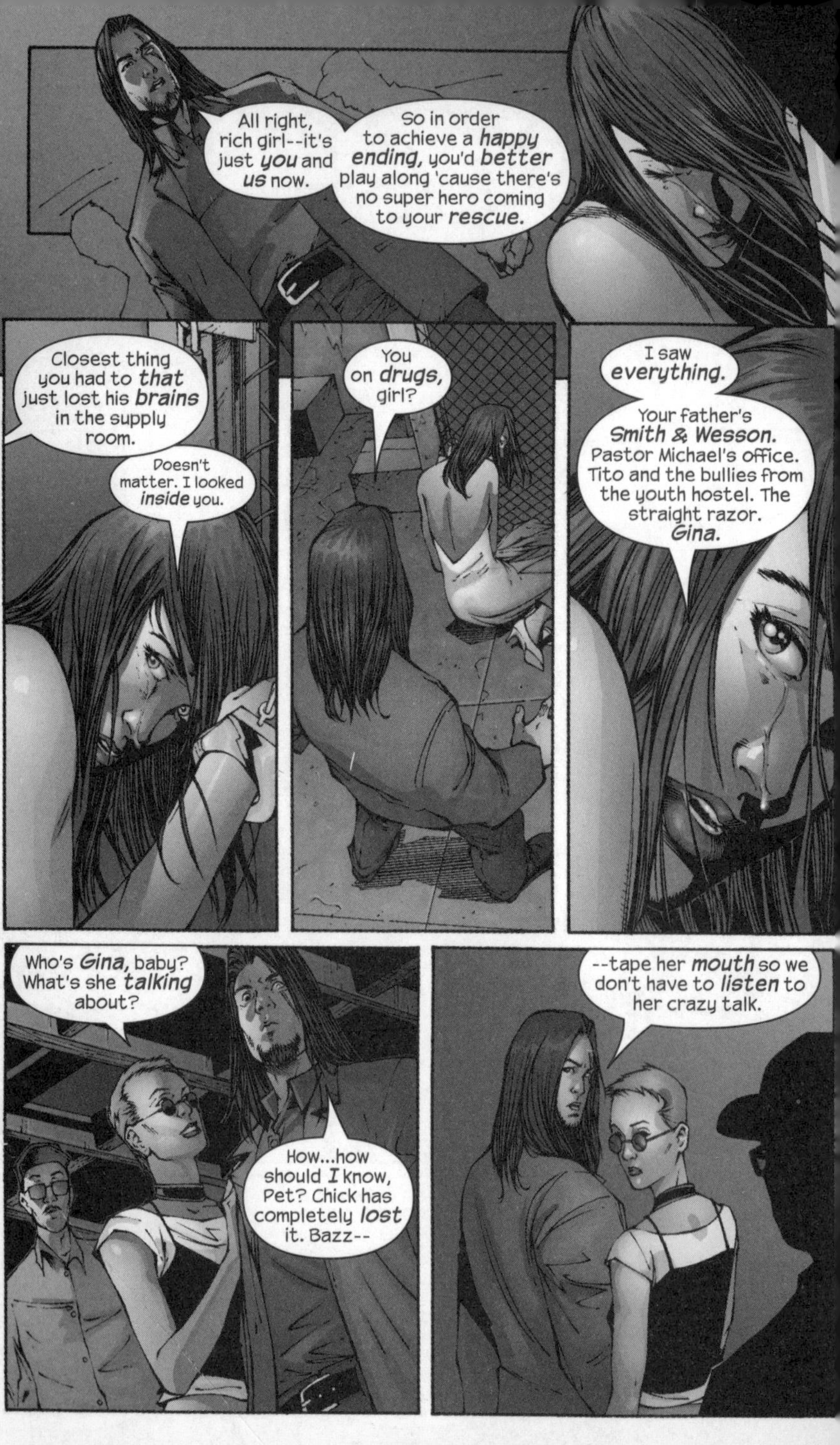
All right, rich girl--it's just you and us now.
So in order to achieve a happy ending, you'd better play along 'cause there's no super hero coming to your rescue.
Closest thing you had to that just lost his brains in the supply room.
Doesn't matter. I looked inside you.
You on drugs, girl?
I saw everything.
Your father's Smith & Wesson. Pastor Michael's office. Tito and the bullies from the youth hostel. The straight razor. Gina.
Who's Gina, baby? What's she talking about?
How...how should I know, Pet? Chick has completely lost it. Bazz--
--tape her mouth so we don't have to listen to her crazy talk.

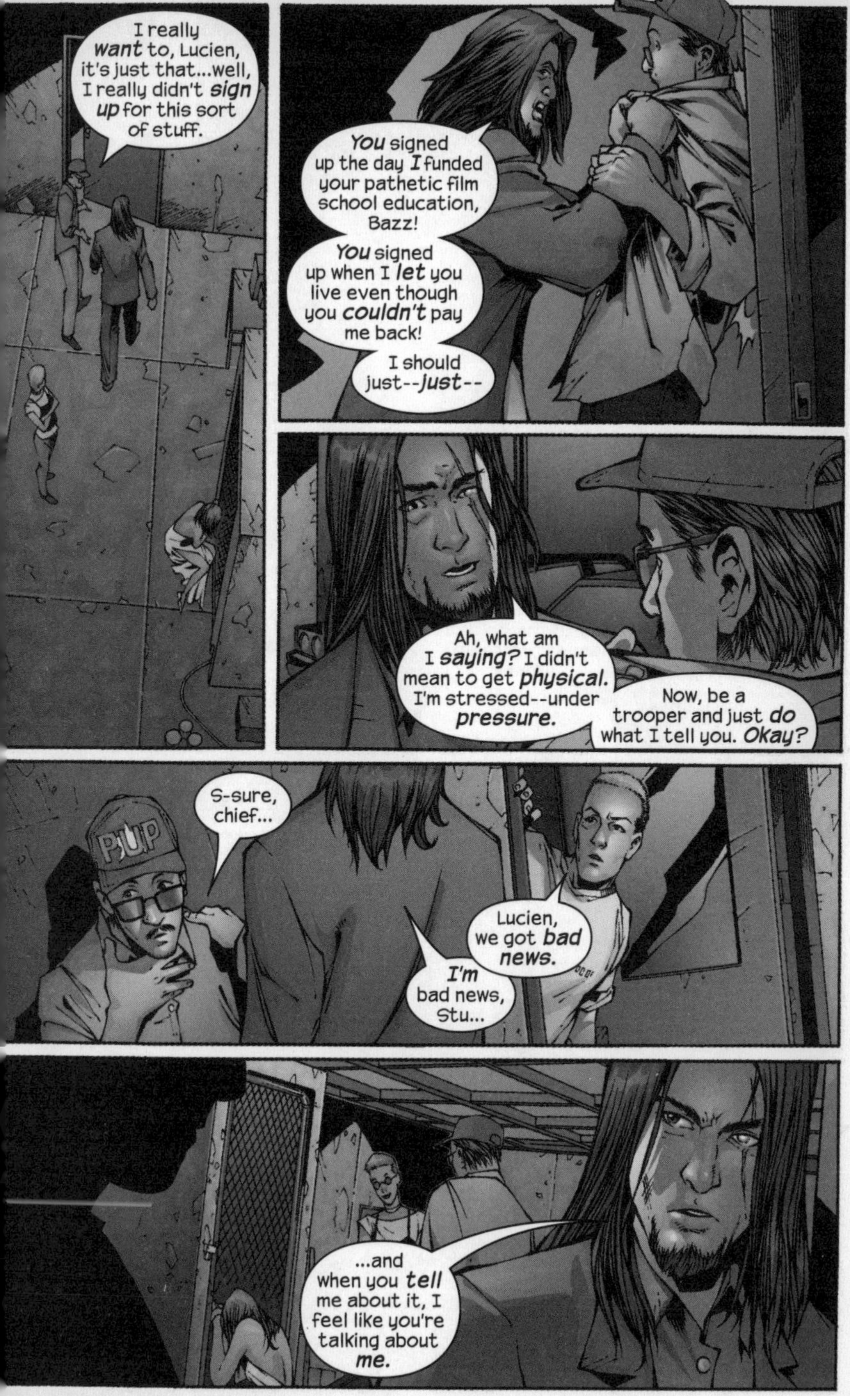
I really *want* to, Lucien, it's just that...well, I really didn't *sign up* for this sort of stuff.
You signed up the day *I* funded your pathetic film school education, Bazz!
You signed up when I *let* you live even though you *couldn't* pay me back!
I should just--*just*--
Ah, what am I *saying?* I didn't mean to get *physical.* I'm stressed--under *pressure.*
Now, be a trooper and just *do* what I tell you. *Okay?*
S-sure, chief...
PUP
Lucien, we got *bad news.*
I'm bad news, Stu...
...and when you *tell* me about it, I feel like you're talking about *me.*

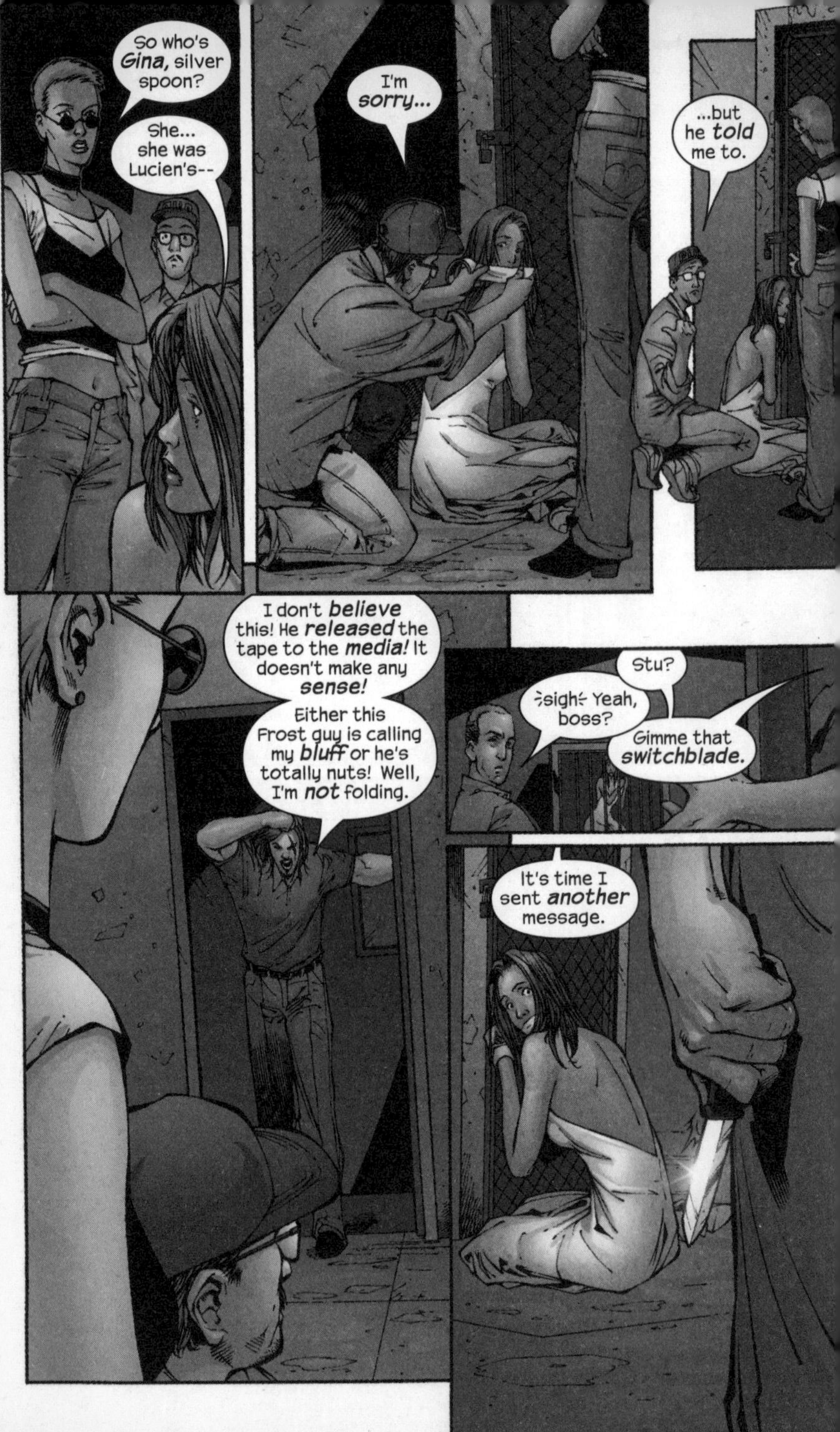
So who's *Gina,* silver spoon?
She... she was Lucien's--
I'm *sorry...*
...but he *told* me to.
I don't *believe* this! He *released* the tape to the *media!* It doesn't make any *sense!*
Either this Frost guy is calling my *bluff* or he's totally nuts! Well, I'm *not* folding.
Stu?
sigh Yeah, boss?
Gimme that *switchblade.*
It's time I sent *another* message.

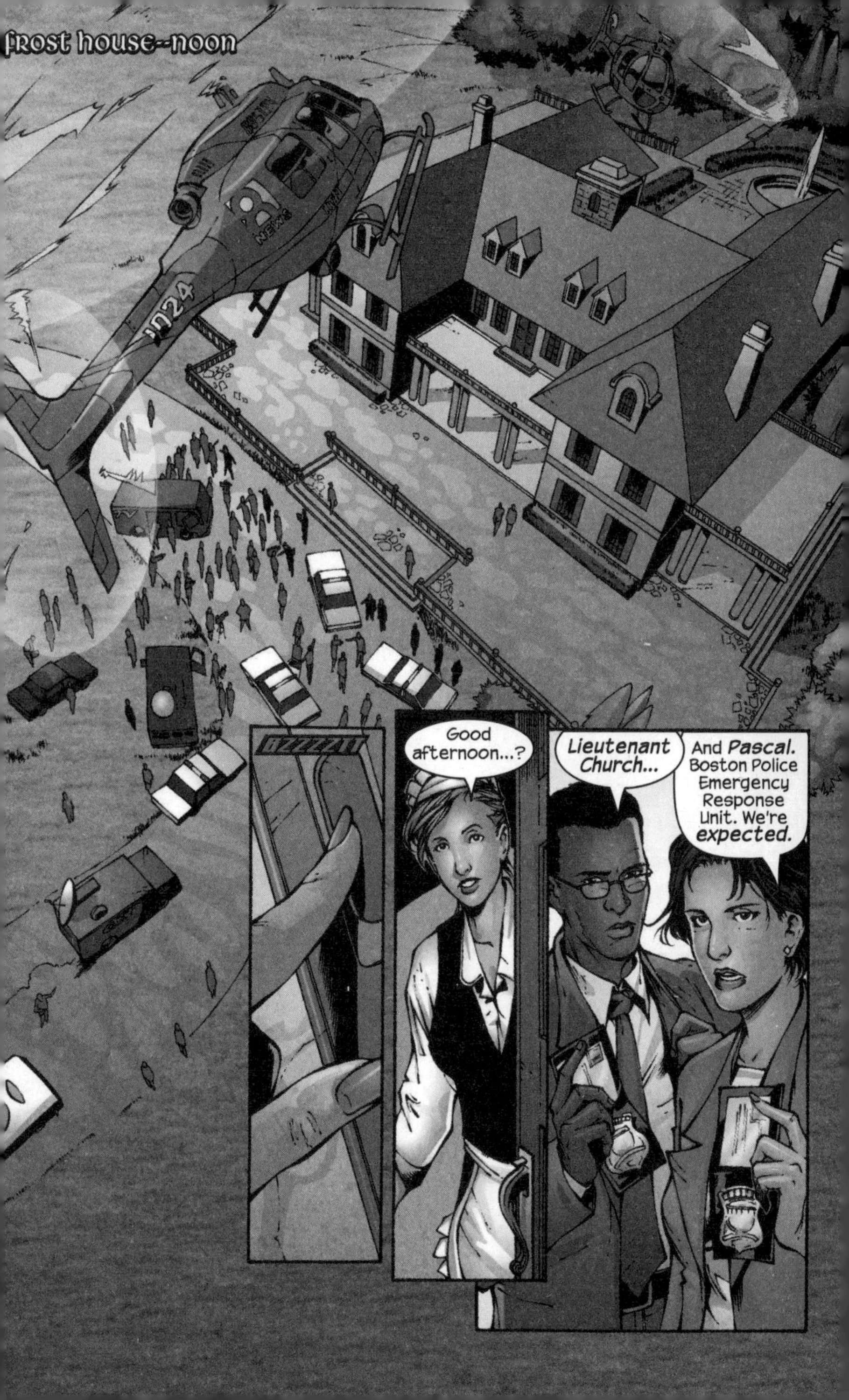
frost house--noon
BZZZZTT
Good afternoon...?
Lieutenant Church...
And Pascal. Boston Police Emergency Response Unit. We're expected.

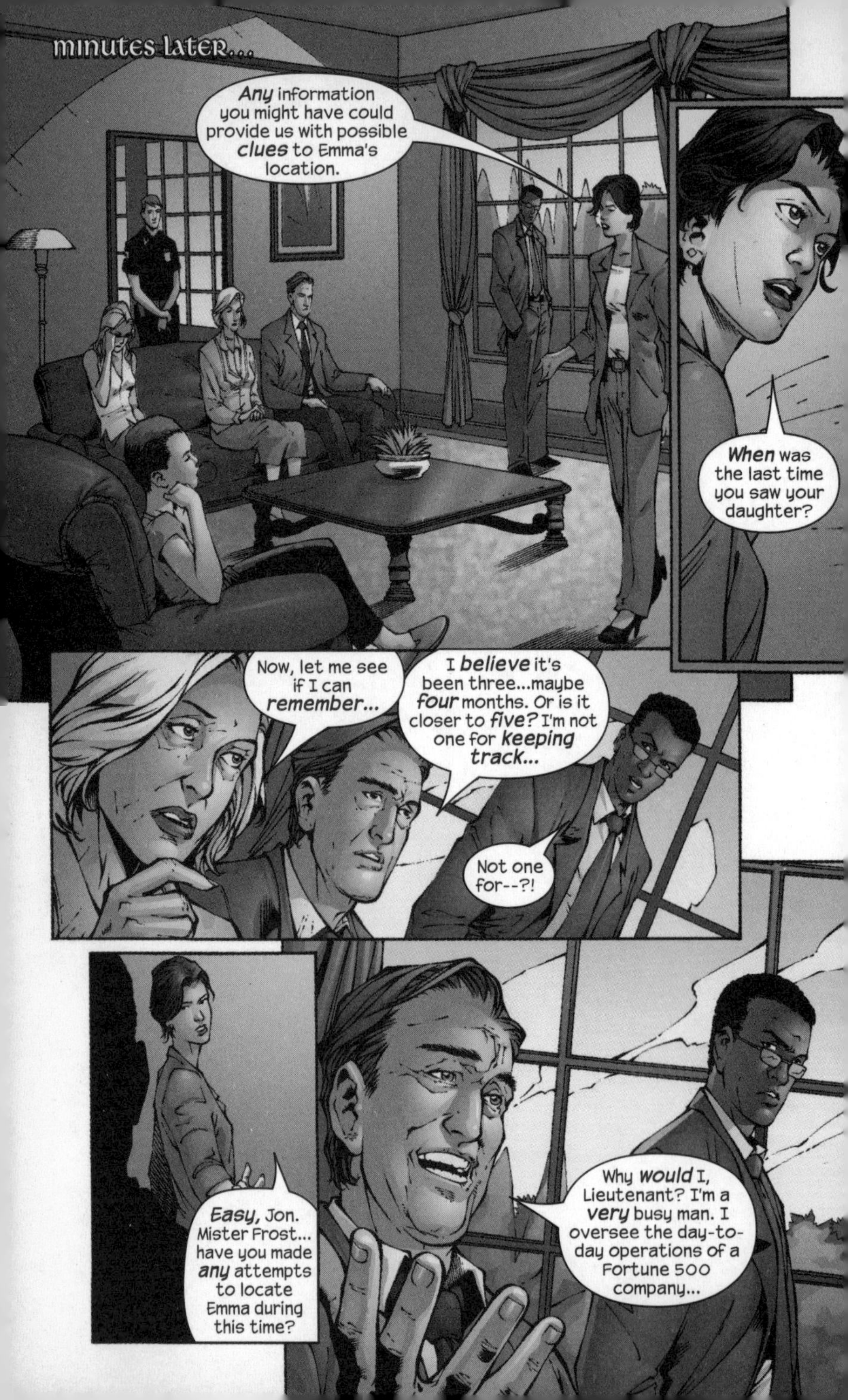
minutes later...
Any information you might have could provide us with possible clues to Emma's location.
When was the last time you saw your daughter?
Now, let me see if I can remember...
I believe it's been three...maybe four months. Or is it closer to five? I'm not one for keeping track...
Not one for--?!
Easy, Jon. Mister Frost... have you made any attempts to locate Emma during this time?
Why would I, Lieutenant? I'm a very busy man. I oversee the day-to-day operations of a Fortune 500 company...

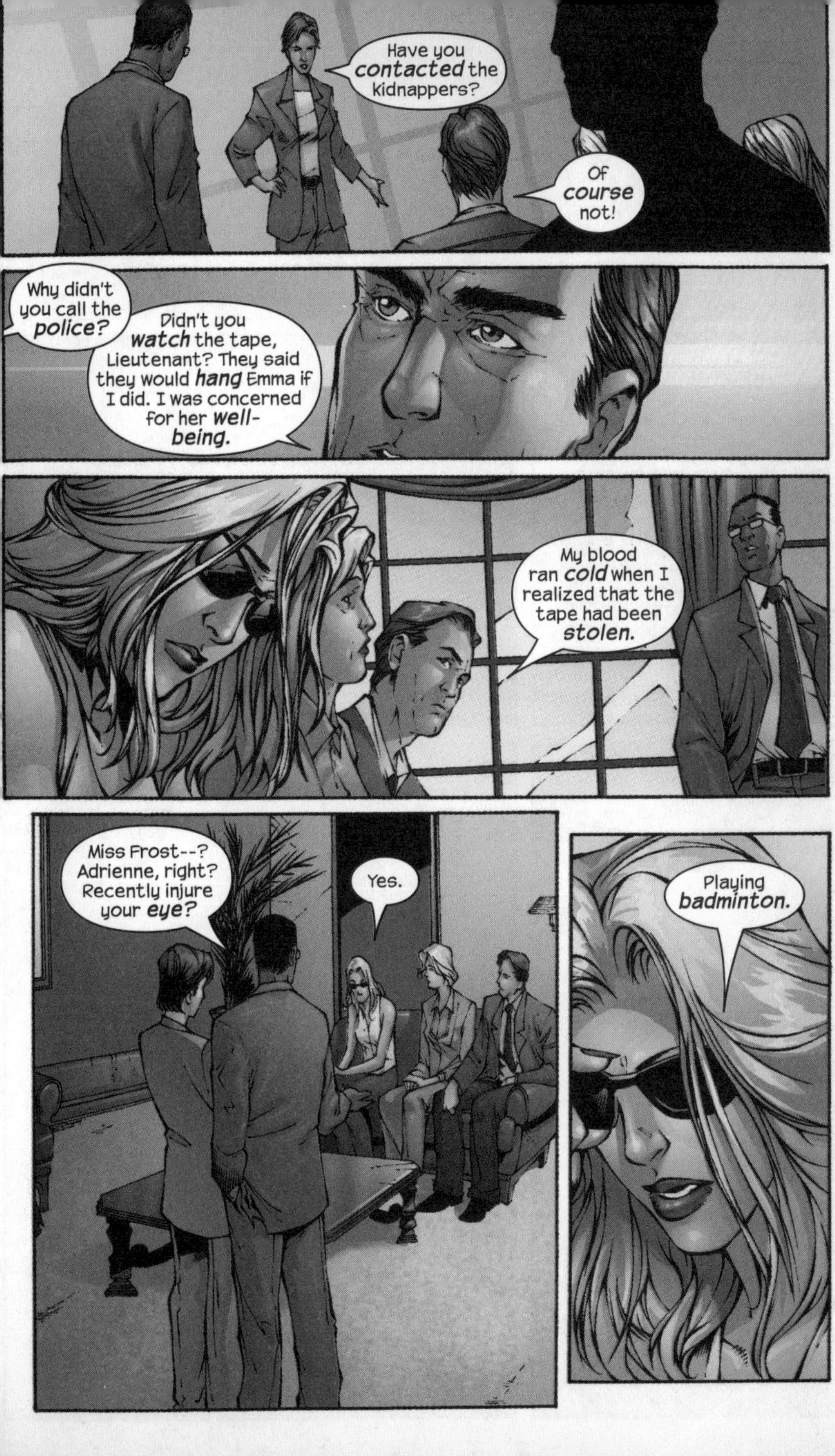
Have you contacted the kidnappers?
Of course not!
Why didn't you call the police?
Didn't you watch the tape, Lieutenant? They said they would hang Emma if I did. I was concerned for her well-being.
My blood ran cold when I realized that the tape had been stolen.
Miss Frost--? Adrienne, right? Recently injure your eye?
Yes.
Playing badminton.

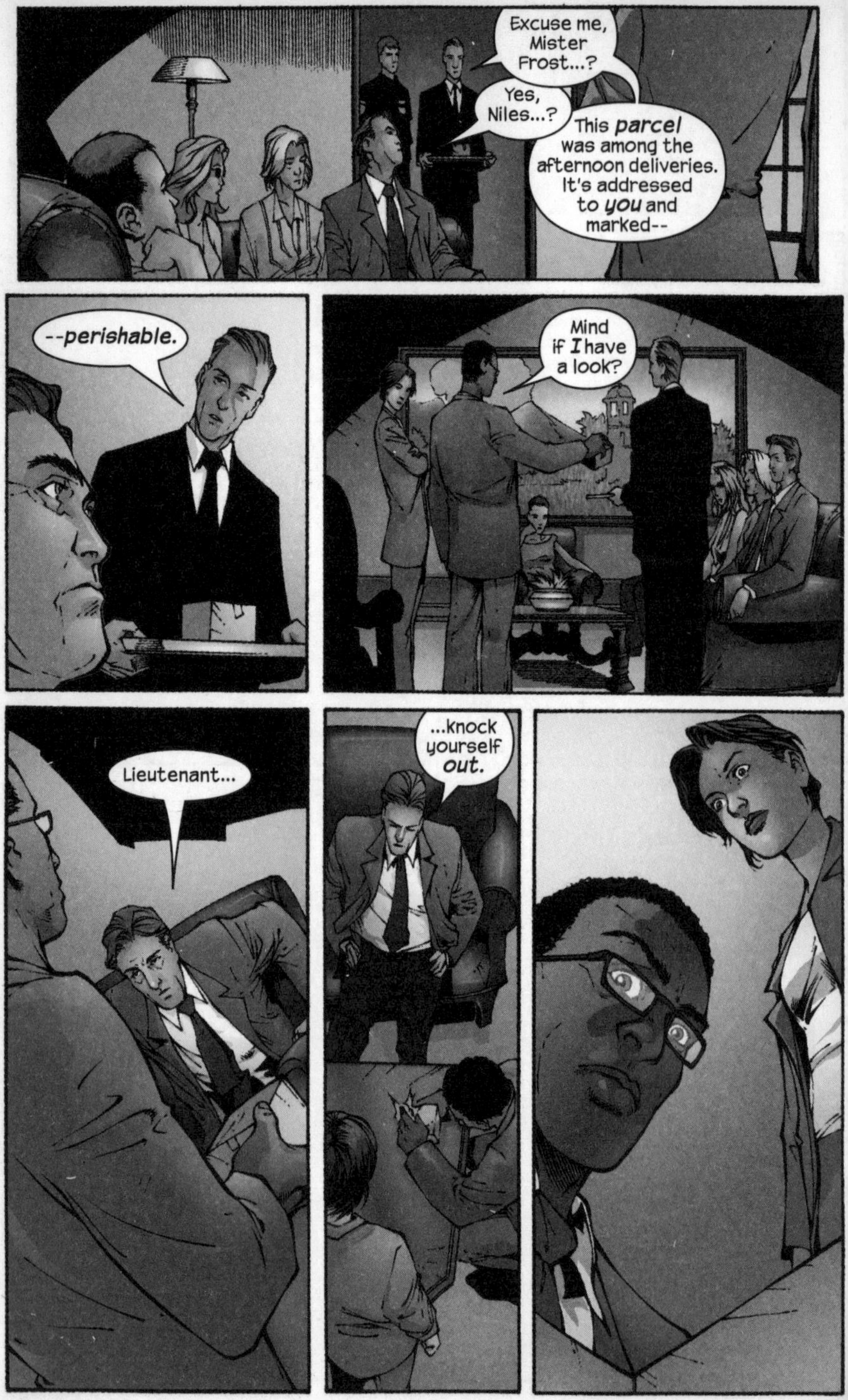
Excuse me, Mister Frost...?
Yes, Niles...?
This *parcel* was among the afternoon deliveries. It's addressed to *you* and marked--
--*perishable.*
Mind if *I* have a look?
Lieutenant...
...knock yourself *out.*

It's a lock of brown hair.

And... and an *ear.*

W-what!?

Is this *Emma's* hair?

Y-yes...

Can... ...can any of you identify the... the...

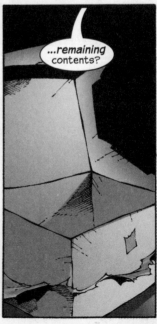

...remaining contents?

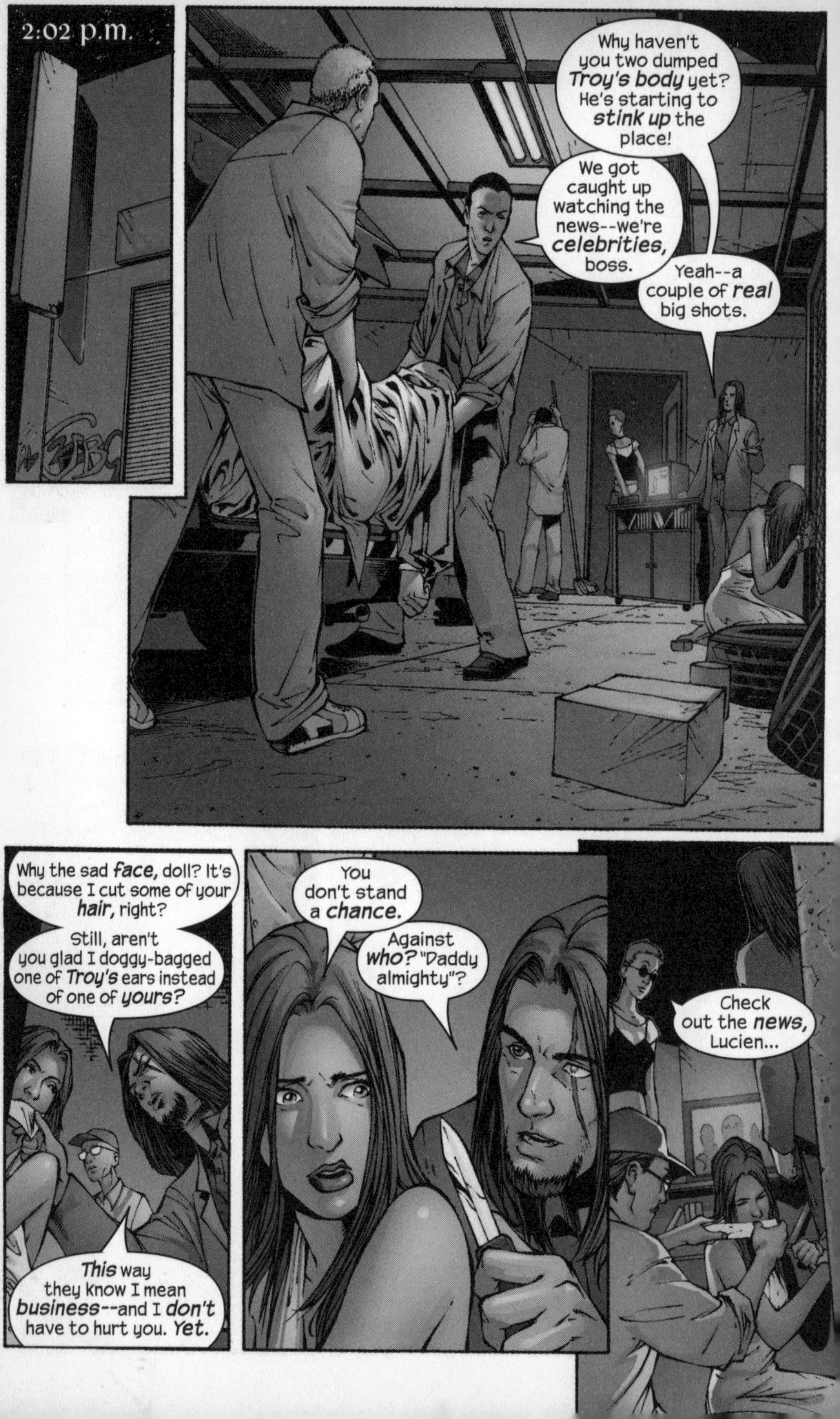
2:02 p.m.
Why haven't you two dumped Troy's body yet? He's starting to stink up the place!
We got caught up watching the news--we're celebrities, boss.
Yeah--a couple of real big shots.
Why the sad face, doll? It's because I cut some of your hair, right?
Still, aren't you glad I doggy-bagged one of Troy's ears instead of one of yours?
This way they know I mean business--and I don't have to hurt you. Yet.
You don't stand a chance.
Against who? "Daddy almighty"?
Check out the news, Lucien...

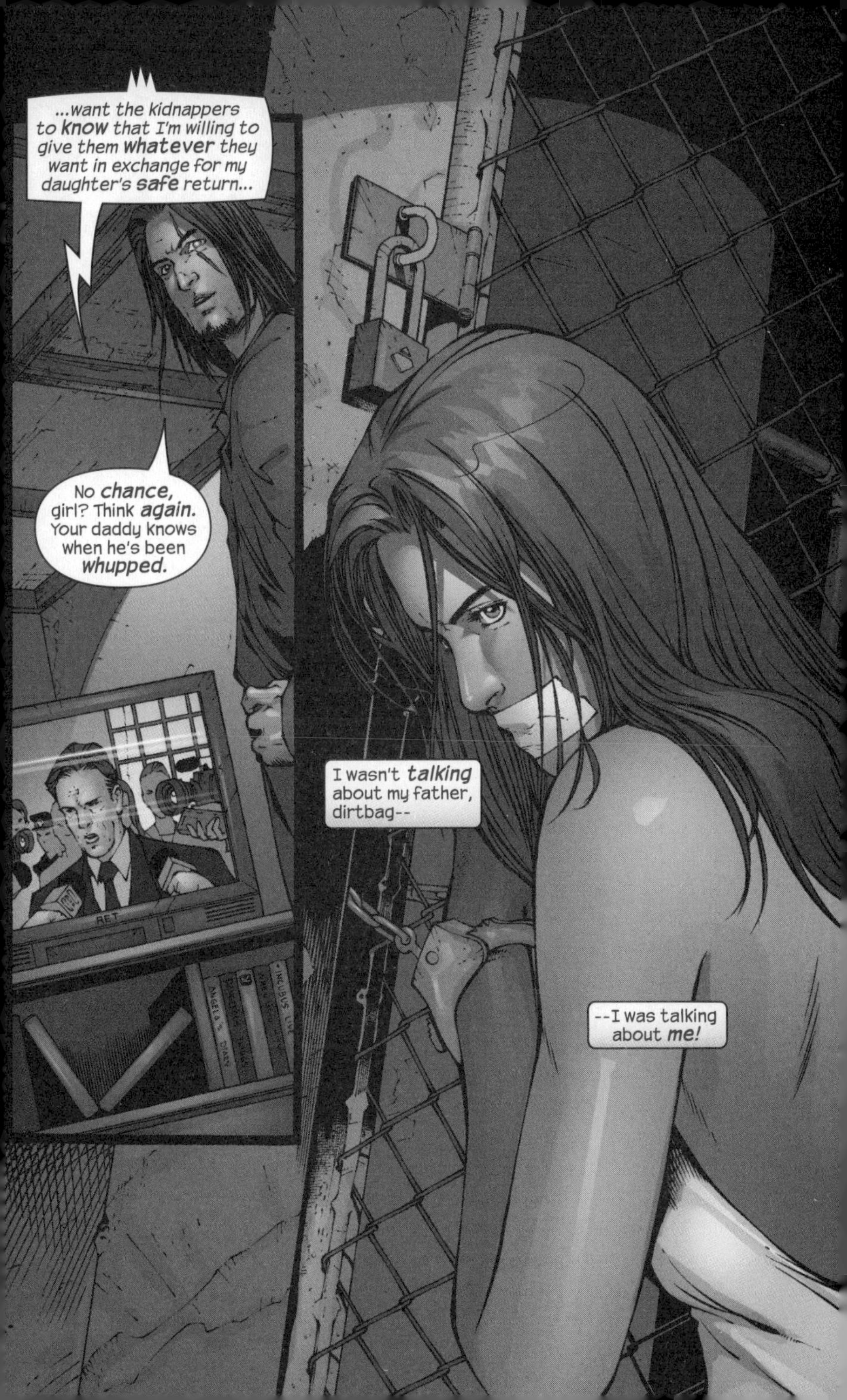
...want the kidnappers to know that I'm willing to give them whatever they want in exchange for my daughter's safe return...
No chance, girl? Think again. Your daddy knows when he's been whupped.
I wasn't talking about my father, dirtbag--
--I was talking about me!

MIND GAMES 6 OF 6

GOING MENTAL

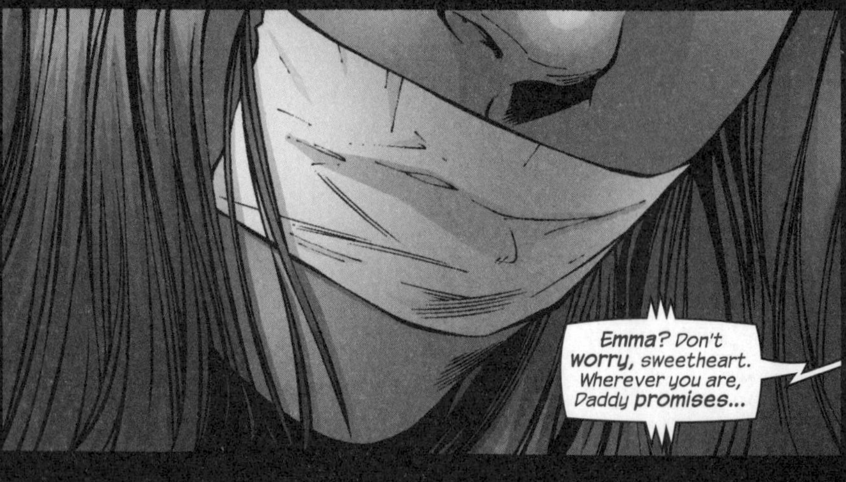
Emma? Don't worry, sweetheart. Wherever you are, Daddy promises...

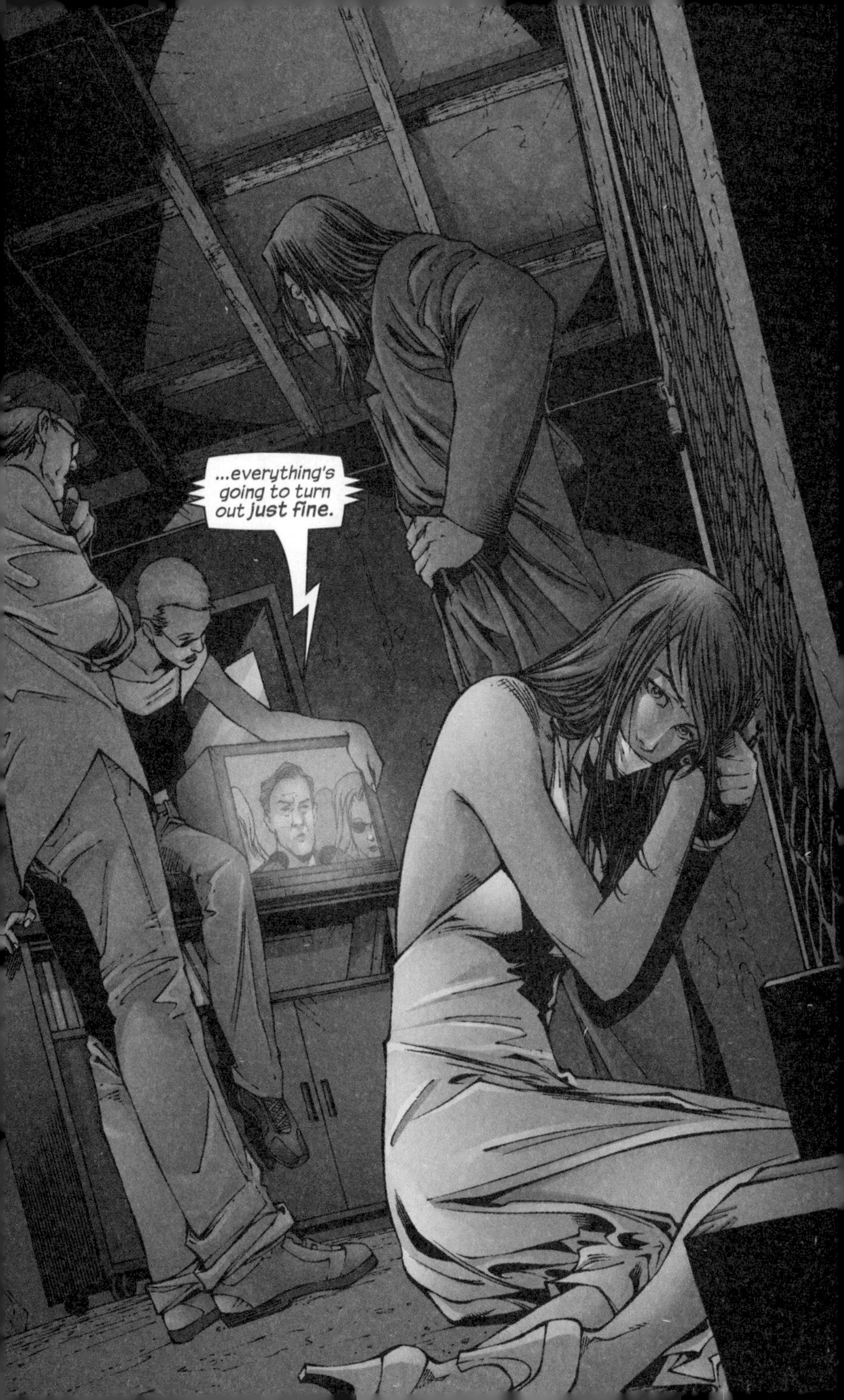
...everything's going to turn out just fine.

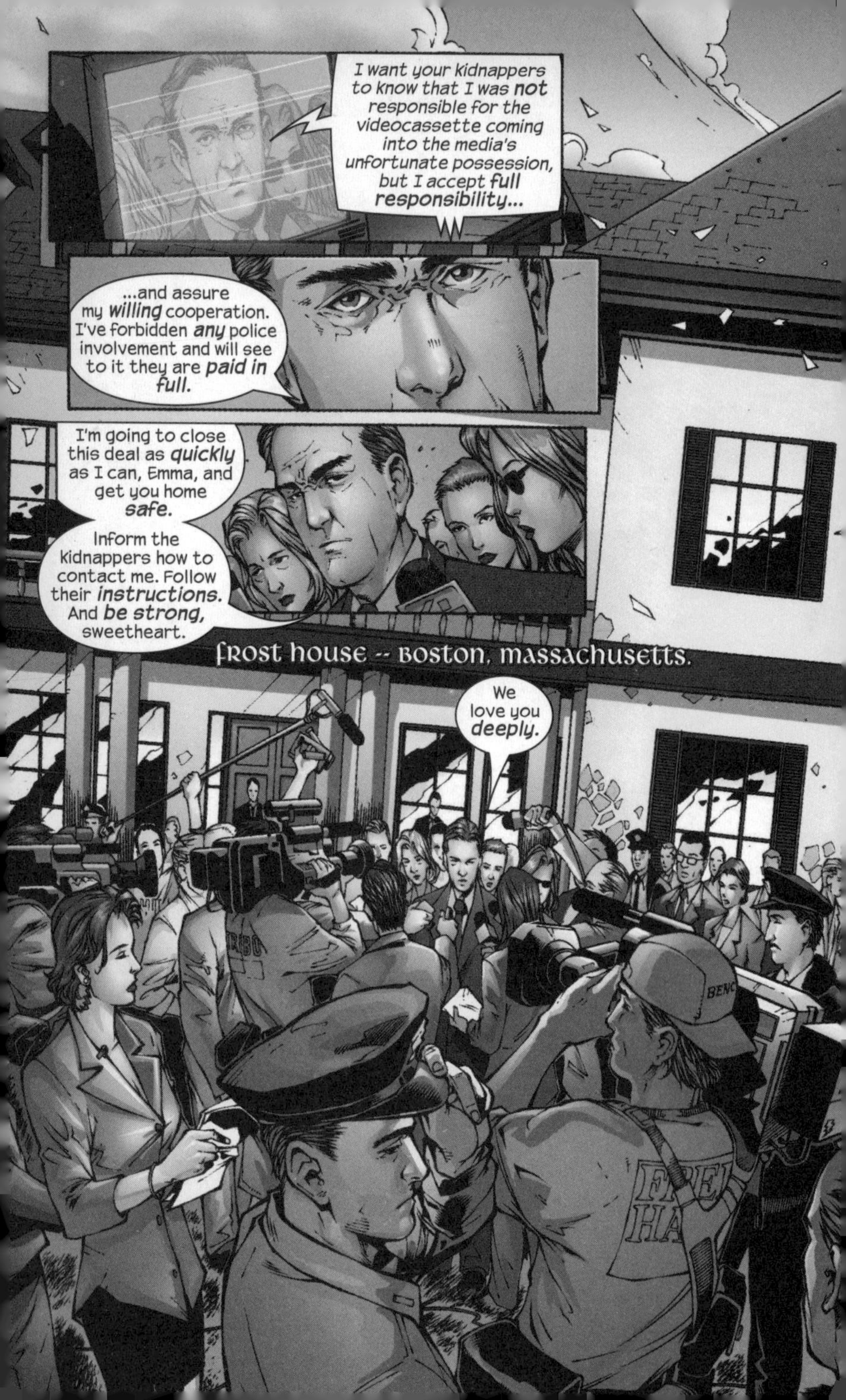
I want your kidnappers to know that I was not responsible for the videocassette coming into the media's unfortunate possession, but I accept full responsibility...
...and assure my willing cooperation. I've forbidden any police involvement and will see to it they are paid in full.
I'm going to close this deal as quickly as I can, Emma, and get you home safe.
Inform the kidnappers how to contact me. Follow their instructions. And be strong, sweetheart.
Frost House -- Boston, Massachusetts.
We love you deeply.

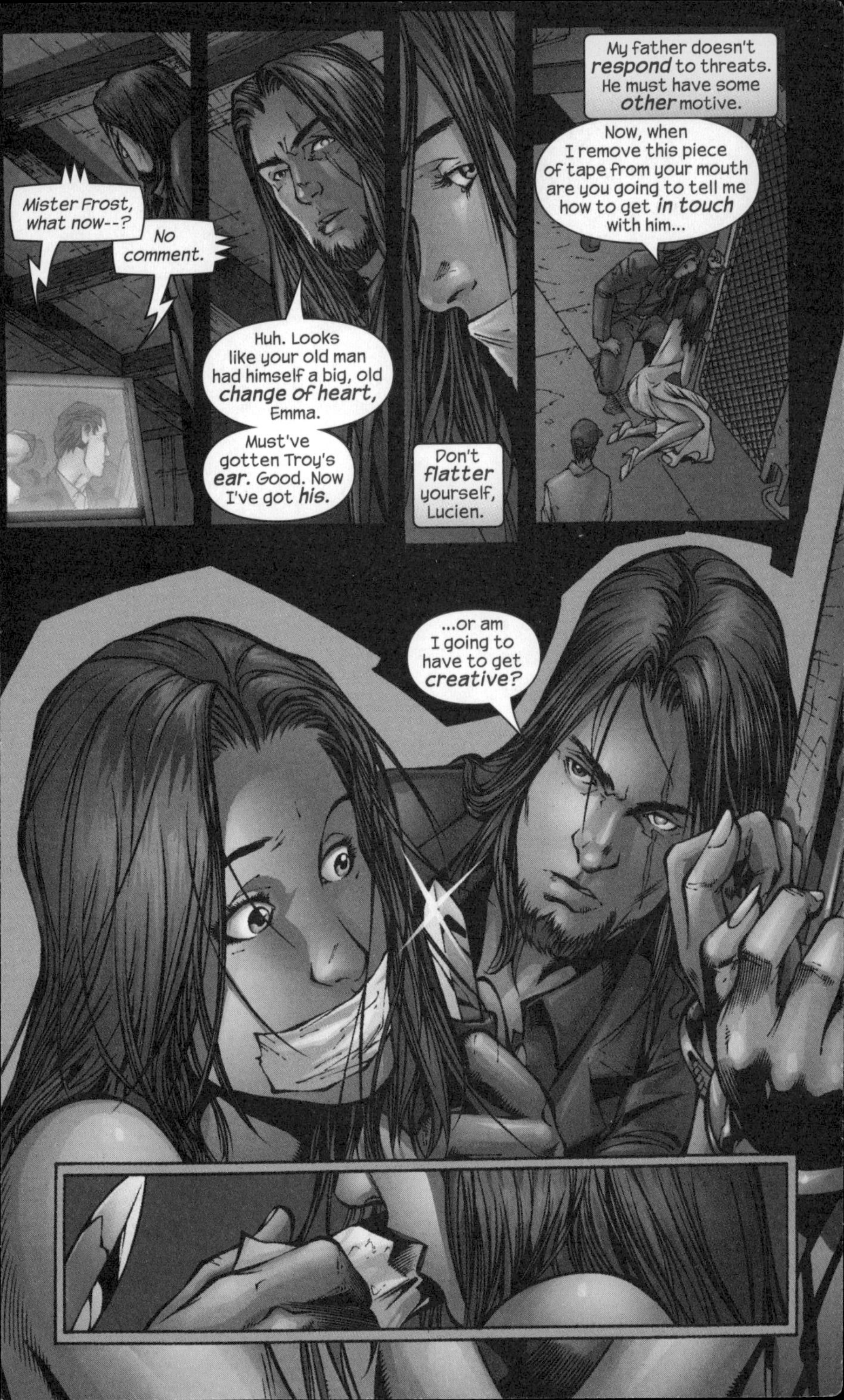
Mister Frost, what now--?
No comment.
Huh. Looks like your old man had himself a big, old change of heart, Emma.
Must've gotten Troy's ear. Good. Now I've got his.
Don't flatter yourself, Lucien.
My father doesn't respond to threats. He must have some other motive.
Now, when I remove this piece of tape from your mouth are you going to tell me how to get in touch with him...
...or am I going to have to get creative?

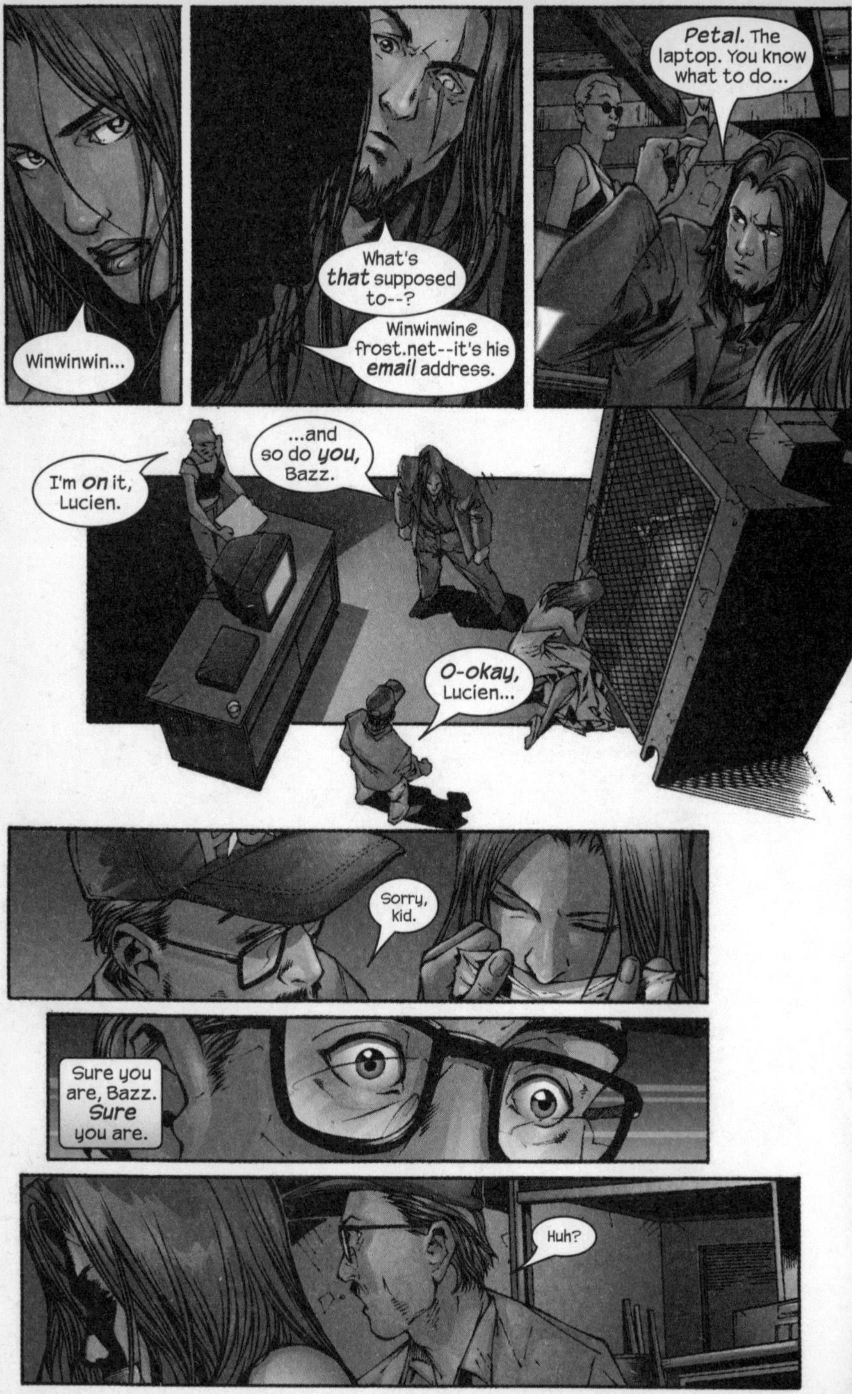
Winwinwin...
What's that supposed to--?
Winwinwin@ frost.net--it's his email address.
Petal. The laptop. You know what to do...
I'm on it, Lucien.
...and so do you, Bazz.
O-okay, Lucien...
Sorry, kid.
Sure you are, Bazz. Sure you are.
Huh?

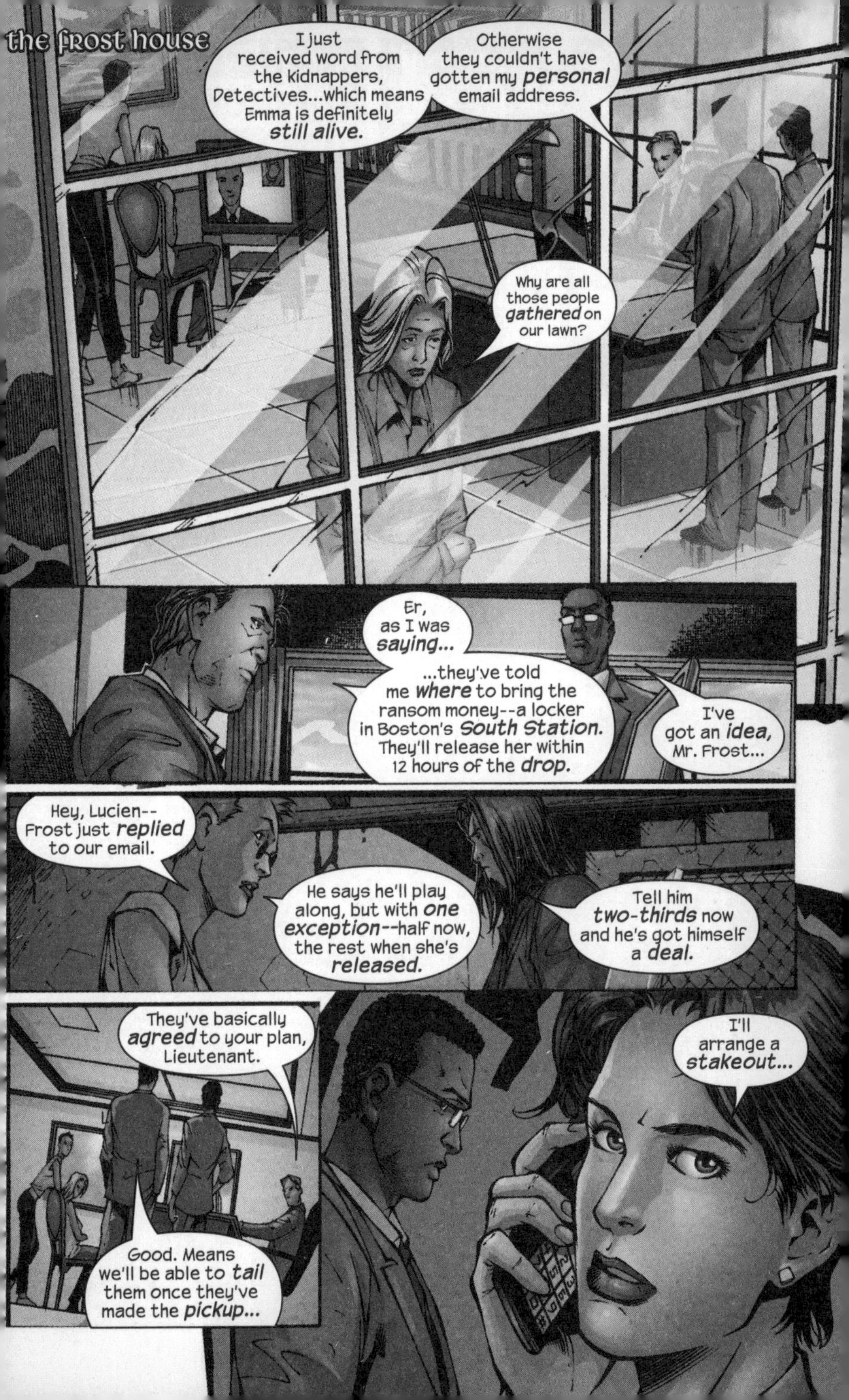
the frost house
I just received word from the kidnappers, Detectives...which means Emma is definitely still alive.
Otherwise they couldn't have gotten my personal email address.
Why are all those people gathered on our lawn?
Er, as I was saying...
...they've told me where to bring the ransom money--a locker in Boston's South Station. They'll release her within 12 hours of the drop.
I've got an idea, Mr. Frost...
Hey, Lucien-- Frost just replied to our email.
He says he'll play along, but with one exception--half now, the rest when she's released.
Tell him two-thirds now and he's got himself a deal.
They've basically agreed to your plan, Lieutenant.
I'll arrange a stakeout...
Good. Means we'll be able to tail them once they've made the pickup...

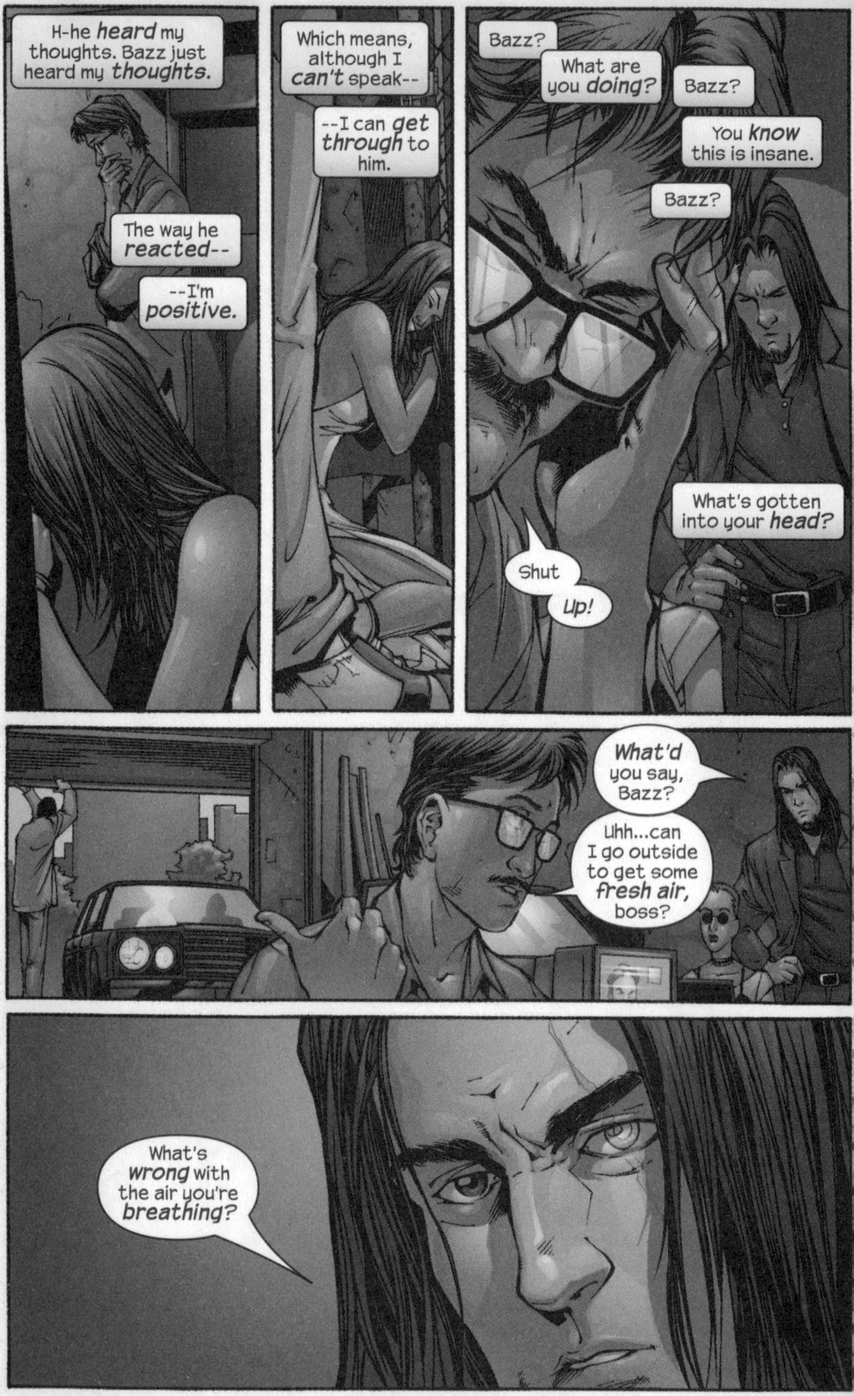
H-he heard my thoughts. Bazz just heard my thoughts.
The way he reacted--
--I'm positive.
Which means, although I can't speak--
--I can get through to him.
Bazz?
What are you doing?
Bazz?
You know this is insane.
Bazz?
What's gotten into your head?
Shut up!
What'd you say, Bazz?
Uhh...can I go outside to get some fresh air, boss?
What's wrong with the air you're breathing?

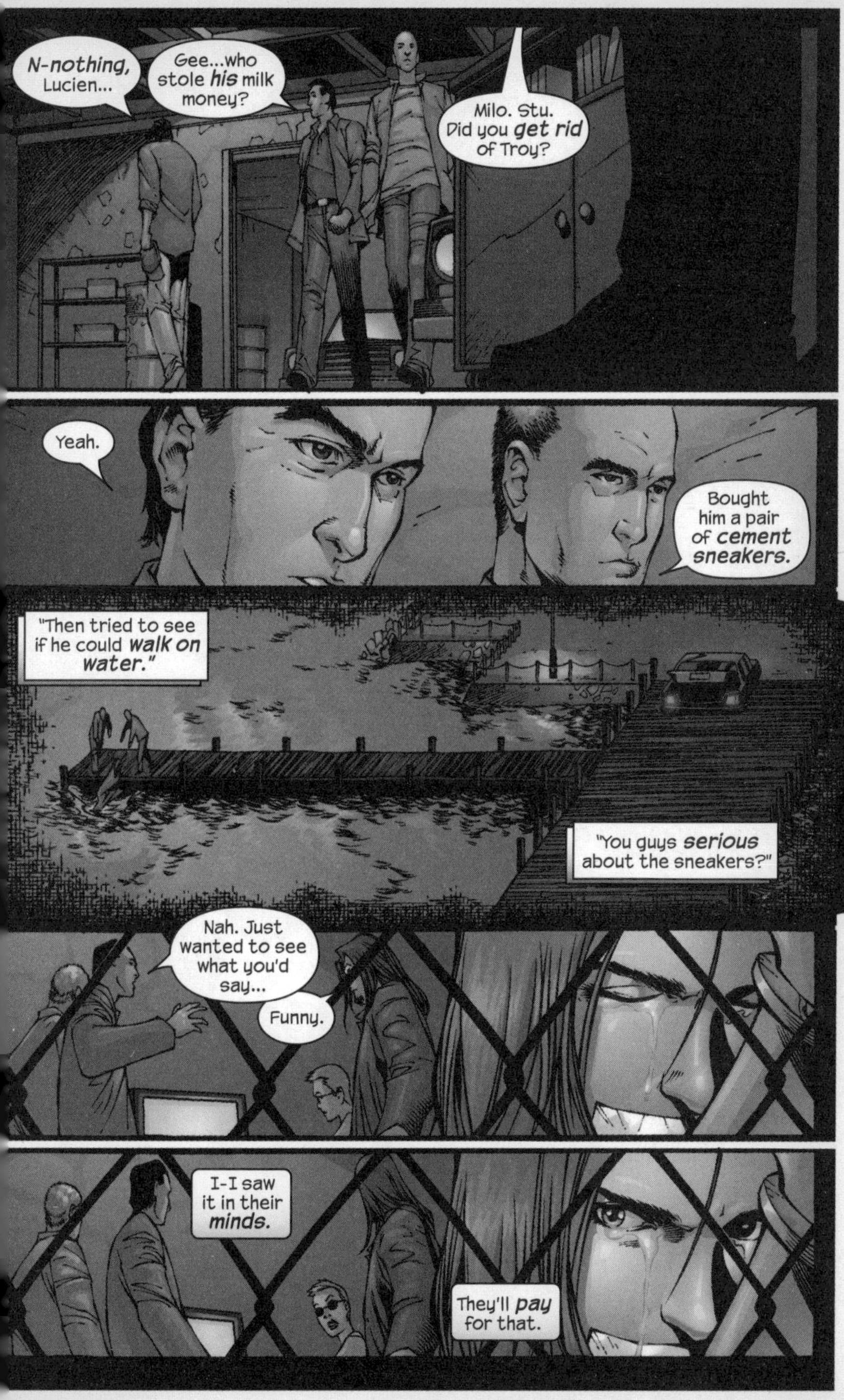

N-nothing, Lucien...
Gee...who stole his milk money?
Milo. Stu. Did you get rid of Troy?
Yeah.
Bought him a pair of cement sneakers.
"Then tried to see if he could walk on water."
"You guys serious about the sneakers?"
Nah. Just wanted to see what you'd say...
Funny.
I-I saw it in their minds.
They'll pay for that.

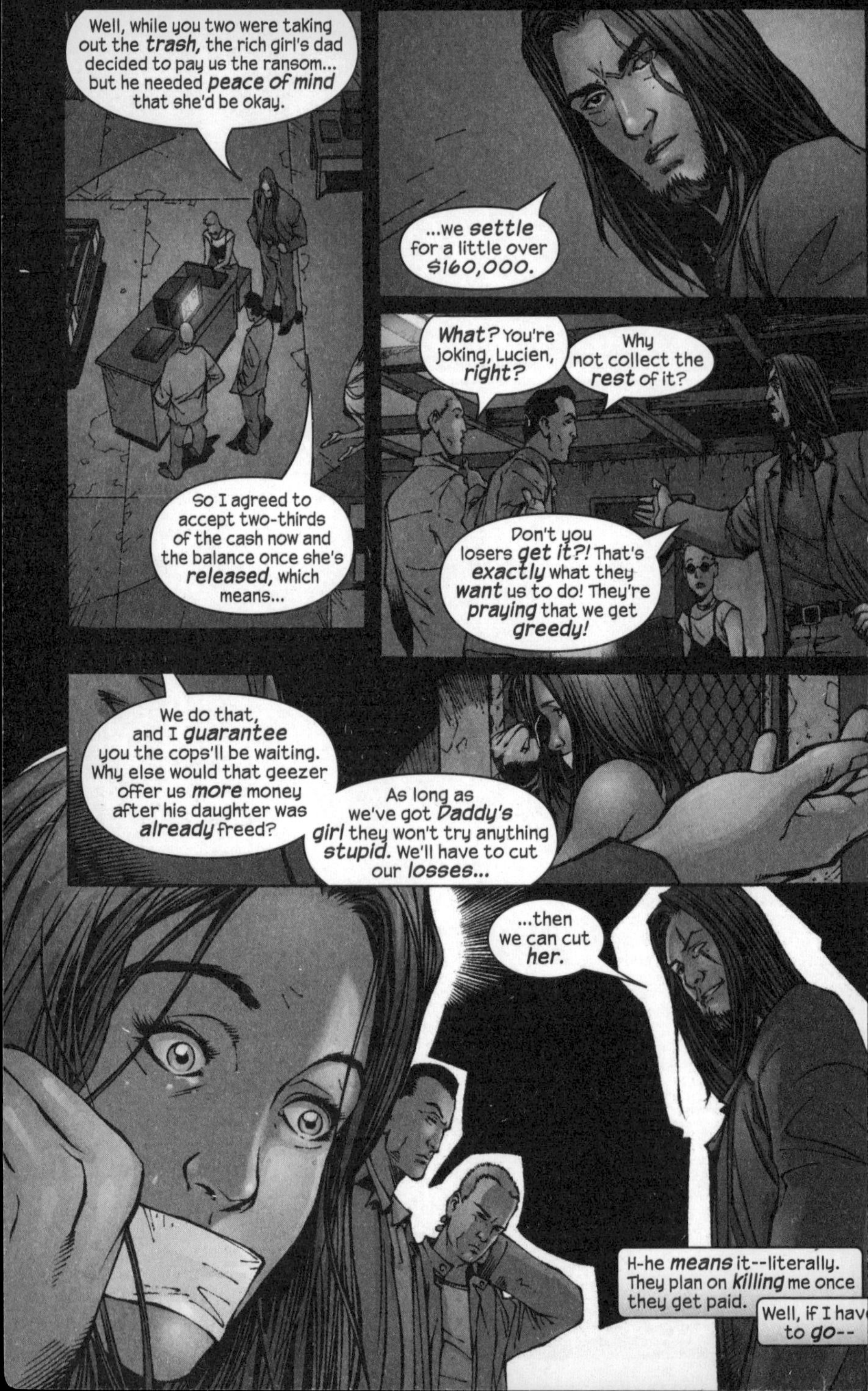
Well, while you two were taking out the trash, the rich girl's dad decided to pay us the ransom... but he needed peace of mind that she'd be okay.
So I agreed to accept two-thirds of the cash now and the balance once she's released, which means...
...we settle for a little over $160,000.
What? You're joking, Lucien, right?
Why not collect the rest of it?
Don't you losers get it?! That's exactly what they want us to do! They're praying that we get greedy!
We do that, and I guarantee you the cops'll be waiting. Why else would that geezer offer us more money after his daughter was already freed?
As long as we've got Daddy's girl they won't try anything stupid. We'll have to cut our losses...
...then we can cut her.
H-he means it--literally. They plan on killing me once they get paid.
Well, if I have to go--

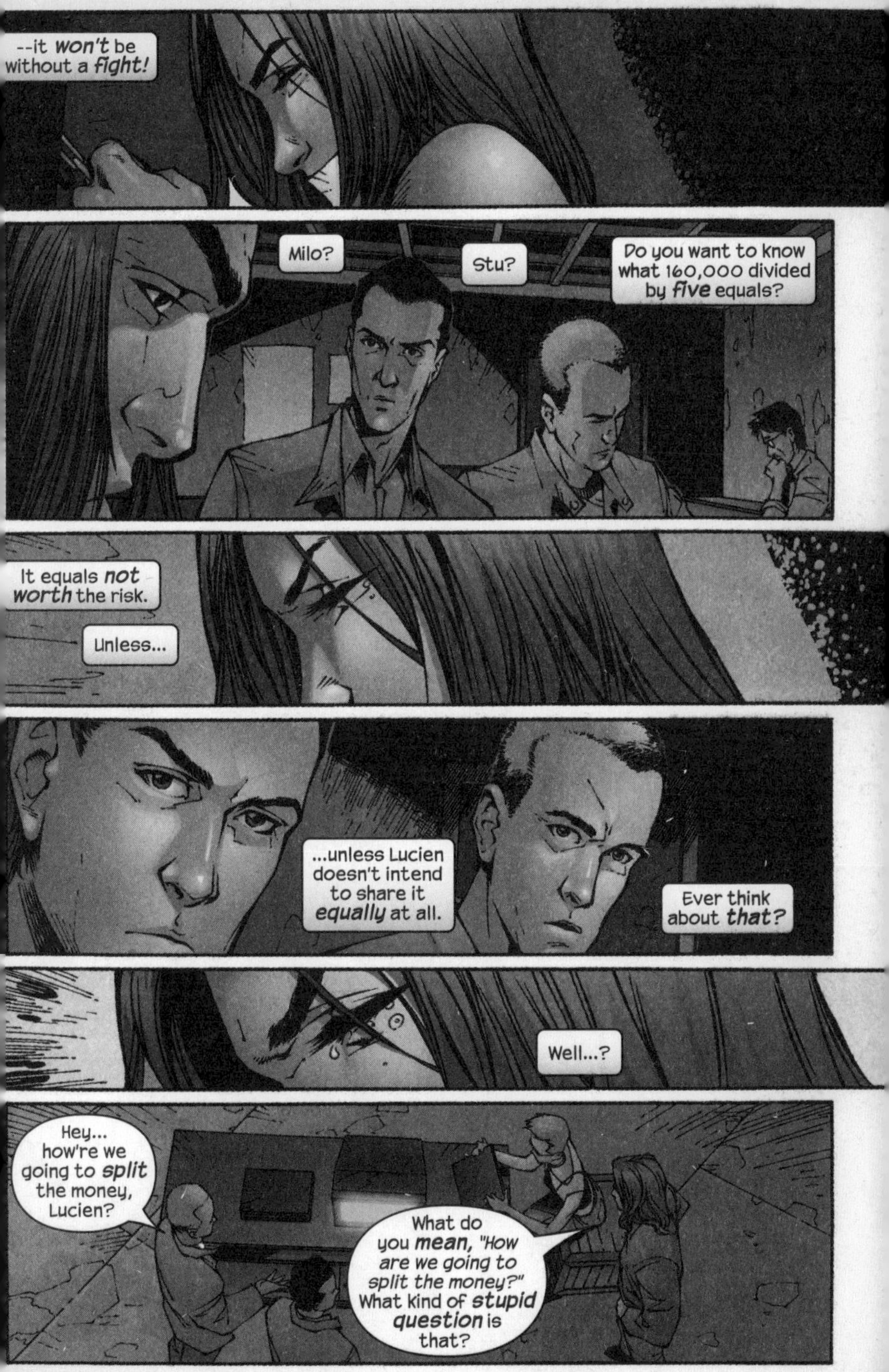

--it won't be without a fight!
Milo?
Stu?
Do you want to know what 160,000 divided by five equals?
It equals not worth the risk.
Unless...
...unless Lucien doesn't intend to share it equally at all.
Ever think about that?
Well...?
Hey... how're we going to split the money, Lucien?
What do you mean, "How are we going to split the money?" What kind of stupid question is that?

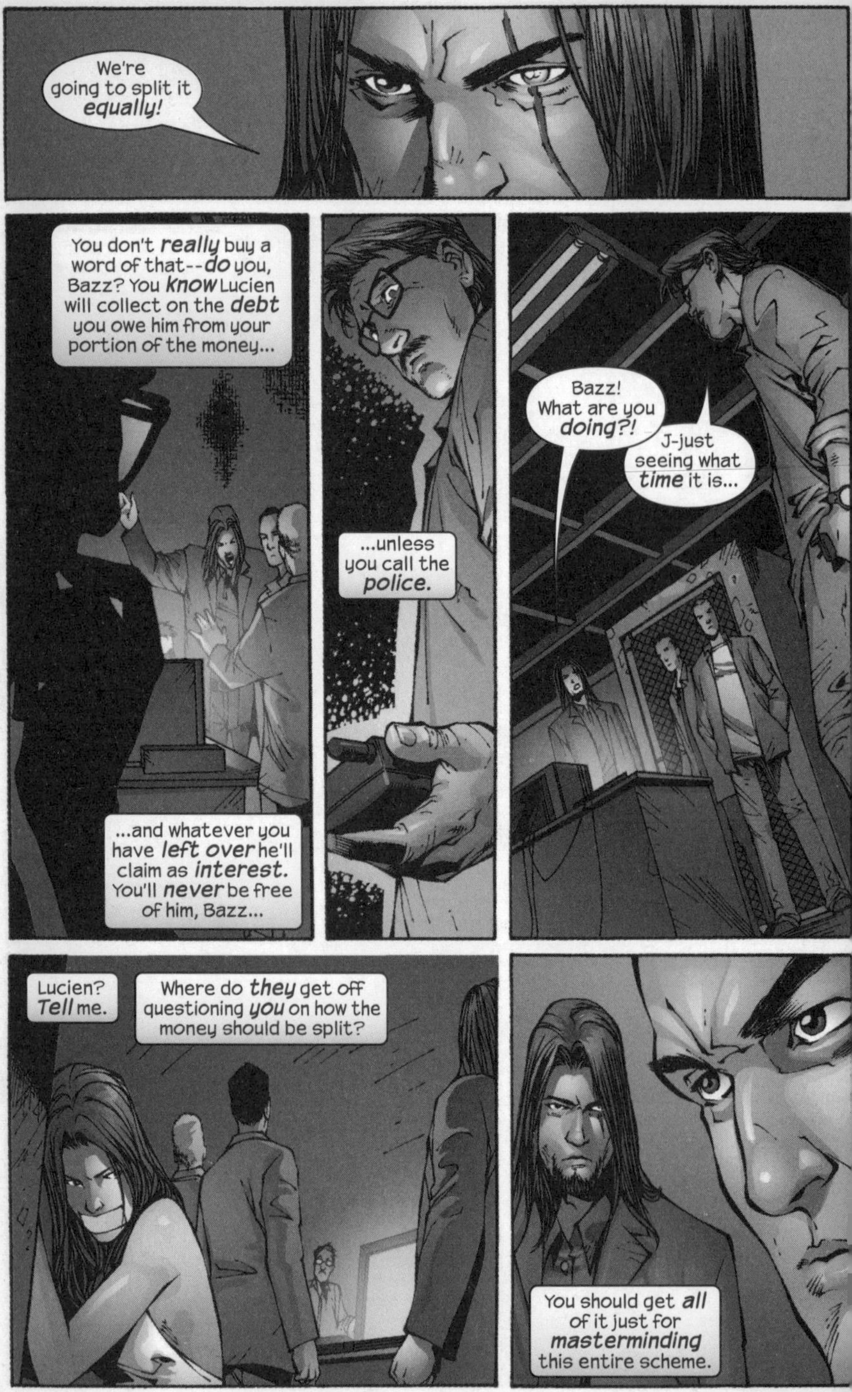
We're going to split it *equally!*
You don't *really* buy a word of that--*do* you, Bazz? You *know* Lucien will collect on the *debt* you owe him from your portion of the money...
...and whatever you have *left over* he'll claim as *interest.* You'll *never* be free of him, Bazz...
...unless you call the *police.*
Bazz! What are you *doing?!*
J-just seeing what *time* it is...
Lucien? *Tell* me.
Where do *they* get off questioning *you* on how the money should be split?
You should get *all* of it just for *masterminding* this entire scheme.

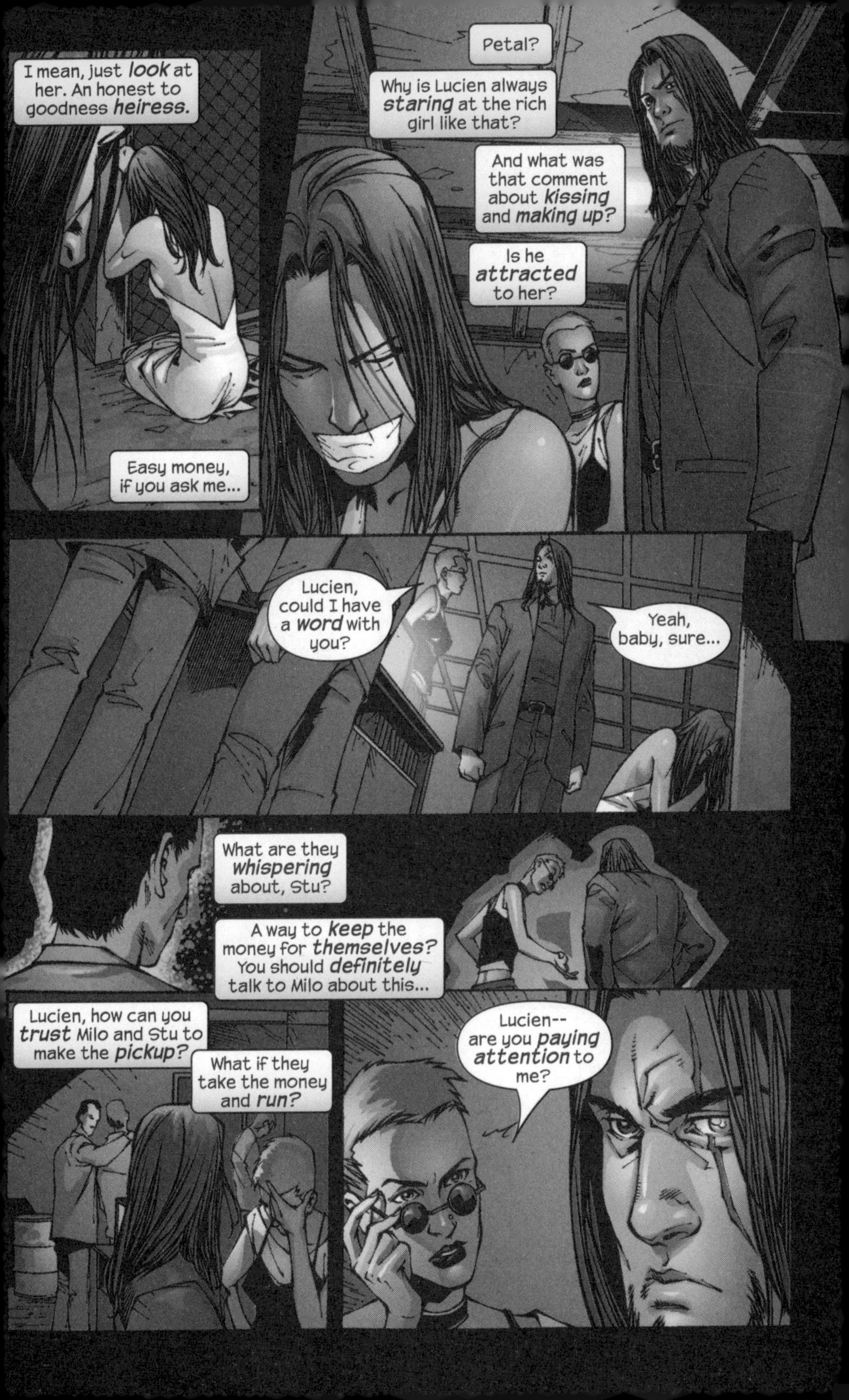
I mean, just look at her. An honest to goodness heiress.
Easy money, if you ask me...
Petal?
Why is Lucien always staring at the rich girl like that?
And what was that comment about kissing and making up?
Is he attracted to her?
Lucien, could I have a word with you?
Yeah, baby, sure...
What are they whispering about, Stu?
A way to keep the money for themselves? You should definitely talk to Milo about this...
Lucien, how can you trust Milo and Stu to make the pickup?
What if they take the money and run?
Lucien-- are you paying attention to me?

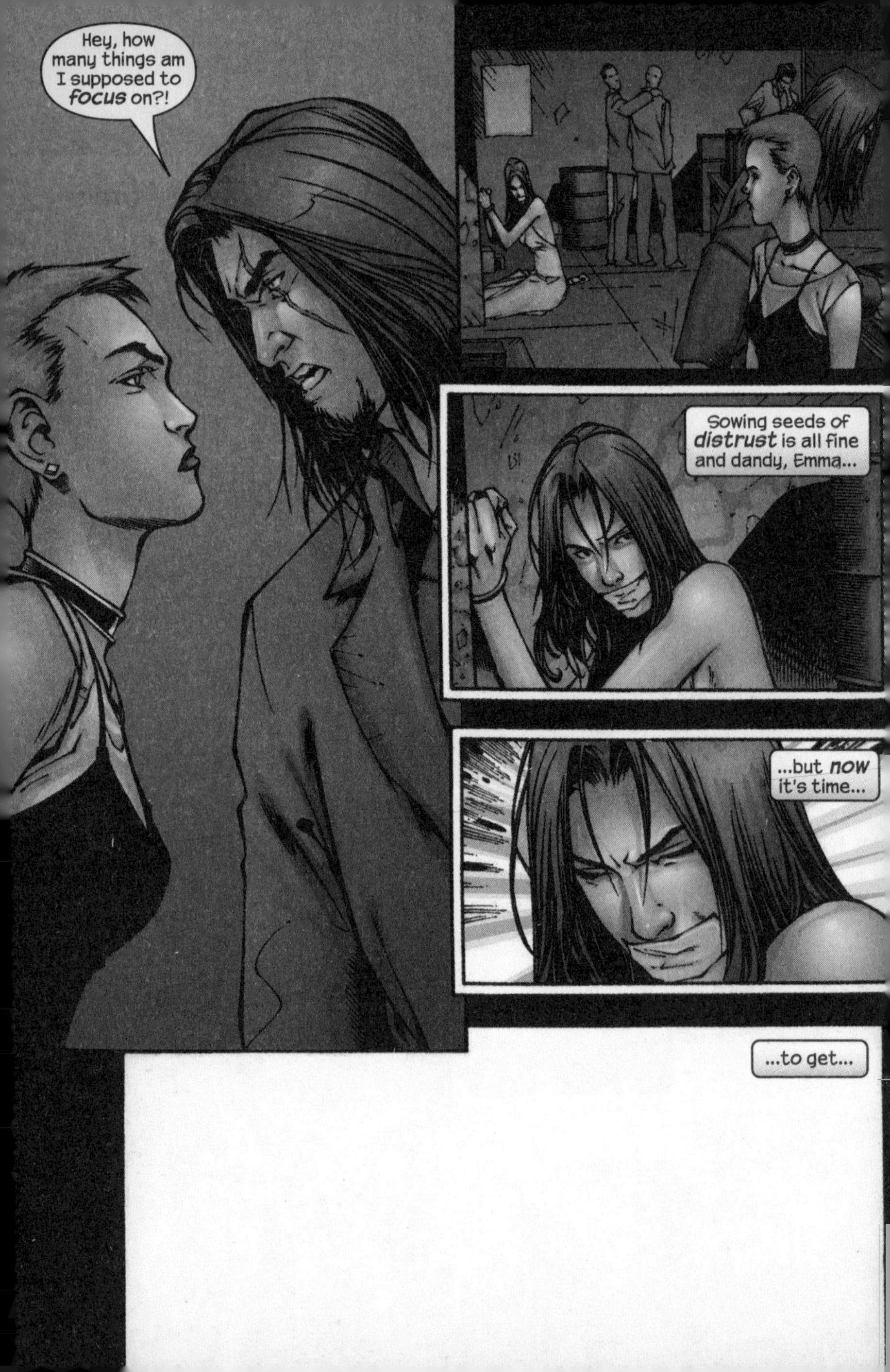
Hey, how many things am I supposed to *focus* on?!
Sowing seeds of *distrust* is all fine and dandy, Emma...
...but *now* it's time...
...to get...

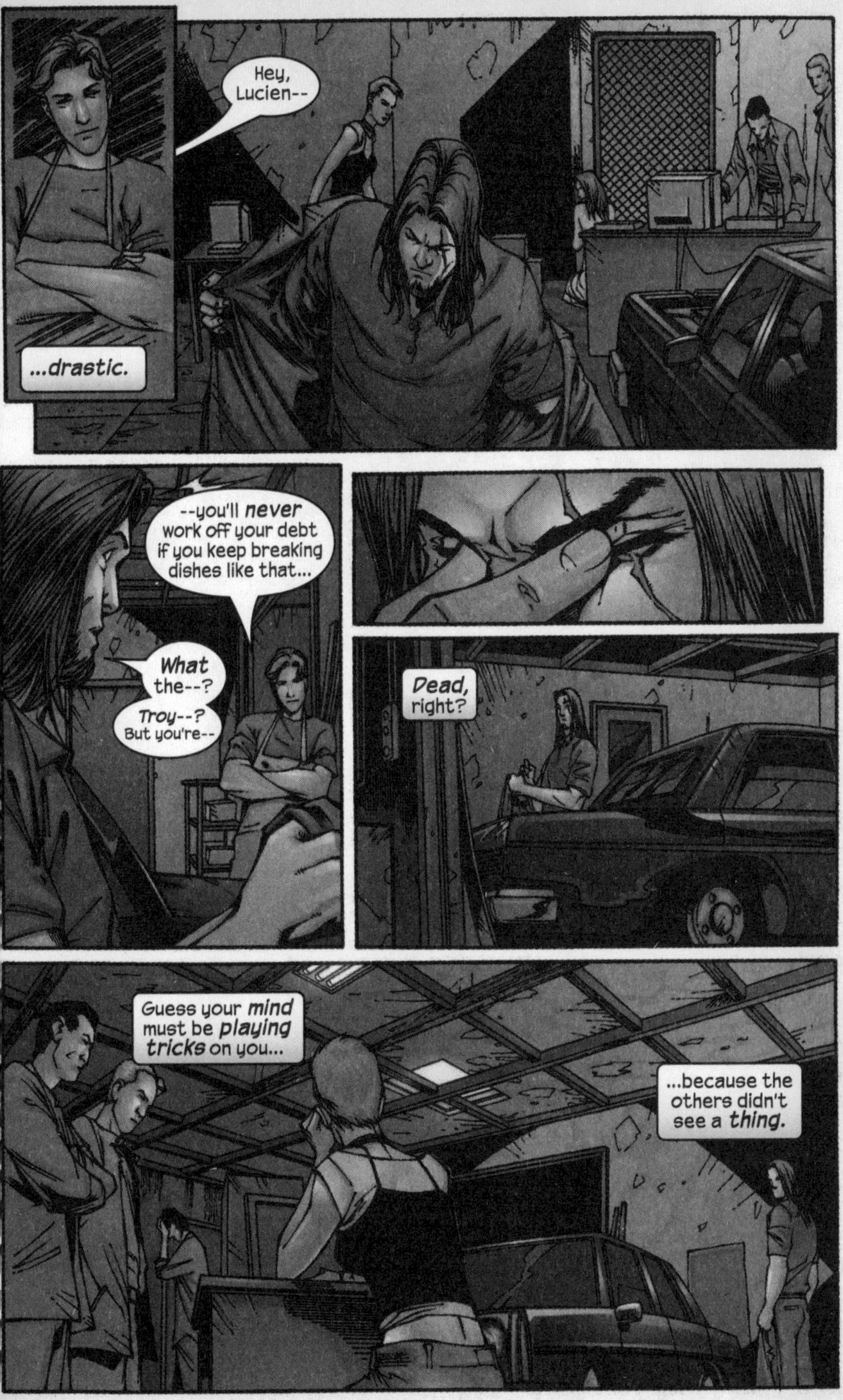

Hey, Lucien--
...drastic.
--you'll never work off your debt if you keep breaking dishes like that...
What the--?
Troy--? But you're--
Dead, right?
Guess your mind must be playing tricks on you...
...because the others didn't see a thing.

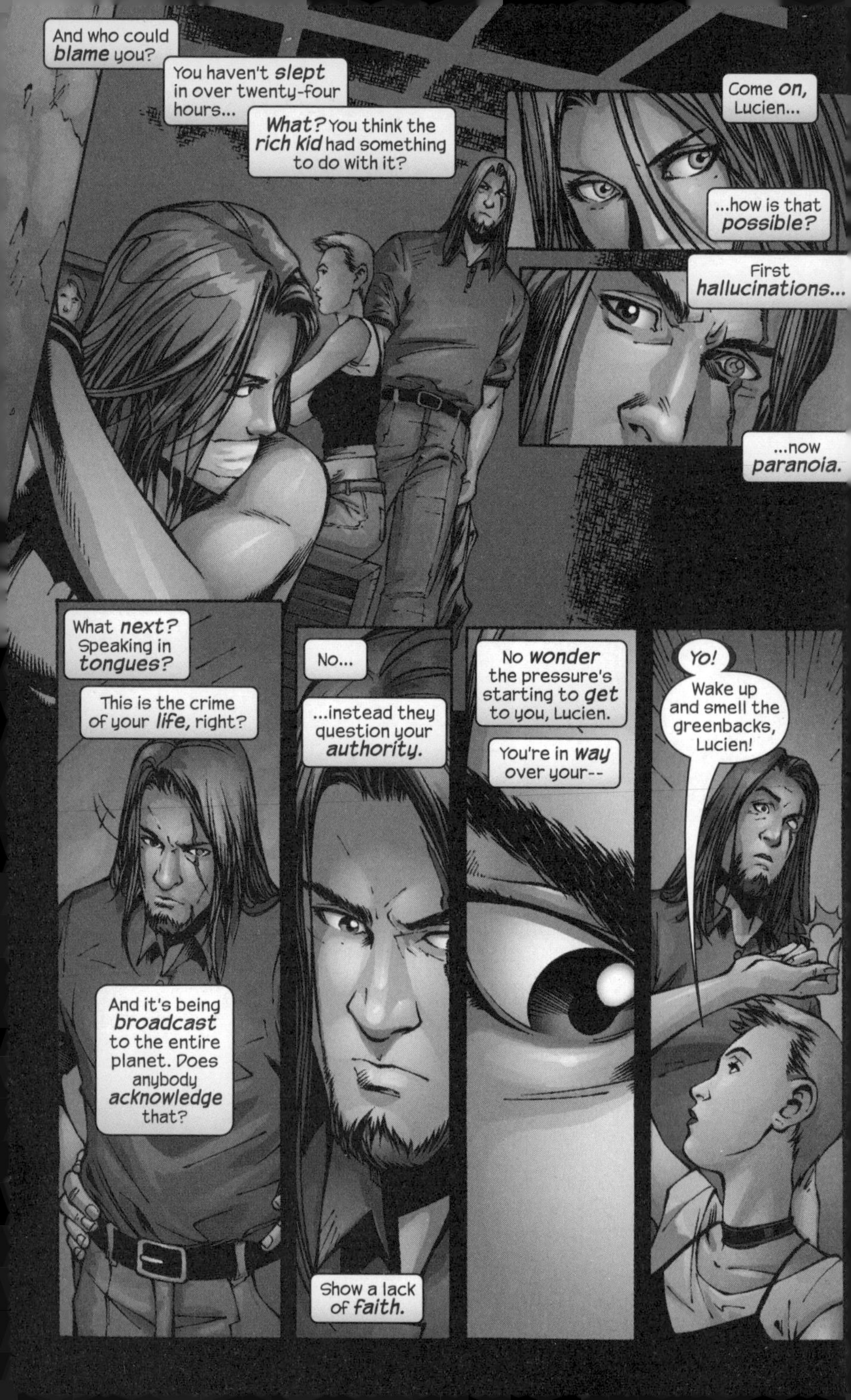
And who could blame you?
You haven't slept in over twenty-four hours...
What? You think the rich kid had something to do with it?
Come on, Lucien...
...how is that possible?
First hallucinations...
...now paranoia.
What next? Speaking in tongues?
This is the crime of your life, right?
And it's being broadcast to the entire planet. Does anybody acknowledge that?
No...
...instead they question your authority.
Show a lack of faith.
No wonder the pressure's starting to get to you, Lucien.
You're in way over your--
Yo!
Wake up and smell the greenbacks, Lucien!

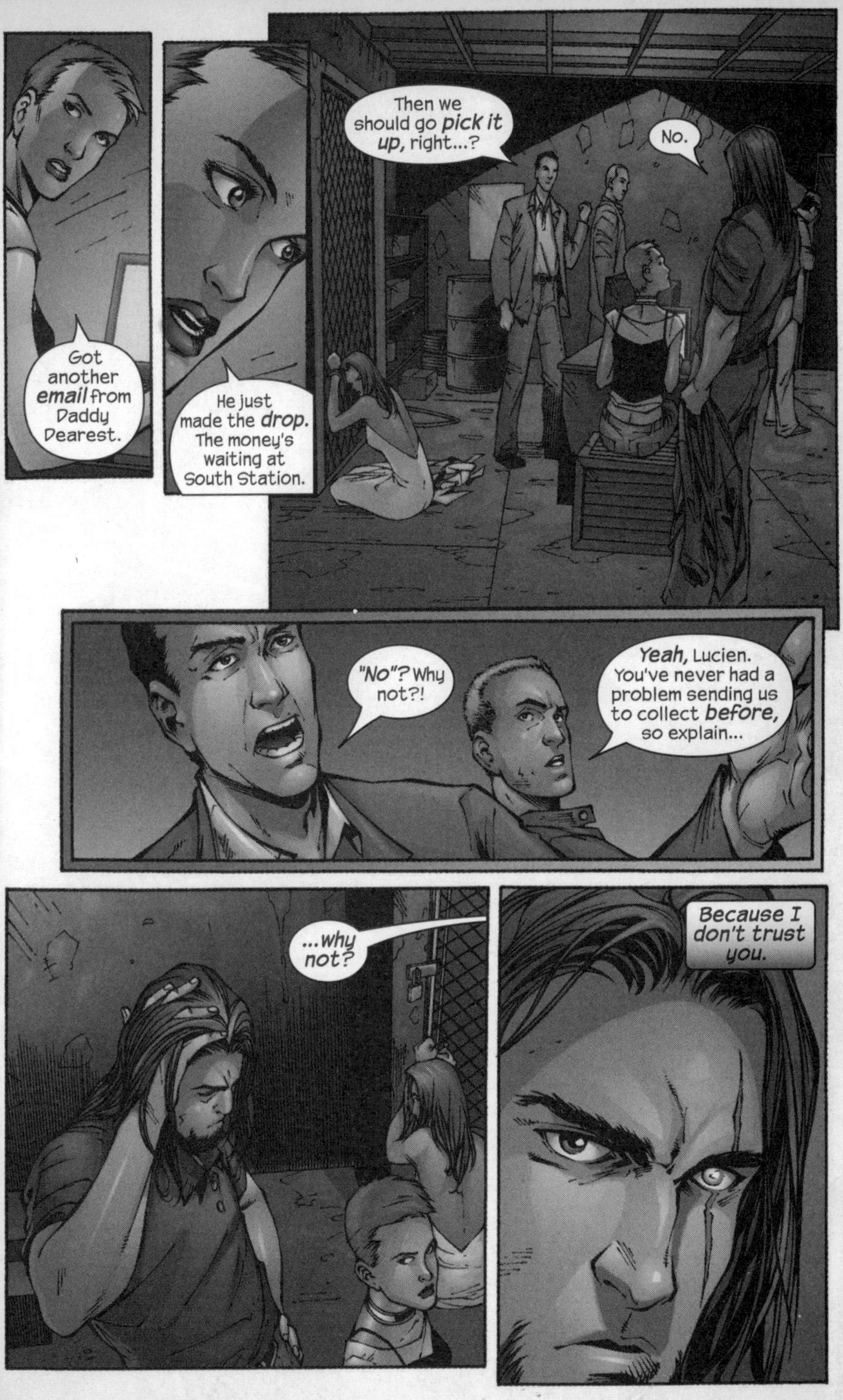
Got another email from Daddy Dearest.
He just made the drop. The money's waiting at South Station.
Then we should go pick it up, right...?
No.
"No"? Why not?!
Yeah, Lucien. You've never had a problem sending us to collect before, so explain...
...why not?
Because I don't trust you.

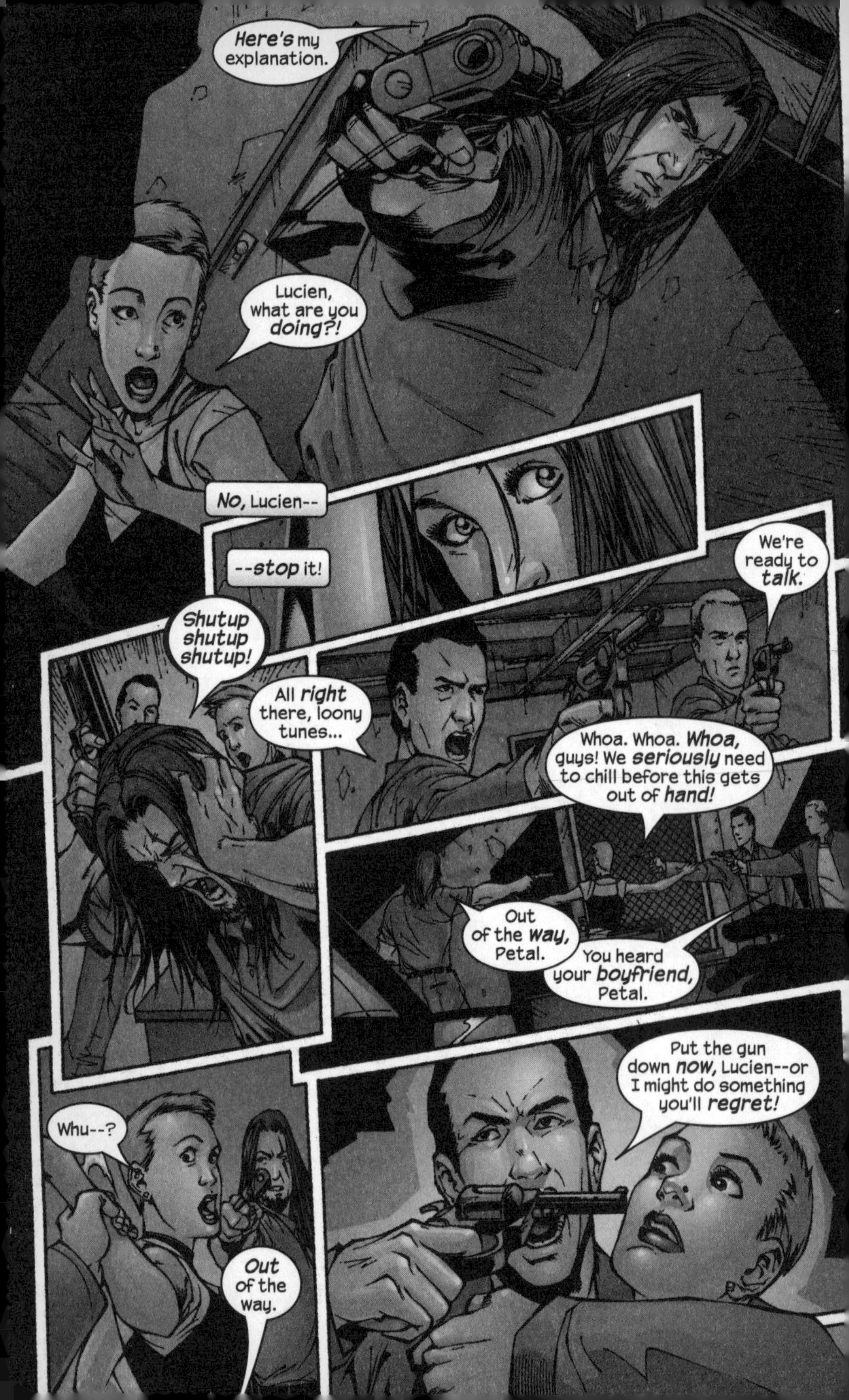
Here's my explanation.
Lucien, what are you doing?!
No, Lucien--
--stop it!
Shutup shutup shutup!
All right there, loony tunes...
We're ready to talk.
Whoa. Whoa. Whoa, guys! We seriously need to chill before this gets out of hand!
Out of the way, Petal.
You heard your boyfriend, Petal.
Whu--?
Out of the way.
Put the gun down now, Lucien--or I might do something you'll regret!

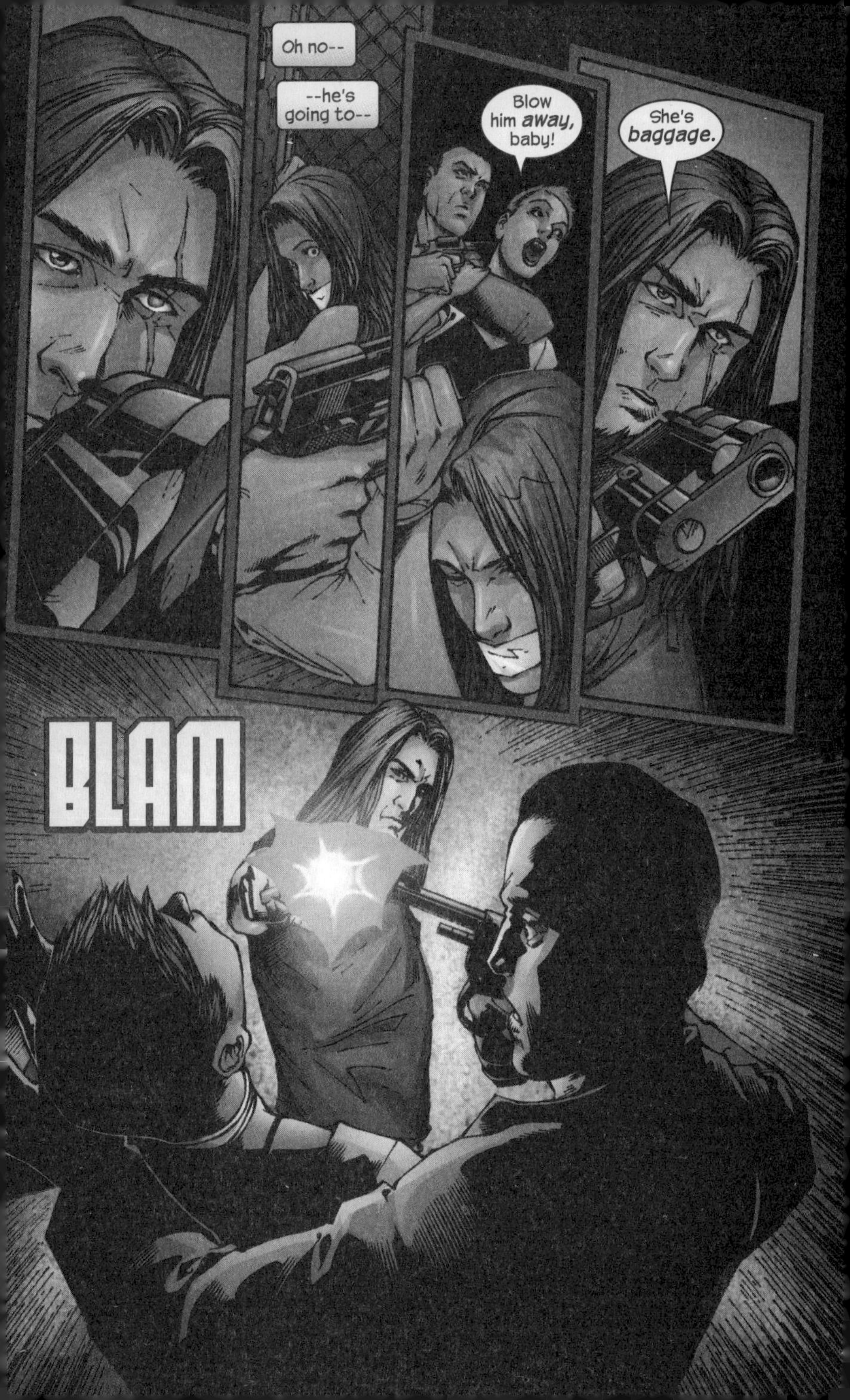

Oh no--
--he's going to--
Blow him away, baby!
She's baggage.
BLAM

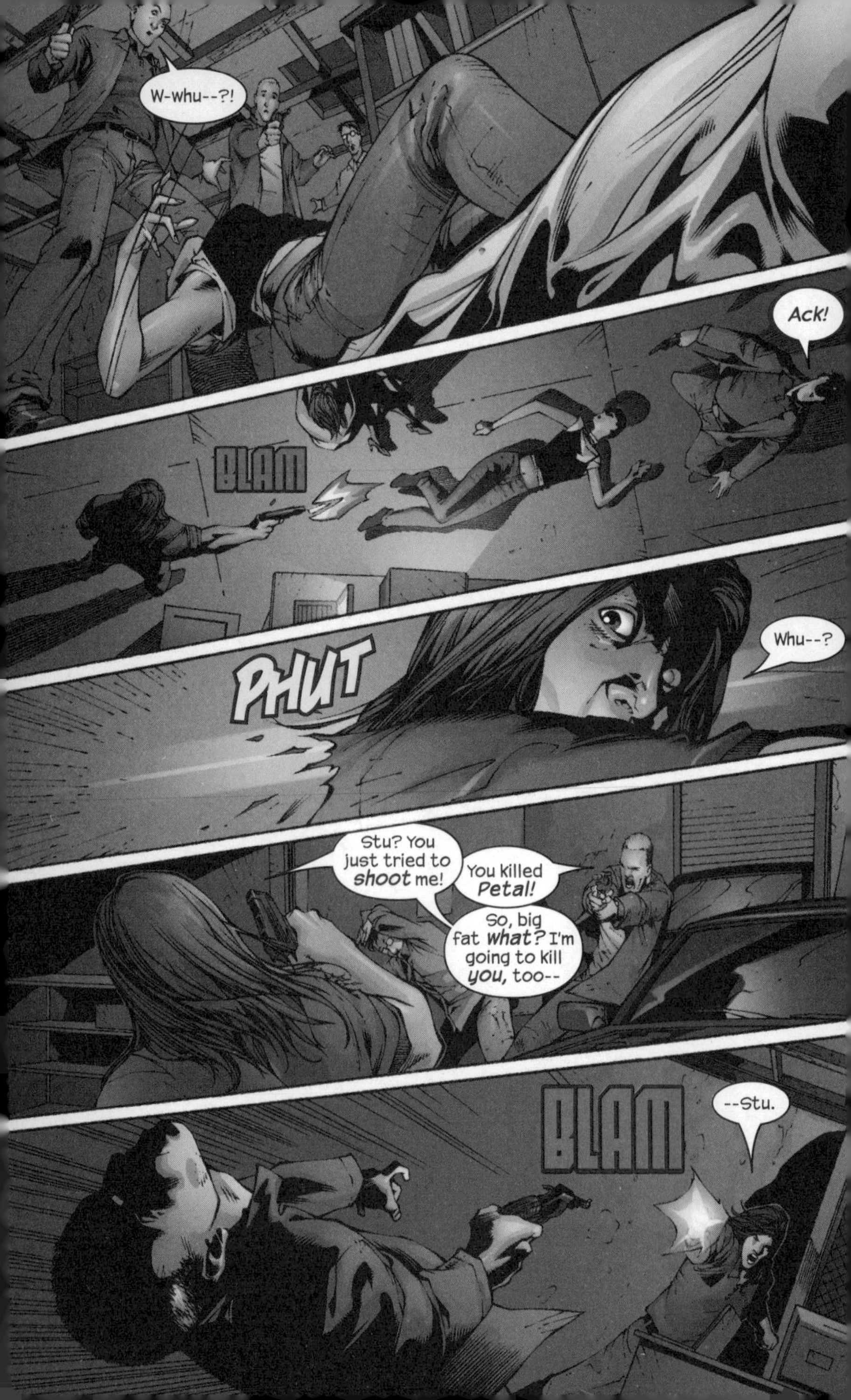
W-whu--?!
Ack!
BLAM
PHUT
Whu--?
Stu? You just tried to *shoot* me!
You killed *Petal!*
So, big fat *what?* I'm going to kill *you*, too--
BLAM
--Stu.

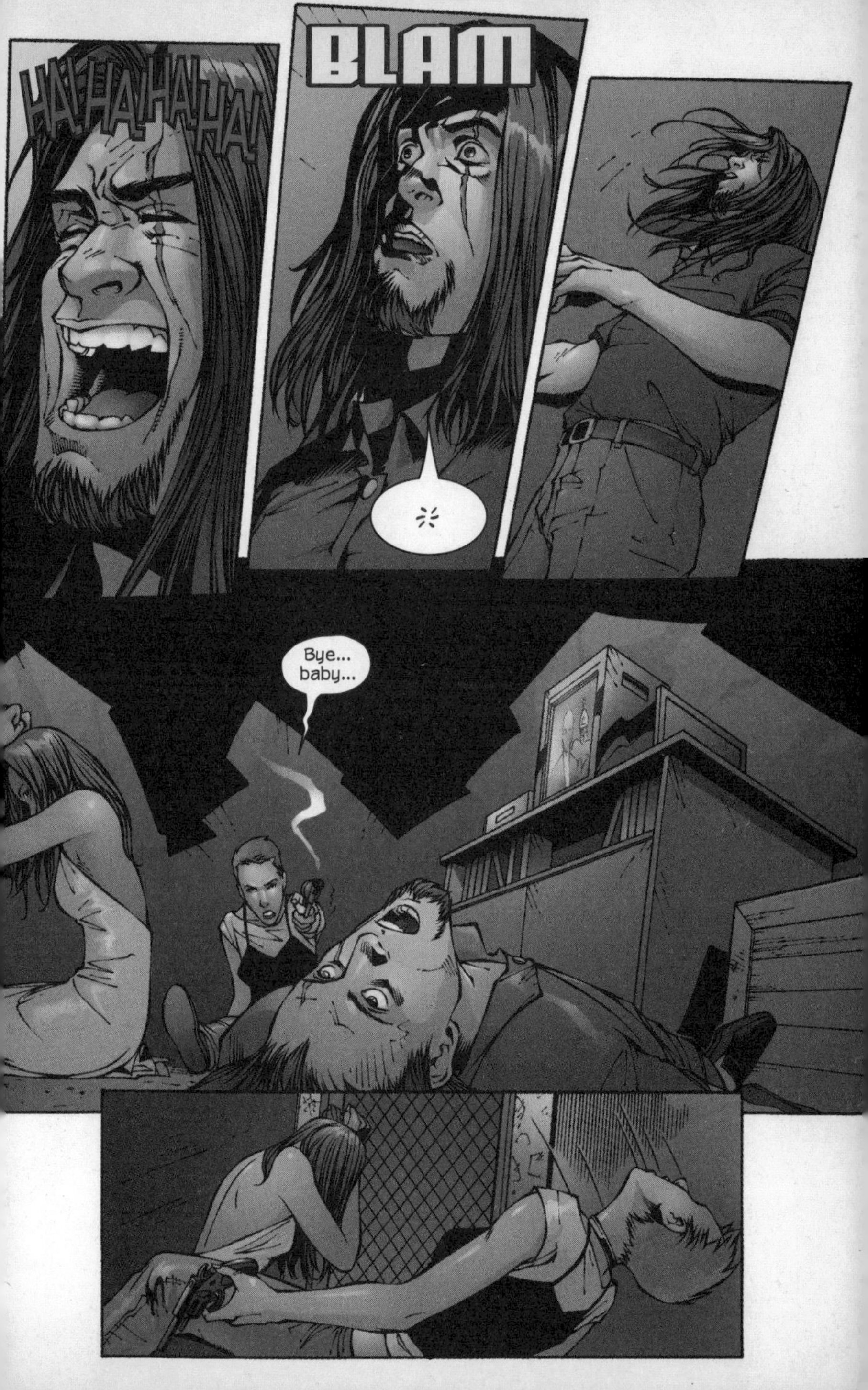
HA! HA! HA! HA!
BLAM
Bye... baby...

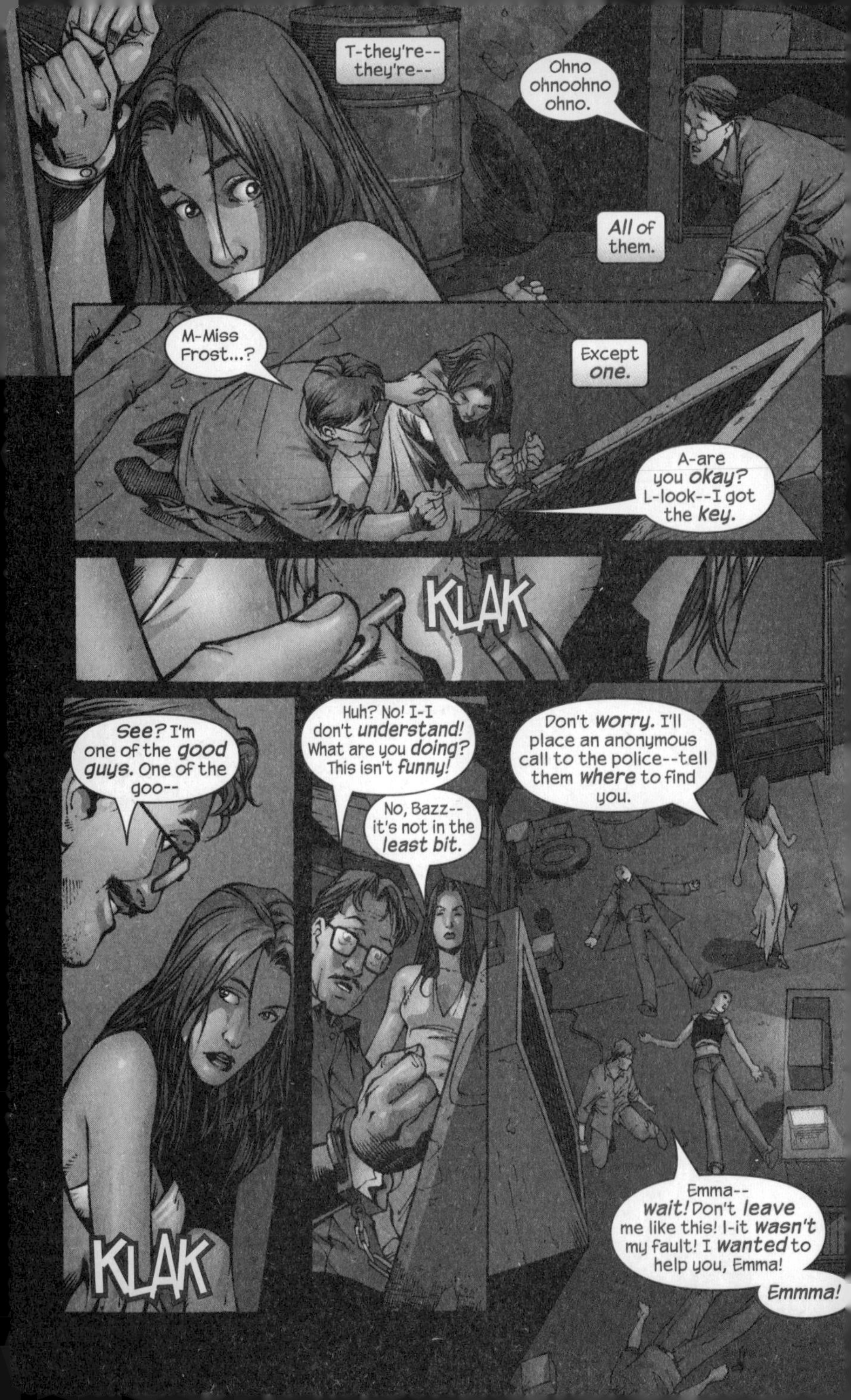

T-they're--
they're--
Ohno
ohnoohno
ohno.
All of
them.
M-Miss
Frost...?
Except
one.
A-are
you okay?
L-look--I got
the key.
KLAK
See? I'm
one of the good
guys. One of the
goo--
KLAK
Huh? No! I-I
don't understand!
What are you doing?
This isn't funny!
No, Bazz--
it's not in the
least bit.
Don't worry. I'll
place an anonymous
call to the police--tell
them where to find
you.
Emma--
wait! Don't leave
me like this! I-it wasn't
my fault! I wanted to
help you, Emma!
Emmma!

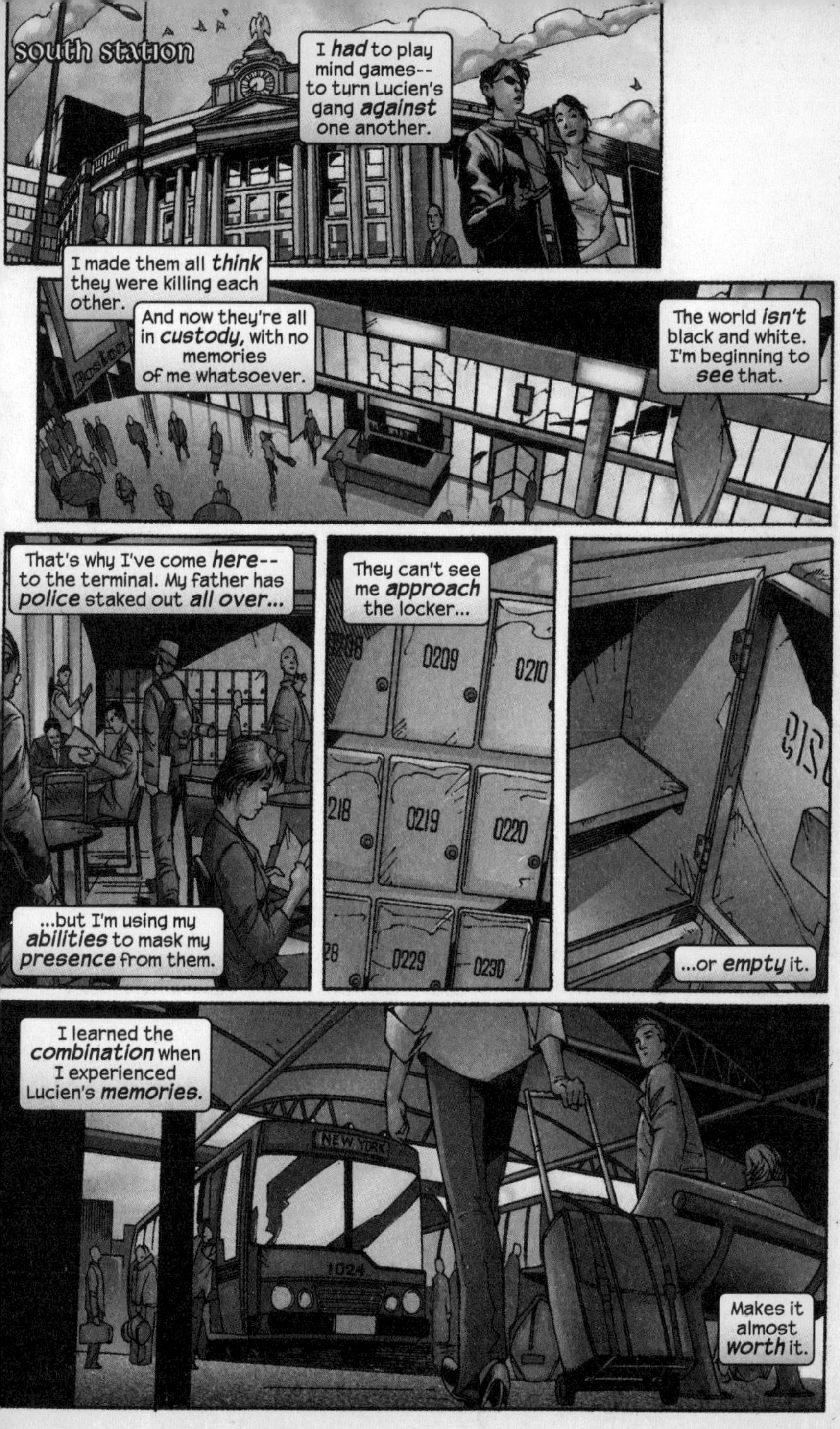
south station
I had to play mind games-- to turn Lucien's gang against one another.
I made them all think they were killing each other.
And now they're all in custody, with no memories of me whatsoever.
Boston
The world isn't black and white. I'm beginning to see that.
That's why I've come here-- to the terminal. My father has police staked out all over...
...but I'm using my abilities to mask my presence from them.
They can't see me approach the locker...
0209
0210
218
0219
0220
0229
0230
...or empty it.
I learned the combination when I experienced Lucien's memories.
NEW YORK
1024
Makes it almost worth it.

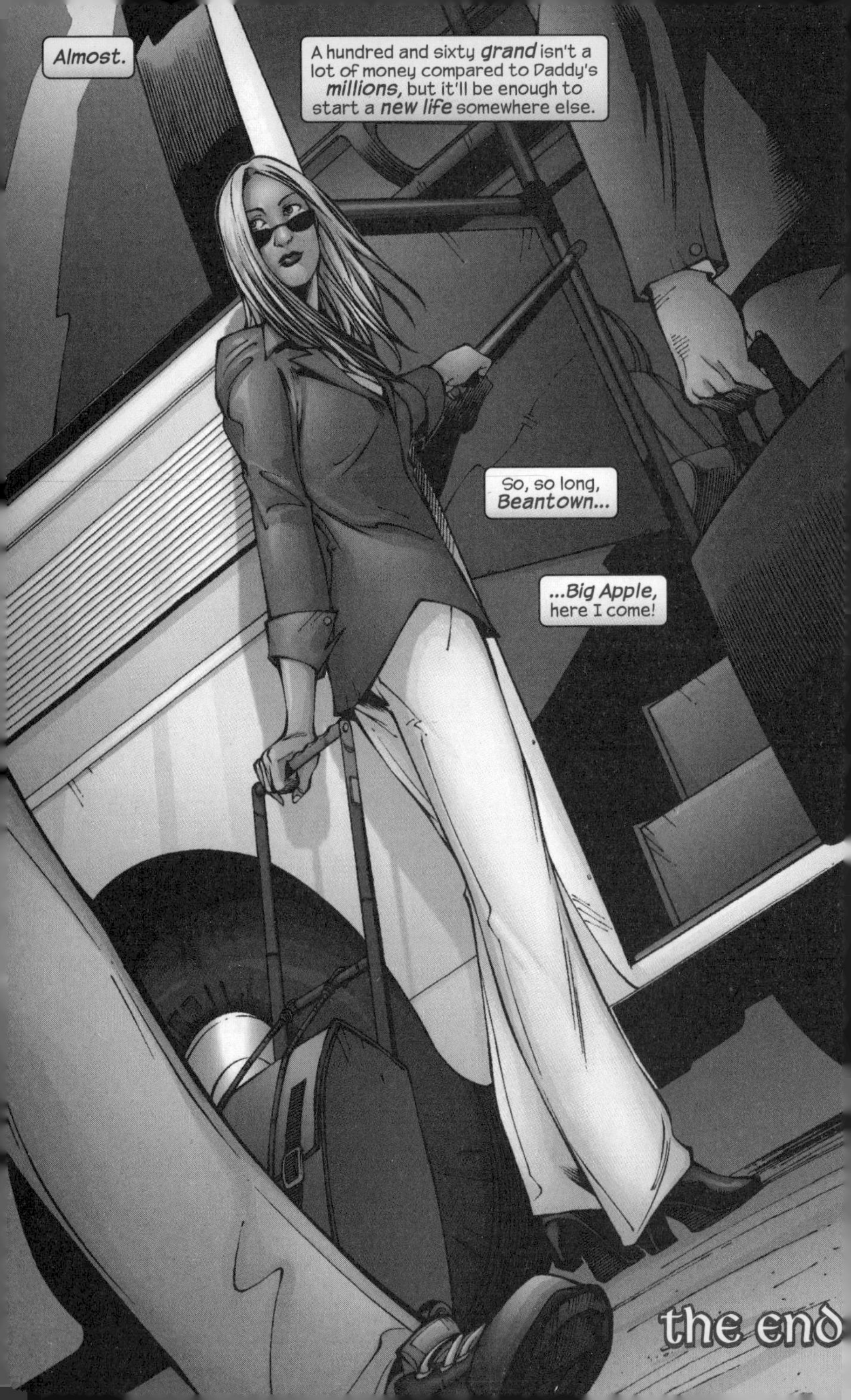
Almost.
A hundred and sixty grand isn't a lot of money compared to Daddy's millions, but it'll be enough to start a new life somewhere else.
So, so long, Beantown...
...Big Apple, here I come!
the end